"It is a sign of laziness to pigeonhole telenovelas as a repository of stereotypes. A complex, multifaceted universe is depicted in them through the prism of melodrama, which the masses, especially in Hispanic civilization, wholeheartedly adore. Frankly, literary classics such as Gabriel García Márquez's *One Hundred Years of Solitude* are melodramatic, too. A less condescending, more sensible approach is to look at melodrama as a tool for understanding social mores, which is what June Erlick does in this practical book. I'm grateful to her for taking a contrarian approach."

—**Ilan Stavans** is Lewis-Sebring Professor in the Humanities,
Latin American and Latino Culture at Amherst College,
author of *Love and Language* and *I Love My Selfie*, and
editor of *The Norton Anthology of Latino Literature*

"A delightful, thoroughly researched and enlightening account of what is perhaps Latin America's most important cultural phenomenon, the telenovela."

—**Alma Guillermoprieto** is a writer for *The New York
Review of Books* and the author of *The Heart That Bleeds*

TELENOVELAS IN PAN-LATINO CONTEXT

This concise book provides an accessible overview of the history of the teleno-vela in Latin America within a pan-Latino context, including the way the genre crosses borders between Latin America and the United States. Telenovelas, a dis-tinct variety of soap operas originating in Latin America, take up key issues of race, class, sexual identity and violence, interweaving stories with melodramatic romance and quests for identity. June Carolyn Erlick examines the social impli-cations of telenovela themes in the context of the evolution of television as an integral part of the modernization of Latin American countries.

June Carolyn Erlick is Publications Director at the David Rockefeller Center for Latin American Studies at Harvard University and Editor-in-Chief of *ReVista, the Harvard Review of Latin America.*

Latin American Tópicos

Series Editor: Michael LaRosa, Rhodes College

Telenovelas in Pan-Latino Context

June Carolyn Erlick

TELENOVELAS IN PAN-LATINO CONTEXT

June Carolyn Erlick

Routledge
Taylor & Francis Group

NEW YORK AND LONDON

First published 2018
by Routledge
711 Third Avenue, New York, NY 10017

and by Routledge
2 Park Square, Milton Park, Abingdon, Oxon OX14 4RN

Routledge is an imprint of the Taylor & Francis Group, an informa business

Library of Congress Cataloging-in-Publication Data
A catalog record for this book has been requested

ISBN: 978-1-138-68174-3 (hbk)
ISBN: 978-1-138-68176-7 (pbk)
ISBN: 978-1-315-54560-8 (ebk)

Typeset in Bembo
by Apex CoVantage, LLC

For the people of Colombia, and, in particular, Micaela and Sara Luna, Manuela, Santiago and Sebastián, who hopefully will live in a world of peace.

CONTENTS

SERIES EDITOR'S INTRODUCTION

Bienvenidos to *Tópicos*, a new series of books for classroom use developed by Routledge. The series is designed to reach a new generation of college students, and the reading public, searching for excellent syntheses of important topics relevant to the Latin American region. The series will offer relatively short, accessible survey books that are based on sound scholarship combined with the particular interest of the author.

The authors writing for this series represent a variety of disciplines; we know that Latin America can only be understood through study and reading across disciplines. Historians, political scientists, anthropologists, literary critics and journalists—among others—have helped expand the understanding of a region that remains somewhat mysterious to the general reading public in the United States, and to college students. In recent days, the Latin American region has lost some of its allure as other areas of the world—East Asia and the Middle East, for example—attract the attention of policy makers, and the funding priorities of think tanks, foundations and universities.

We want students to study the history and culture of Latin America, and the books in this series are designed to support that initiative. Many students graduate from college never having formally studied Latin America, and our hope is that, with this series that connects the Latin American region to cultural and historic themes globally, we can challenge students to focus on a critically dynamic region of the world.

Our first book, authored by journalist June Erlick, focuses on *telenovelas*, and June's clear, captivating prose helps the reader contextualize *telenovelas* in a Latin American and world context. In preparing this book, June watched a lot of hours of Latin American *telenovelas* and her determination allows the reader to see the political, economic and cultural relevance of this critical Latin American cultural manifestation. I'm very grateful to June Erlick for helping us kick off this series and hopeful the series helps promote a new, fresh conversation based on relevant topics and exciting, enticing writing.

Michael J. LaRosa
Series Editor
March, 2017
Coral Gables, Florida

ACKNOWLEDGMENTS

Acknowledgments are terrifying. Or I should say, writing acknowledgments is terrifying. I'm always afraid I'll leave someone out, put the thanks in the wrong order or thank someone who would rather remain anonymous.

So when Routledge indicated that acknowledgments were optional, I almost took up the offer. But how could I? This book has been a collaboration of many, many friends and scholars who shared their telenovela experiences with me. It's been an almost daily obsession of mine at the office, parties and other social events. Instead of "How are you?" or "Isn't the weather terrible?" it would be "Tell me about the first telenovela you ever saw," or "Do you watch such and such?" And I'd get a smile and almost always a long and fertile answer. So here goes, and if you are not here, but should be, know that you are a part of that wonderful collective of shared experiences.

First and foremost, a great big acknowledgment to my series editor Michael LaRosa, who saw a book before I did in my incessant babbling about telenovelas. And then, a hearty thanks to Eve Mayer and Theodore Meyer, my editor and assistant at Routledge, who had utmost patience with my trivial pursuit questions about capitalizations and serial commas. And thanks to my copy editor, Sharon Tripp.

I work in a wonderful academic center, the David Rockefeller Center for Latin American Studies at Harvard, headed up by Brian Farrell and Ned Strong (thanks for your patience and support!). This community allowed me to chat on a daily basis with scholars and practioners from all over Latin America. A special thanks to Abby Cordova from El Salvador, Liza Paravisini from Puerto Rico, Esther Hamburger from Brazil, Geydis Fundadora from Cuba, María Vázquez from Argentina, Ana María Reyes from Colombia and Boris Muñoz from Venezuela. Your suggestions and stories have shaped this book.

To political scientist Jorge Domínguez and historian Alejandro de la Fuente for taking seriously my questions about Cuban radionovelas (I thought you might not), to Aldo Panfichi, Neida Jímenez, Patricia Borja, Yadira Rivera, Margarita Martínez, Gabriela Farrell and Isabel Espinosa and many, many more who made this book possible with contacts, recommendations and anecdotes, thanks and more thanks.

My colleague Edwin Ortiz was a wonderful and understanding sounding board for some of the complicated themes in the book. And so many of my fellow staff members—many of whom grew up in Latin America or in Latino households—shared their experiences with telenovelas with enthusiasm.

A special thanks to Giuliana Cassano, who generously shared her contacts with the Ibero-American Observatory of Television Fiction (Obitel), which led to my attendance at the 2016 meeting in São Paulo with the hospitable leadership of Maria Immacolata Vassallo de Lopes and Guillermo Orozco Gómez. And to all the Obitel members who participated in this process of understanding telenovelas.

Immense words of gratitude are in store for Humberto Delgado and Carmen Dorado, who managed to collect the images for this book with dedication and persistence. And who, in the midst of the task, were constantly feeding me materials from the Mexican press about telenovelas.

Thanks to Azriel Bibliowitz for fishing out his college thesis about telenovelas—which has weathered the test of time very nicely. And sincere gratitude to Omar Encarnación, who endured e-mail after e-mail of questions about the chapter on gays in this book, for his patience and inspiration (and also to Joyce Murdoch for insisting that gays warranted a chapter of their own).

I could go on and on, but as I said in the beginning, this was all a collective effort and if your name isn't here, it is in spirit if you think it should be. But one more thanks, even if she isn't here to read it. I don't know if Margot Adler, my dear late friend and journalism school classmate, ever saw a telenovela. I certainly never saw one with her, but it was Margot who made me see the beauty and power of popular culture. It was Margot who was there when something new and exciting was on television. It was Margot who erased the differences between highbrow and lowbrow culture for me. So thank you, Margot, wherever you are, and thank you again to all who made this collective experience popular. Gracias.

June Carolyn Erlick
Somerville, MA

1

DISCOVERING TELENOVELAS

The world's eyes were on Nicaragua, the small Central American country that had toppled a dictator and set up a revolutionary government. U.S. president Ronald Reagan had deemed the small nation a threat to national security. As journalists in Nicaragua, we found that there were certain hours we just couldn't get interviews—even if we were on deadline.

In 1986, while U.S. congressional representatives were debating whether to provide support to the anti-revolutionary forces known as Contras, Nicaraguans were debating whether María Elena would marry Jorge Luís and if Don Rafael Del Junco would regain his voice.

Telenovela hour, when *El derecho de nacer* (The Right to Life) came on, was sacred and shut the country down. It's not that the bloody Contra war, which had been devastating Nicaragua for five years, wasn't a reality for most Nicaraguans. Most of the telenovela buffs had lost some relative, had a son in the army or had simply watched their living standards decline as the war ate up almost half the government budget.

But in Nicaragua's highly polarized society, it was only the telenovelas that seemed to cut through both class and political barriers.

El derecho de nacer, a 1981 Mexican remake of a 1952 Cuban telenovela, tells the story of an illegitimate boy rescued by the family's black maid. The wealthy grandfather had sent an employee to kill the infant to save the family honor, but the man relents and Mama Dolores comes to the rescue. The boy, Albertico, grows up to be a successful doctor and, without knowing it, rescues his half-brother from alcoholism and falls in love with his cousin (who fortunately turns out to be adopted).

In Nicaragua at the time, more than half the population was born out of wedlock, so many could identify with the theme. But the suffering, the division in the

Del Junco family, love, religion, ethics, class and even alcoholism were also issues with a direct appeal in revolutionary Nicaragua.

"It's a mirror image of society," Martín Vega of the North American Desk of the Foreign Ministry told me then. "Different people identify with different characters."

I remember when former U.S. president Jimmy Carter received an honorary degree from the Jesuit University, the ceremony was delayed while Carter met with government officials. Commandante Dora Tellez, Nicaragua's health minister, looked at her watch impatiently. "If this guy doesn't get here soon," she fretted, "I'm going to miss the telenovela."

In Lenin Fonseca Hospital, surgery was not performed during the telenovela hour.

"We're all young doctors, and we all identify with Albertico's professionalism," a 22-year-old internist told me.

For a sociology professor, the show's real hero was the black maid who raises Albertico as her own child: "All the poor people, all the people for whom this revolution was made, identify with Mama Dolores. They're out there saying, that's me, that's me."

Horacio Ruíz Sr. of the opposition newspaper *La Prensa* saw the telenovela a different way. "The message is basically anti-Sandinista, anti-class struggle," he explained to me. "The values that are extolled are bourgeoisie values, and Albertico gets ahead in a bourgeoisie world of pretty clothes and pretty landscapes."

Not only did the program cut across class and political barriers, but it also evoked a curiously pan-Nicaraguan nostalgia for the pre-Sandinista past. The radionovela version was first heard in Nicaragua in the early 1950s. "Everyone was tuned to the radio, when there was no earthquake, when there was a downtown," Ruíz from *La Prensa* reminisced. The city center was destroyed in a devastating 1972 earthquake, and even the most anti-Somoza Nicaraguans tended to long for that time before war and rubble.

The mother of Jaime Wheelock, one of the nine members of the powerful Sandinista directorate at the time, played María Elena in the Nicaraguan radio version. A Nicaraguan baseball pitcher was remembered by his nickname of María Dolores because his wife played that role in the radio version.

For war-torn Nicaragua, telenovelas were not only a national institution, but also a connection with other countries that export their telenovelas there—particularly Mexico, Venezuela and Brazil.

The guest of honor at the 1986 anniversary celebration of the Sandinista revolution was the Brazilian actress who played the role of the "Slave Isaura" in a popular telenovela. "Here I am not a slave," she told the cheering crowds.

I wrote about the Nicaraguan telenovela phenomenon for the *Wall Street Journal*. It was clear to me from my interviews that viewers found more than a mere distraction; in a revolutionary wartime society, the series was providing identity and unity—even if the interpretations of the telenovela were different. It was something the entire nation did for an hour each evening and then talked about incessantly the following day.[1]

Ever since then, I've heard anecdote after anecdote of how telenovelas are the routine of public life, uniting citizens for fleeting moments in a collective activity of watching. Abby Cordova, a political science professor from El Salvador at the University of Kentucky, recalls how during the guerrillas' final offensive in San Salvador in 1989 she huddled with her grandmother watching telenovelas in their hilltop home while helicopters buzzed overhead and bullets grazed the walls of their home. "My grandmother was not going to miss the telenovela," she recalled, "and I was always there to watch it with her."

Laura, a singer from Colombia living in Boston, recalls her childhood in Medellín, where she attended a very conservative Catholic private school. The school used to send home lists of specific telenovelas the girls should not watch because they treated subjects like sex out of wedlock or divorce. Laura was enterprising though, she recalls. She saved her allowance and when her parents were out, she bribed the maid to let her watch the telenovelas. She wanted to share the experience—to know what everyone else (including most of the girls at school, who managed to find their own ways to watch) was talking about.

In today's Cuba, telenovelas are a different type of collective experience: knowing the endings before anyone else provides bragging rights about how up-to-date one is. Many Cubans watch national telenovelas and not so recent imported ones on state-owned national television. But those who have more money, whether it's because they have relatives abroad or run small private businesses, subscribe to something called the *paquete*—the package. The package provides recorded television programs, mostly from Miami-based Spanish language television, and comes in the form of a memory stick with news, telenovelas and other shows. The more you pay, the quicker you get the package and can tell all your friends about the telenovela endings (Cubans apparently don't mind spoilers).

"Knowing the end of a telenovela—whether it's a Brazilian or Turkish one—is definitely a status symbol in Cuba nowadays." Geydis Fundadora, a Cuban sociologist who works at the Latin American Faculty of Social Sciences (FLACSO) in Havana, told me.

Telenovelas were even mentioned in Fidel Castro's November 2016 obituary in the *Miami Herald*, the newspaper that serves the world's epicenter of Cuban exiles. Journalist Glenn Garvin, in discussing Castro's legendary long public speeches, recalled that the day in 2008 when Castro officially resigned the Cuban presidency, a biologist in Havana sighed with relief and told a *Miami Herald* reporter, "Now I can watch my Brazilian telenovelas without worrying that they're going to be interrupted by a six-hour speech."[2]

Not the Soaps

When I wrote my article for *The Wall Street Journal* about the furor caused by *El derecho de nacer*, the headline writer entitled the article, "TV: Soaps for Sandinistas." It would be many, many years before I would discover that telenovelas really weren't the same as soap operas.

It's true that Colgate-Palmolive, the U.S. soap company, sponsored early telenovelas, just as they did in the United States. But the creative roots of Latin American telenovelas are much deeper than their corporate sponsorship. They have a different history and form than their American cousins.

For one thing, telenovelas have an ending—usually a happy one resulting in a wedding or a big celebration. They generally run from 120–180 episodes. Unlike soap operas, telenovelas air in prime time—usually after the evening news. And everyone watches telenovelas: men, women and children, often in family groups. Telenovela watching often cuts across age groups, with grandparents watching with their grandkids, and across classes, as children watch with their maids or babysitters. In some rural communities, even today, large groups of fans watch the telenovelas at community centers or in the plaza. The habit was formed when televisions were scarce because of their high cost, and continues until the present day, even with the abundance of low-cost television sets throughout Latin America. In contrast, soap operas broadcast on daytime television, have a largely female audience and are watched in isolation or perhaps with a preschool child.

"It's important to emphasize that telenovelas are seen by all audience targets and have enormous differences from soap operas," writes Colombia's Caracol vice president Juana María Uribe Pachón, in a Spanish-language e-mail. "In the first place, telenovelas always have a storyline with a clear start and finish and with a definite goal, whether it be love or the overcoming of some obstacle … for example, in the *Ronca de Oro* [The Voice of Freedom: Helenita Vargas], it's discrimination and machismo; in *Diomedes*, it's poverty."

Statistics provided by Caracol, Colombia's leading television station, show how audience share spreads across race and class. For example, in the case of *Ronca de Oro*, almost half the viewers from January 27 to April 25, 2014, were women, while 30.7 percent were men. Children under 12 made up 8.2 percent of the audience; those in the 12–17 category made up 10.9 percent, and from 18–24 9.6 percent. The network also categorized viewing by three social classes, with each commanding about a third of the audience, with the lower class leading slightly.

Diomedes, which follows the travails of a popular Colombian musician, showed a similar participation, with 45.8 percent female viewers, 38.6 percent male, and the rest youth. However, the show—perhaps because it focuses on poverty—drew slightly over half its viewers from what Caracol characterizes as lower class. The statistics, provided by Caracol, cover the period from January 13 to March 19, 2015.[3]

According to a Nielsen Ratings spokesperson, who gave me the information informally, women account for more than 70 percent of U.S. soap opera viewers, based on ten telecasts of four separate soap operas in 2015.

Telenovelas did not originate in the laundry rooms of suburban U.S. homes, but in the gritty cigar factories of prerevolutionary Cuba. To keep workers concentrated on the mechanical task at hand, readers called *lectores* perched on a high platform and read to entire factories from newspapers and literary works ranging from translations of Balzac and Dickens to Cuban authors such as Félix B. Caignet.[4]

Caignet's immensely popular *El derecho de nacer* may have first been heard in cigar factories, but it soon became popular over the entire island in the form of a radionovela. And like the telenovelas to come, it soon obtained international fame, with versions adapted and transmitted in Venezuela, Mexico and beyond.

The radionovela did not develop in a vacuum. In addition to its cigar factory roots, the stories told in serialized newspaper novels and graphic comic books influenced the new genre. In Argentina, the *folletín* or newspaper novels, taking their inspiration from European serialized newspaper novels, came in the form of so-called "gaucho-novels," distributed through loose-leaf pamphlets or weekly newspapers. Later, these "gaucho-novels" made their way to radio, where they drew on longstanding dramatic traditions and added music and sound effects. Telenovela theorist Jesús Martín-Barbero notes that the "open structure" of the newspaper serial constituted one of the key elements in today's telenovela, "both in its configuration as a genre and in its widespread success."[5]

In Mexico, the evolution took place from episodic graphic comic books. Indeed, the 1930s were known as "the Golden Age of Comic Books" there. The stories were narrative, with a compelling storyline. For example in 1937, Mexican newspaper cartoonist Gabriel Vargas invented *La Familia Burrón*, a comic that revolved around the life of a lower-class Mexican couple with two teenaged children and a younger adopted child. The comic narrative details their daily struggles in an impoverished neighborhood. One can easily see how such a story is only one step away from a radionovela and eventually from telenovelas.

One, of course, could look even further back to the theatre traditions, which inspired the narratives of serial newspaper novels, comic narratives and, most blatantly, telenovelas. Again, Martín-Barbero has a lot to say on the subject, finding theatre roots in "the forms and styles of entertainment in the popular fairs and in the oral story-telling traditions [of the 19th century] that emphasized fear, mystery and terror" that attracted a predominantly, if hardly wholly, illiterate audience. But although the theatre tradition influenced the printed narratives and the radionovelas, the difference was that the latter were episodic: they kept the audience coming back time after time.[6]

Television came to Latin America at the beginning of the 1950s. Cuba and Brazil vied for the very first telenovela, with *Sua vida me pertence* (Your Life Belongs to Me) appearing in Brazil in 1951 and *Senderos de amor* (Paths of Love) airing in Cuba the same year. Mexico was not far behind with *Ángeles de la calle* (Angels of Love) later in 1951. These three telenovelas were shown once or twice a week, and Mexico was the first to show a telenovela in 1958 in its modern daily form: *Senda prohibida* (Forbidden Path) by Fernanda Villeli, who later would adapt the radionovela *El derecho de nacer* to television.

Like the Cuban telenovelas, Brazilian telenovelas found their roots in very popular radionovelas. Radio São Paulo aired its first radionovela in June 1941 with an adaptation of a Cuban original, *In Search of Felicity*. The radio station was soon broadcasting 22 radionovelas daily.[7]

In the early years of the telenovela, the performance was broadcast live, with actors who memorized their lines and acted with the impromptu flourishes of theatre. Later, telenovelas became more of an industrial production, with actors relying on teleprompters. Scenes were filmed in quick sequence, and actors often worked in a variety of telenovelas at the same time or in quick succession, spawning a star system.

The history of Latin American telenovelas was firmly rooted in Latin America, rather than being an imported product from the United States. Like Latin Americans themselves, the genre could look toward Europe for some of its theatrical and comic serial narrative inspirations, but the programs were by Latin Americans and about Latin Americans and for Latin Americans.

Researching the history of telenovelas and realizing that my initial assumptions about their relationship to soap operas had been incorrect, I discovered a quote from Venezuelan scriptwriter José Ignacio Cabrujas that would summarize all I had been learning.

"We [scriptwriters] are responsible for the only possibility that 95 percent of the population has for seeing itself on the screen, because the only story Latin Americans hear about themselves is the telenovela," he told young screenwriters at a workshop.

> Telenovelas are the only stories that connect Mexico with Argentina; the telenovela is an instrument of cohesion in Latin America. It is a fabulous instrument of communication that we have invented—and that belongs to us. It is our creation and we are talking to all the Latin Americans when we write a telenovela.[8]

He added that telenovelas have managed to achieve what endless meetings of Latin American economics ministers could not—to provide a sense of integration to the continent.

As the telenovelas became more popular and more of them were produced, Latin American television channels showed fewer U.S. series and movies (often reruns). For example, in Chile in the early 1970s, each television channel showed an average of three U.S. movies daily and many series, according to Chilean media scholar Valerio Fuenzalida. By 1977, each channel was showing one U.S. movie daily and many fewer series, replaced by three telenovelas daily on each channel. The pattern was similar in other Latin American countries, Fuenzalida observed. The telenovela touched collective cultural memories that the U.S. productions did not.[9]

"The telenovela genre has developed as a complex cultural project with generic, social and cultural roots far back in Latin American history," observes University of Leicester media and communication professor Thomas Tufte.[10]

The telenovelas featured—and still do—music identified strongly with each country, whether it's rancheras in Mexico or vallenato in Colombia. They evoke daily life, whether at a ranch or in a poor neighborhood or an elegant mansion. Love is most often the common denominator and sometimes ambition, but the country-focused nature of the telenovela can be identified with by those from elsewhere, as they too are carried along by the emotionally dramatic stories. The winning formula is a strong local flavor with universal themes.

Despite the strong local overtones of the telenovela, the programs often mixed actors from different countries (although viewers of Netflix, Telemundo and Univision productions might have assumed that this was a more recent phenomenon as represented by the Brazilian star of the Colombian-themed *Narcos*). But even in 1969, in the extremely popular *Simplemente María* (Simply María), the role of María's best friend and eventual business partner Teresa was played by well-known Colombian actress Mariela Trejos. Braulio Castillo, an archetypically handsome Puerto Rican telenovela star, played Esteban, the male protagonist. Both Trejos and Castillo helped the telenovela on its path to international recognition, particularly in Colombia, Central America and the Caribbean, where the actors already had many fans.

It's as if we are looking at a series of concentric circles; a Mexican telenovela would allow Mexicans to see themselves and their society, to hear their music, to enjoy their landscapes while at the same time projecting to the rest of the world what it is to be Mexican and what it is to be Latin American.[11]

Telenovelas gave Latin Americans a chance to see themselves and their problems and challenges, their identities and concerns, on the small screen night after night and to talk about what they were seeing day after day.

And one of those concerns was the transition to modernity. Latin America was becoming a more urban society, a more modern society, as it industrialized, drawing traditional farmers from the rural countryside to become workers. So it's no surprise that the first daily telenovela in Brazil was actually named after a telephone line. Like the television, the telephone was a symbol of the move into the modern world. Although *2-5499 Ocupado* was adapted from an Argentine story, the telenovela scriptwriter Ivani Ribeiro of *2-5499 Ocupado* also wanted to write realistic Brazilian telenovelas, rather than importing and adapting scripts from Mexico and other Latin American countries. She considered other telenovelas "too weepy," and thus began a particular type of telenovela, grounded in local Brazilian reality. Modernity wasn't just a matter of newfangled contractions for Ribeiro and other scriptwriters: it was a way of seeing the world, taking on subjects such as gender and class. Telenovelas presented to the viewers subjects they didn't ordinarily talk about and sparked conversations among viewers.[12]

Telenovelas produced in different Latin American countries took on distinct personalities. Mexicans tend to be more romance-focused and classically melodramatic. Colombians incorporated humor into their telenovelas. Argentines portrayed the middle class long before any other Latin American country. Yet, despite these distinctions, the telenovelas have from a very early date moved from one country to another with ease, often through lucrative exports. The flow of telenovela scripts among Latin American countries began in the 1950s. By 2005, the telenovela had become a $2 billion business, of which $1.6 billion came from exports within Latin America and the Caribbean and $341 million to Europe, Asia, Africa and the Arab world. Brazil, Mexico and Venezuela became powerful hubs of telenovela production and exports. Many books and articles have been written on telenovelas as a business, and that is not the focus of this book.

Yet media businesses are successful because they build audiences, and I began to wonder how it is that telenovelas moved so easily from one country to another. For those readers who have always lived in the United States, you might think of Latin America as one unified continent. That's far from true. For many, many years (and to some degree even now), the easiest way to get from Argentina to Mexico, or from Peru to Nicaragua, was to fly through Miami and back out again to Latin America. Books published in Mexico or even neighboring Venezuela didn't make their way to Colombia, and Peruvians had no idea what Argentines were writing. The advent of the Internet and transnational Latin American-owned airlines have brought the continent together to a degree, but still not as much as an outsider might assume.[13]

Telenovelas are rooted in transnationality. The industry was strong and thriving in prerevolutionary Cuba, in part because of its experience with radionovelas and in part because U.S. soap company Colgate-Palmolive was willing to finance productions there and use advertising space on the popular series. Scripts from telenovelas circulated from country to country; radionovela scripts had previously been imported from Mexico, Argentina and Cuba to Brazil, being translated from the Spanish for the growing Brazilian market. The process continued with telenovelas; one of Brazil's most popular early telenovelas, *Eu compro esa mulher* (I Will Buy This Woman) in 1966, was developed from a Cuban script.

But with the triumph of the 1959 Cuban revolution, it was not just scripts but people that began to circulate. Many Cuban writers and producers branched out in exile from the island to work in other countries. They brought with them not only their know-how, but also an exile's eye, an immigrant's perspective, a way of being and adapting to a country but seeing it in a slightly different light. Cuban writer Gloria Magadan went to Brazil where she brought to TV Globo her experience in making telenovelas. Magadan had emigrated from Cuba to Puerto Rico, working first for Telemundo and then for Colgate-Palmolive; after that, she went to Venezuela, where she worked in the telenovela industry and finally ended up in Brazil, where she developed and directed the international telenovela department.

Delia Fiallo, who is often called "the mother of the Latin American telenovela," was another Cuban exile telenovela writer with a tremendous impact on the international scene. Fiallo left Cuba for Venezuela, producing such classic hits as *Cristal* and *Leonela*, strong women's tales. Fiallo had long been aware of the social impact of telenovelas. In 1957 in Cuba, while the Cuban rebels were fighting to overthrow the dictator, she wrote *Soraya*, which takes place in India. In a 2013 interview, she noted that she had incorporated a subtext in favor of freedom in that telenovela and in *Cuando se quiere a un enemigo* (When One Loves One's Enemy): "In these novelas, I expressed an oppressed people's desire for freedom."[14]

Another "global" writer, Caridad Bravo Adams, brought Latin America what might have been its first classic of overt social change, the Peruvian telenovela *Simplemente María*. Bravo Adams was the Mexican-born daughter of Cuban parents, who adapted the script from an Argentine version by Celia Alcántara. The telenovela was remade in Brazil, Venezuela, Argentina (again) and Mexico, as recently as 2015. Bravo Adams moved back to Cuba with her parents and, like Magadan and Fiallo, left again after Fidel Castro came to power.[15]

Not all of the international scriptwriters leaving their imprints on other Latin American telenovela industries were Cuban exiles. One important figure was Valentín Pimstein, a Chilean immigrant who ventured to Mexico at an early age. He became a scriptwriter and eventually an executive producer for the television network now known as Televisa, producing 97 telenovelas, including a remake of Bravo Adams's *Simplemente María* in 1989. And he also "discovered" the work of Delia Fiallo, whose abundant production of telenovelas in Venezuela then became popular in Mexico. Telenovelas were creating a kind of informal globalization long before the term was popularized.

So it was fitting that the first telenovela to really capture Brazil was the Portuguese version of the same telenovela we mentioned at the beginning of this chapter, *O direito de nascer* (El derecho de nacer/The Right to Life), a 1964 version of the Cuban radionovela by Félix Caignet. "This was an unprecedented television event, where just five months after the military coup, the country was united in front of the television set to watch a live broadcast of its final episode."[16]

Isaura also eventually led the way in the late 1980s, when telenovelas began circulating beyond the Spanish- and Portuguese-speaking market. In China, for example, some 450 million viewers followed the fate of the beautiful slave as she tried to escape from her vengeful master. And seven out of ten Russians watched Mexico's *Los ricos también lloran* (The Rich Also Cry), one of Pimstein's productions (Figure 1.1), and the Venezuelan series *Cristal* (written by Delia Fiallo) drew 11 million viewers worldwide for its final episode.

Paula Andaló, in the Pan American Health Organization magazine, observes:

> Telenovelas' larger-than-life story lines may be exaggerated renditions of real-life dramas, but many viewers see their own lives reflected in those of their favorite stars . . . and are drawn in by the compelling twists and turns of overwrought plots. Thus, modeling a behavior they see on screen is almost natural.

Colombians may see themselves, and Latin Americans may see themselves, but the universality of these stories of love and betrayal, rags to riches, means that

FIGURE 1.1 Promotional Image for *Los Ricos También Lloran*. *Los Ricos También Lloran,* 1979, Produced by Valentin Pimstein, Image: Verónica Castro.

others around the world can identify (ironically, this identification can function in reverse, so Turkish and South Korean telenovelas are gaining popularity recently in Latin America).[17]

The globalization through traveling scriptwriters did not stop in the Cuban postrevolutionary era. Indeed, history seems to be repeating itself with a recent exodus of telenovela writers and producers from Venezuela, under the tottering socialist government and a collapsing television industry there.

One of those writers was Perla Farias, a Venezuelan scriptwriter and producer. She's now senior vice president of scripted development at Telemundo, the Miami-based Hispanic television network (at the same time, another Venezuelan exile, Carmen Urbaneja, was promoted to senior vice president, scripted productions, from vice president, novela production.)[18]

Farias is a key figure in our continued story of globalization and putting subjects on the table that viewers don't usually talk about. Farias descended from that pan-Latino telenovela world. She is the daughter of Daniel Farias, one of those Cuban exiles who went to Venezuela; he directed the hit *Cristal*, written by fellow Cuban exile Delia Fiallo. Her mother was telenovela actress Gioia Lombardini, the daughter of Italian immigrants to Venezuela.

In an interview on National Public Radio, Perla Farias describes how when she first came to Miami in 2003, she was looking for telenovela projects to develop for her then-job at Telemundo as vice president and happened to be reading *La Reina del Sur* (Queen of the South), a novel by Spanish author Arturo Pérez-Reverte.[19]

The first episode of *La Reina del Sur* attracted 2.4 million viewers, the highest-rated premiere in the network's history, according to Telemundo. By its second month, the telenovela was No. 1 in prime time, beating out not just Univision, the Spanish-language rival, but also English-language programming.

"We had a female protagonist that was completely opposite to the typical novela protagonist," Farias told NPR:

> I mean, she killed people. She was a lesbian in the character. And that, for a protagonist, is huge. I mean, imagine coming from our telenovelas, or classical telenovelas, could you ever imagine having that kind of possibilities, you know? It was a big risk.

So a Venezuelan, who happened to be the daughter of a Cuban exile and an Italian immigrant, managed to transform pan-Latino television in the United States.

But the pan-Latino influence doesn't stop there; it's also having its impact on English-language television in the United States. Back in Venezuela, Perla Farias wrote a successful telenovela called *Juana la vírgen*. A 17-year-old woman gets artificially inseminated by accident in a hospital and becomes pregnant. When Mauricio, the biological father, finds out, he falls in love with the teenager, who happens to be a virgin, despite the fact he is married to Carlota, who does everything in her power to keep them apart. Eventually, after a lot of twists and turns, Juana and Mauricio escape to a mountainside retreat with the newborn.

Does it sound familiar? Some of you may have watched *Jane the Virgin*, the once-a-week romantic comedy/telenovela that airs on The CW (and can be accessed on Hulu and Netflix). My interns—both Latinas—at Harvard watch it, and when I asked the 60-ish mother of a Colombian-American journalist friend of mine if she knew about the show, she regurgitated the plot to date. The series has an addictive telenovela quality, and indeed Jane Villanueva's dad Rogelio de la Vega plays a vain telenovela star. The series doesn't fulfill the definition of a telenovela, as it's gone on for several seasons and shows no signs of ending—like a soap opera. But it's definitely not a soap opera: it takes its cues from the melodrama of the telenovela, with romantic triangles and accompanying musical cues for each character. It also relies heavily on the interwoven story of three generations of women in the Villanueva family, grandmother, mother and daughter, strong women all.

In the U.S. version, Jane is 23, not 17, and the biological father is a fabulously rich (but married) cancer survivor. Like Carlota, Rafael's wife Petra does everything she can to keep them apart. Jane is a budding writer and graduate student, although motherhood and crushes often prove to be distractions. Like its telenovela inspirations, *Jane the Virgin* brings up subjects that its viewers might not otherwise have conversations about: sexuality, faithfulness, parental relations.

Jane the Virgin is far from the only U.S. series with telenovela roots. There's also *Narcos*, the popular Netflix-Telemundo series that tells the story of druglord Pablo Escobar. The series was set and filmed in Colombia, and in keeping with the pan-Latino flavor of telenovelas, was written and directed by Brazilian filmmaker José Padilha; the actor who plays Pablo Escobar, Wagner Moura, is also Brazilian, and the musical theme was written and composed for the series by singer-songwriter Rodrigo Amarante. *Narcos* follows on the heels of a successful Colombian telenovela, *Pablo Escobar: El patrón del mal*, also about Escobar, but manages to make U.S. Drug Enforcement Agency agents into the heroes and center of the story.

Like *Jane the Virgin*, which is basically English language with some Spanish dialogue with subtitles, *Narcos* uses bilingual dialogue so the Colombian characters don't end up speaking English to each other. It's aimed at both a Hispanic and U.S. audience (and is also watched by many of my friends still living in Latin America). It's not a telenovela, again because it continues to stretch on for many seasons, but it's a definite example of how the telenovela culture is now influencing U.S. culture.

Before *Jane the Virgin* and *Narcos*, there was *Ugly Betty* (2006–10) (Figure 1.2), a remake of the Colombian *Yo soy Betty, la fea* (commonly know as *Betty la fea*), another hybrid that was aired weekly, but carried strong traits of its Latin American origins. The heroine was a Mexican Latina from Queens, Betty Suárez, who uses her wits to get ahead at a trendy New York fashion house.

Before *Betty*, MyNetworkTV, a division of Fox, was experimenting with telenovela-style programming for an American audience. A 2006 television series,

FIGURE 1.2 America Ferrera Stars as Ugly Betty in the American Television Adaptation of *Yo soy Betty, la fea*. *Ugly Betty*, 2006, Created by Silvio Horta, Image: America Ferrera.

Desire, was loosely based on the 2004 Colombian telenovela *Mesa para tres* (Table for Three). Two brothers run from a New Jersey crime family and end up in Los Angeles running a restaurant. They are both in love with the same woman, and their involvement leads to complex intrigues of murder and betrayal. Wikipedia calls the series "an American telenovela." The same year, *Fashion House*, a short-lived telenovela about a corporate takeover of a fashion house, which was based on a Cuban script *Salir de noche* (Out in the Night) that was sold to MyNetworkTV, and which aired nightly, just like a Latin American telenovela, had mixed results; viewers did not want to watch every night.[20]

Yet the telenovela influence is still holding strong in the United States. Sony Pictures Television has announced the development of *El Comandante*, a telenovela about the late Venezuelan strongman Hugo Chávez that aired on Telemundo with English-language subtitles. The biopic's refrain, "El poder de la pasión y la pasión por el poder" (the power of passion and the passion for power), evokes the melodramatic power of the telenovela. Chávez is played by a Colombian actor, Andrés Parra, who starred as Pablo Escobar in *El patrón del mal* (let's hope that the Venezuelan accent is easier for Parra than Spanish Colombian was for Brazilian Moura in *Narcos*; telenovelas may be pan-Latino, but accents vary greatly from region to region).

Angelica Guerra, Sony Pictures Television's senior vice president and managing director, production, Latin America and the United States, told *Variety* magazine that the biopic, like all telenovelas, would air nightly, but she added, "It's a hybrid, using the telenovela format, albeit shorter, but with the look and feel of a U.S. drama."[21]

Samantha Nogueira Joyce observes, "For more than thirty years, now, telenovelas have dominated prime time programming on most Latin American televison. . . [covering] a culturally constructed region from the southern tip of Latin America to the Hispanic communities of the United States." Now we can safely say that telenovelas and their hybrids are moving beyond the Hispanic communities and into the U.S. mainstream.[22]

Telenovelas have also propelled stars from Latin America into the U.S. orbit. They are increasingly gaining popularity not only among Latinos and Spanish-language television such as Univision and Telemundo, but in their reinvention for the American market; they are also becoming a vehicle for Latin American actors and actresses to make it into U.S. television and film. Just a couple of examples are the Brazilian Sofía Vergara, the highest-paid actress in U.S. television, and the Mexican Selma Hayek, who produced *Ugly Betty*. Such influence from the telenovelas is diversifying the U.S. television industry.

Discovering Telenovelas (Over and Over Again)

Colombian Nobel Prize recipient Gabriel García Márquez once said he thought telenovelas were a much more effective way of reaching people than books.

Sitting on a rocking chair in tropical Cartagena in 1987, the author of *A Hundred Years of Solitude*, can still be seen in a YouTube image on the Internet proselytizing for the genre.

Wearing his trademark white guayabera shirt, he tells the unseen interviewer,

> I've always wanted to write a telenovela. They're wonderful . . . the problem is we're accustomed to think that a telenovela is necessarily in bad taste, and I don't believe this to be so. . . . In Colombia alone, in one single night, one episode of a telenovela can reach ten to fifteen million people . . . It's only natural that someone who wants to reach people is attracted to telenovelas like a magnetic pole. He cannot resist it.[23]

García Márquez, who at one time was the president of the International Film and Television School, actually ran a 1989 workshop at the film school at San Antonio de los Baños, Cuba, about writing telenovela scripts using one of his short stories as raw material: *Me aquilo para soñar* (I Rent Myself Out to Dream). That was as close to writing a telenovela as he ever got.[24]

García Márquez's comments shouldn't have surprised me (although they did) since he was a master at invoking the very specific and local to create universal stories, collapsing fantasy and reality as good telenovelas do. Yet, trained as I was to draw a false and hard line between high culture and popular culture, it surprised me not only that he thought it, but also that he admitted it to a wide public audience.

Another discovery was learning that telenovelas were museum-worthy. And again, that should not have surprised me, because García Márquez had already erased the distinction between high and low culture for me. Colombia's National Museum, housed in an impressive old fortress prison, featured an exhibit in 2010 called "A Country of Telenovelas." Here one could find all sorts of artifacts, from the hat used by actor Adam Corona in *Pero sigo siendo el rey* (But I'm Still the King) to the Latin prayer book with leather covers used by Carlos Muñoz in his portrayal of Father Pío Quinto Quintero in the telenovela *San Tropel* to the accordion played by musician Egidio Cuadrado in *Escalona*. Here one could also hear and watch segments of telenovelas from the previous 30 years of Colombian history.

And that was the significance of having a telenovela exhibit in this world-class museum in downtown Bogotá, one that is primarily dedicated to history and the visual arts. Journalist Mauricio Bernal observed, "[The National Museum] is a history museum, and that's not irrelevant because the exhibit is precisely that: an exhibition of history. The National Museum exalts the telenovela, recognizes its transcendence and proclaims that it is something much more than the patrimony of bored housewives and maids looking for companionship while they iron clothes."[25]

Telenovelas (and soap operas) also form an integral part of the displays at the Chicago-based Museum of Broadcast Communications. The Paley Center for

Media, with offices in New York and Los Angeles, also devotes attention to the genre (and an image from *Ugly Betty* is prominent on its website).

And a traveling exhibition of "Under the Mexican Sky: Gabriel Figueroa—Art and Film" shown at the Los Angeles County Museum of Art (LACMA) and at the Museo del Barrio in New York, among others, featured four large color film stills shot by photographer Ángel Corona Villa depicting scenes from *El amor tiene cara de mujer* (Love Has a Woman's Face), a telenovela Figueroa made with director Tito Davison in 1971 (and the producer was Valentín Pimstein, the Chilean immigrant who became a Mexican telenovela tycoon, and the telenovela itself was a remake of a 1964 Argentine telenovela).[26]

The presence of telenovelas in museums is a salute to their importance in Latin American society, and many scholars have dedicated themselves to figuring out why and how.

The Thinkers

It suddenly seemed as if I could not escape the world of telenovelas, even when I wasn't watching them. I was returning to Boston from Colombia, where I usually spend my Christmas holidays. Tired, but not quite tired enough to doze off, I browsed the Avianca airline magazine. My eyes lit on a special feature by Universidad de los Andes media scholar Omar Rincón discussing telenovelas. Illustrated by a passionate couple locked in a serious embrace with a television camera rolling on one side, the article contained eloquent and thoughtful ideas.

"In Latin America, we are the telenovela," he writes.

> And we are because the telenovela has been in charge of our sentimental education, how we love and how we live passion, tragedy and comedy. The telenovela has taken charge of our identities and traumas; to know who we are, we must see ourselves in its stories. The result is a continent whose common memory is a melodrama, a struggle for recognition, a search to find out from whence we came and who we are, a desire for social mobility.[27]

So it was on that long trip home that I first began to discover the philosophers of the telenovela, the thinkers who were not trying to figure out what made a profit, but why and how the telenovela is the medium that allows Latin Americans to see themselves and to project that identity to the world at large. These were the philosophers who saw that in the movement from country to country, telenovelas were carving out universal themes on a continent separated by mountains, rivers, jungles and sometimes even language.

First and foremost, I learned, was the work of Jesús Martín-Barbero, a Spanish intellectual who has lived in Colombia since the 1960s. And it started, as many things do in Colombia, with an examination of violence. In the 1980s, the Jesuit think tank CINEP began a study of television as a form of popular participation, which led to the study "La telenovela en Colombia: televisión, melodrama y vida cotidiana" (The Telenovela in Colombia: Television, Melodrama and Daily Life), spearheaded by Martín-Barbero. The telenovela emerged as the crossroads of modernity, the place where popular narratives intersected with technological transformation and national content converged with transnational global formats.

Martín-Barbero saw that telenovelas—through the genre of melodrama— sought to know or reknow (*reconocer*, which can also mean "recognize"), to take us beyond mere appearances. The successful telenovela, he wrote, "looks to fight against all wrongdoing, the appearances, against everything that hides and disguises reality: *it is a struggle to make oneself known*."[28]

In his book *Drugs, Thugs, and Divas*, O. Hugo Benavides, another one of the intellectuals who theorizes telenovelas, talks about the importance of Martín-Barbero's work. He cites Martín-Barbero's exploration of the history and role of melodrama, which emerged as a contrary force to the established theatre reflecting the views of the elite class.

Benavides observes in discussing Martín-Barbero's work:

> These historical characteristics of the melodrama—overdramatization, emphasis on emotion rather than logic, use of music to mark key relationships, characters as symbols of ethical values—are still the key elements of telenovelas throughout the Americas and therefore are part of these telenovelas' cultural and historical representation as well.[29]

Melodrama, according to Martín-Barbero, allows the recuperation of popular memory; it becomes a "drama of recognition."

> Whether it takes the form of a tango, a soap opera, a Mexican film or a cheap crime story, the melodrama taps into and stirs up a vein of collective cultural imagination. And there is no access to historical memory or projection of dreams into the future which does not pass through this cultural imagination.[30]

It was almost as if Martín-Barbero was giving permission with his prolific in-depth analyses to a cadre of telenovela scholars approaching the subject from many vantage points and academic disciplines. Argentine media scholar Nora Mazziotti, for example, contends that the telenovela is "a type of collective and generational glossary that can be shared and activated at any moment." The telenovela, for Mazziotti, shows different ways of expressing affection, social norms in regards to the family and significant other and gender relationships. Many academics specialized in a particular country or business aspects or relationships between telenovelas and political trends.[31]

In Madrid, Spain, in 2009, a group of Latin American academics, telenovela directors, scriptwriters, journalists and musicians got together in a week-long conference to discuss the telenovela as an expression of popular culture. Panels, with probably the best titles in the academic world, ranged from "A Baby Is Abandoned on the Doorstep" to "Carlos Jesús Is Your Brother. You Can't Marry Him" to "Music to Iron by with the Flavor of a Telenovela." The conference was widely covered by the press in Spain and Latin America.[32]

After reading the work of many telenovela specialists (many of whom are cited in this book) and learning about the Spanish conference, I discovered that there is actually an official Latin American network of telenovela studies. In a quiet corner of the lush tropical college campus of the University of São Paulo in Brazil, the Center for Telenovela Studies serves as the informal world headquarters for the Ibero-American Observatory of Television Fiction (Obitel). The organization, which monitors all types of television fiction in Latin America, the United States, Spain and Portugal, hones in on telenovelas simply because they are the most popular form of television fiction to date.

In 2016, the monitoring covered programs on 77 open television channels—53 private channels and 24 public channels—in 12 different countries. Under the leadership of Obitel general coordinators Guillermo Orozco Gómez from the University of Guadalajara in Mexico and Maria Immaculata Vassallo de Lopes from the University of São Paulo, Obitel produces a yearbook in three languages and organizes a yearly seminar about what's new in the world of television fiction. Obitel has operated since 2005 as an international research network. Since 2008, Globo, the Brazilian television network, has provided resources for the network's projects, which stretch from Brazil to the United States to Spain.

"[Obitel] is, therefore, an intercultural project that allows to identify and interpret the representations that these countries make of themselves and of others in the television narratives, through which people build and rebuild their cultural identity," the 2016 yearbook explains. "These approaches facilitate the Observatory constructing, at the same time, a comprehensive overview about the cultural and economic strength that fiction has gained in the Ibero-American television and in the life of these countries."[33]

Each yearbook is like a little encyclopedia with the country-by-country report listing the most popular television fiction works (usually telenovelas), and focusing on a theme—in 2016, it was "(Re)Invention of Television Fiction and Genres." The yearbook looks at who's producing what and who's importing what (and even takes on the sensitive theme of "the Turkish conquest," the popularity of imported Turkish telenovelas). It examines audience trends, market shares, social merchandising and government regulations. The list of social merchandising themes ("social merchandising" is used for socially oriented themes people don't often talk about) is fascinating. For example, Argentina's 2016 report listed "environmental contamination, search for justice, homosexuality, unwanted/teenage pregnancies, child abduction, institutional corruption, class relationships and discrimination, depression, alcoholism, mental illness, gender-based bias, infidelity, infertility, domestic abuse, tension between tradition and modernity, male chauvinism and rape." And that's just for the ten most-watched titles in one country!

At an August 2016 seminar in Brazil, country coordinators discussed their findings in panel discussions and expressed their enthusiasm for telenovelas in the corridors. James Dettlief, one of the regional coordinators for Peru, recalls how as a young boy he would watch telenovelas until his parents came home. One was about a blind girl threatened by a stalker. The telenovela only showed one side of his face, but then one night it showed the other side, deeply ravaged by burns. His parents came home and he told them all about it. "Telenovelas are part of our lives, and they were a big part of my life then too. I felt proud of having that information to tell my parents."

Added co-coordinator Guillermo Gómez Orozco, "I've always thought telenovelas are just another way of recounting reality."

The Obitel researchers are both a diligent and committed bunch, but in terms of sheer enthusiasm and participation, the award for academic involvement goes to Carolina Acosta-Alzuru, an associate professor at the Grady College of Journalism and Mass Communication at the University of Georgia. Originally from Venezuela, Acosta-Alzuru teaches a course called "Telenovelas, Culture and Society" and maintains a class blog.

"The fascination with Latin American telenovelas is worldwide," she explains in her personal blog about telenovelas.

> Huge audiences that transcend nation, class, culture, age and gender differences sit daily in front of their television sets to watch these melodramatic serials. I'm a Latin American woman. Therefore, telenovelas have never been far away from my life. I'm also a scholar and telenovelas have been my chosen object of study since 1999.[34]

In the class blog, students wax poetic, enthusiastic and thoughtful in a blend of absorbing class lessons, Skype guest lectures with writers and directors, and following "their" telenovelas. Each student chose a telenovela to watch during the course of the semester.[35]

One student named Mary writes in the blog (November 11, 2016),

> I started to pick up watching *La Reina de Sur* as well the last few weeks. I realized that the way the writers on Thursday explained how they write the stories matched with the emotionally psychology of my brain. As the end of the shows have to have a cliffhanger to grab the audience, I experienced this heavily.
>
> I found myself watching 4–5 episodes of *La Reina de Sur* when I told myself I only would watch one. It finally got to the point where I would stop the show within 15 minutes of the show because I had to get it to a

slower part of show—which there is not very many slow points throughout a telenovela.

And another student named Cory comments (November 10, 2016), after a lecture on the history of restrictions on Venezuelan media, and Skype interviews with two Venezuelan telenovela writers,

> I appreciate how the writers of Venezuelan telenovelas were able to deal with the constraints they were under. For example, it's really cool that the writers of *La mujer perfecta* were able to raise awareness about the conditions of Asperger's disease through their telenovela. I remember some weeks back in class we read responses by parents of children who have Asperger's and how having a telenovela with characters like Micaela was so inspiring to their families. But now understanding a little more context from the writer's position of governmental restraints, I see the abilities of these writers from an even deeper perspective. I guess what I mean is that they probably felt a threat to their freedom of expression if they wrote anything that puts the government in a bad light. But despite those restraints they were able to use their platform to address other issues.

And a student named Ashley summed up the whole telenovela experience as effectively as any trained media observer:

> From Cote de 'Ivoire [*sic*] to Cuba and Canada to Colombia, with men and women, rich and poor, old and young. Telenovelas simply appeal to a wider range of people than most mainstream entertainment media. So a message presented in a telenovela will, hypothetically, reach a wider range of people than a message presented in some other form of mainstream entertainment media.

Students are not immune to the traditional dichotomy between "high" and "low" culture. One student relates how she was dining with some of her parents' friends, when one, a professor, asked her how she could be studying something so "strange" for class credit. She simply replied that she had learned more about Latin American culture from the class than from any "old" literature or grammar class.

Telenovelas, as she aptly entitled her blog post, are a "window" to Latin American society.

A Window: Continuing Conversations

During a recent theatre performance in Boston of *Mala* by Cuban-American actress Melinda Lopez that deals with the subject of getting old and death, Lopez mentioned how her mother watched telenovelas frequently. At a post-theatre discussion, an audience member asked Lopez how to broach the subject of final health directives with his elderly parents. She responded that he could begin by talking about having gone to the play; I couldn't help thinking that her words of advice had been inspired by conversations discussing telenovelas with her mother.

Like the students in Acosta-Alzuru's class, telenovela viewers not only engage passively with what they are viewing, but also yearn to communicate with others—sometimes subjects that are not easily broached, but sometimes the mere sharing of a common experience.

Martín-Barbero stressed in several of his works that the pleasure to be encountered in watching telenovelas did not take place just in the moment of sitting in front of the television, but in the subsequent discussion with the family, in the office, in the neighborhood and among friends.

Jorge A. González, a professor at the National Autonomous University in Mexico, calls telenovelas "one of the most important symbolic forms used in everyday life."

He carried out ten months of detailed ethnographic research on telenovela watching.

González observed:

> One of the most important findings both in the survey and in the ethnography was that the cultural experience of the telenovelas does not "begin" with the episode and does not end with the conclusion of the single daily showing. All the evidence points towards an *extended universe* of telenovelas.

For one thing, it's the men, as well as the women, who are doing this communicating. He found that 40 percent of the men observed admitted to watching telenovelas, and that the 60 percent who said they didn't were familiar with the plots.[36]

Ana B. Uribe, another Mexican telenovela scholar, points out that watching telenovelas both serves as a structuring activity for the family, usually after dinner, or as background noise while performing other tasks, usually a bit earlier.

> [M]embers of the family use television to create social practices, to reinforce roles at home, and as a way to facilitate conversation through what is seen on the screen; the audience uses the stories, its characters and themes to increase physical contact [by watching together], family solidarity and conflict reduction.[37]

Obitel in its 2012 yearbook discussed how the world of telenovelas extends far beyond the living room screen:

> The telenovela begins to be commented even while it is being watched. It is discussed in every home, with the husband, the mother, the children, the domestic help, with the neighbors, friends, at the work place. Telenovelas

are commented by magazines specialized in commentaries and gossip; in daily newspaper columns, in prestige publications as well as in the popular ones; in the public opinion polls; in the readers' letters to newspapers and magazines; in television and radio programs that broadcast with telenovela actors, and in humoristic programs where they are satirized.[38]

The yearbook comments that music in the form of CDs from specially composed soundtracks, clothes and jewelry popularized by the telenovelas and even furniture and cars work their way into daily life through a merchandising circuit, becoming visible symbols that one is also watching the same telenovela.

Discussion of telenovelas actually seems to be increasing. While in 2012, Obitel focused on family and workplace discussion, by 2014, it was seeing a boom in different forms of discussion (and viewing). The so-called second screen, cell phones and tablets, are becoming means to extend the conversations beyond one's immediate friends and family, a trend Obitel calls "social television." Obitel cites a 2013 Nielsen study that found 80 percent of people with "second screens" use them to communicate about the programs, sometimes through Twitter, sometimes blogs, sometimes YouTube, sometimes Facebook or websites.[39]

Some telenovela scriptwriters and actors maintain their own blogs. The first to do so in Brazil—and most likely in Latin America—was Aguinaldo Silva, the journalist scriptwriter of the 2007 telenovela *Duas Caras* (Two Faces), which deals with controversial race issues. He reported that his blog received 700 comments per post, with readers looking at the blog more than 130,000 times daily while the show was running.[40]

"The trend of integrating social media to television is on the rise, so that TV channels are encouraging users' participation, for which they establish hashtags in the programs or advertisements for the programs," the 2014 report observes. It gives the example of Ecuavisa, an Ecuadoran television network, which hosts "Zona Tuitera" (Twitterers' Zone) and uses several social media accounts to preview 40-second scenes from episodes both on television and YouTube.

Viewers are not always watching on television either; some watch the programs on their cell phones or tablets, others on computers. There are also viewers who watch (or binge watch) through sources such as Netflix or Hulu. And an enormous quantity of telenovelas—both old and almost current—have found a home on YouTube.

This means that young people are becoming more involved in the viewing of telenovelas and their discussion. Magazines, such as *TVyNovelas*, which focuses entirely on telenovelas, have a substantial presence on the web with an abundance of videos and photos. Readers get a chance to vote for their favorite actors and actresses, their favorite telenovelas, even their favorite villains.

Brazilian's TV Globo created a frenzy—fueled by the social media—when it released a sticker album "Fifty Years of Telenovelas" in 2015 for Globo's 50th anniversary. Obitel observed that the release of the album "sparked a veritable collecting fever among fans."[41]

The reception of telenovelas, whether in the living room or through Twitter, might start with gossip, but most telenovela experts say the conversations don't stop there.

The 2013 Obitel report sums up this tendency:

> [T]he debate that telenovelas encourage in society brings to the surface important issues that are not always dealt with in other television programs or even other media. This scenario highlights the social role of fiction as an instance of public debate and of representation of national identity.

And it adds,

> Television is a powerful instrument to narrate the past and influence the way of thinking of the public, especially through the telenovela, which is considered a cultural phenomenon in Latin America. The telenovela, as a popular genre, creates a public space to share a nation's experiences and discussions.... [R]epresentation of telenovelas tends to draw a parallel between social and political realities. In this way, themes acquire importance and start to influence audiences, since ... living the nation through the telenovela is a concrete possibility.[42]

Whether it's thinking about race, gender, class or even the impact of drug trafficking, telenovelas open the door for conversation. The medium may have changed over the years—from living room and water fountain chats to Twitter and blogs—but the message provokes a discussion about social change.

Notes

1 I first wrote about telenovelas in the July 26, 1986, issue of the *Wall Street Journal*. They have been a fascination for me ever since.
2 Glenn Garvin, "Fidel Castro Is Dead: How will history remember Fidel Castro?" *Miami Herald*, November 16, 2016, www.miamiherald.com/news/nation-world/world/americas/fidel-castro-en/article117186483.html.
3 E-mail response to author request by Juana Uribe, March 24, 2015.
4 Diana L. Ríos and Mari Castañeda, eds., *Soap Operas and Telenovelas in a Digital Age: Global Industries and New Audiences* (New York: Peter Lang, 2011).
5 Jesús Martín-Barbero, *Communication, Culture and Hegemony: From the Media to Mediations*, Translated by Elizabeth Fox and Robert A. White (London: Sage, 1994), 113.
6 Ibid., 112.
7 Nico Vink, *Telenovela and Emancipation: A Study on TV and Social Change in Brazil* (Amsterdam: Royal Tropical Institute, 1988), 23.
8 José Ignacio Cabrujas, *Y latinoamérica inventó la telenovela* (Caracas, Venezuela: Alfadil Ediciones, 2002), 135. My translation.
9 Valerio Fuenzalida, *Televisión y Cultura Cotidiana: La influencia social de la TV percibida desde la cultura cotidiana de la audiencia* (Santiago, Chile: Corporación de Promoción Universitaria, 1997), 127.

10 Thomas Tufte, *Living With the Rubbish Queen: Telenovelas, Culture and Modernity in Brazil* (Luton, England: University of Luton Press, 2000), 82.

11 Arvind Singhal and Everett M. Rogers, *Entertainment-Education: A Communications Strategy for Social Change* (Mahwah, NJ: Lawrence Erlbaum Associates, 1999), 35.

12 Esther Hamburger, "Politics and Intimacy in Brazilian Telenovelas," (unpublished dissertation, University of Chicago, 1999), 81. Professor Hamburger was a 2015–16 Peggy Rockefeller Visiting Scholar at the David Rockefeller Center for Latin American Studies, working on an entirely different project. We spent much time discussing telenovelas. She generously shared her thesis with me, and it was a while before I realized she had an ample amount of published material on the subject.

13 Frank J. Lechner and John Boli, eds., *Globalization and Media* (West Sussex, England: Wiley Blackwell, fifth edition, 2015), 380.

14 Yeidy M. Rivero, *Broadcasting Modernity: Cuban Commercial Television, 1950–1960* (Durham, NC: Duke University Press, 2015), 127.

15 El Perro, "Simplemente María, la novela que conquistó América en 1970," *Cínicos de Sinope*, http://cinicosdesinope.com/cine-y-series/simplemente-maria-la-novela-que-conquisto-america-en-1970/.

16 Samantha Nogueira Joyce, *Brazilian Telenovelas and the Myth of Racial Democracy* (Lanham, MD: Lexington Books, 2012), 1–17.

17 Paula Andaló, "Love, Tears, Betrayal . . . and Health Messages," *Perspectives in Health Magazine*, the magazine of the Pan American Health Organization, Volume 8, No. 2, 2003, www.populationmedia.org/wp-content/uploads/2008/03/paho-article-on-pmc-perspectives-in-health-magazine-1122003.pdf.

18 TV News Desk, *Broadway World*, "Telemundo Promotes Perla Farias to SVP, Scripted Development," www.broadwayworld.com/bwwtv/article/Telemundo-Promotes-Perla-Farias-to-SVP-Scripted-Development-20160504.

19 "Episode 722: The New Telenovela," *Planet Money: NPR.* www.npr.org/sections/money/2016/08/31/492123182/episode-722-the-new-telenovela, August 31, 2016. Also see: Jasmine Garsd, "Former Telenovela Actress Changed Landscape of Spanish-Language TV," September 5, 2016, www.npr.org/2016/09/05/492674813/former-telenovela-actress-changed-landscape-of-spanish-language-tv.isten.

20 The first thing I tell my journalism students is "Don't rely on Wikipedia as a source," so this is not a source! I just loved that the online encyclopedia referred to the series as an "American telenovela." https://en.wikipedia.org/wiki/Desire_(TV_series).

21 Anna Marie de la Fuente, "Hugo Chavez Drama Series 'El Comandante' Set at Sony Pictures TV Latin America," May 9, 2016, http://variety.com/2016/tv/news/hugo-chavez-el-comandante-andres-parra-drama-series-1201769203/.

22 Samantha Nogueira Joyce, *Brazilian Telenovelas and the Myth of Racial Democracy* (Lanham, MD: Lexington Books, 2012), 10.

23 Open Culture, "Gabriel García Márquez Describes the Cultural Merits of Soap Operas, and Even Wrote the Script for One," September 28, 2015, www.openculture.com/2015/09/gabriel-garcia-marquez-describes-the-cultural-merits-of-soap-operas.html.

24 Gene H. Bell-Villada, *Conversations with Gabriel García Márquez* (Jackson: University Press of Mississippi, 2006), 150.

25 Mauricio Bernal, "Museo Nacional Colombia reconoce con una exposición interés histórico las telenovelas locales," *El Periódico*, February 19, 2010, www.elperiodico.com/es/noticias/internacional/museo-nacional-colombia-reconoce-con-una-exposicion-interes-historico-las-telenovelas-locales-104815. Translation is mine.

26 Ryan Linkof, "The Telenovela in the Art Museum," January 9, 2014, http://unframed.lacma.org/2014/01/09/the-telenovela-in-the-art-museum/.

27 Omar Rincón, "Telenovela," *Avianca en revista*, December 2015, 146.

28 Jesús Martín-Barbero, *De los medios a las mediaciones: Comunicación, cultura y hegemonía* (México, DF: Gustavo Gili, 1987), 244. Translation is mine; the italics are his.

29 O. Hugo Benavides, *Drugs, Thugs, and Divas: Telenovelas and Narco-Dramas in Latin America* (Austin: University of Texas Press, 2008), 10.
30 Jesús Martín-Barbero, *Communication, Culture and Hegemony* (London: Sage), 1993a, cited in Thomas Tufte, *Living with the Rubbish Queen: Telenovelas, Culture and Modernity in Brazil* (Luton, UK: University of Luton Press, 2000), 7.
31 Nora Mazziotti, *Telenovela: industria y prácticas sociales, Enciclopedia Latinoamericana de Sociocultura y Comunicación* (Bogotá: Grupo Editorial Norma, 2006), 24.
32 América Latina Portal Europeo, "Jornadas Telenovela. ¿Cultura sentimental latinoamericana?" March 23–31, 2009, www.red-redial.net/america-noticia-3039.html.
33 Maria Immacolata Vassallo de Lopes and Guillermo Orozco Gómez, eds., *(Re)Invention of TV Fiction Genres and Formats*, Ibero-American Observatory for Television Fiction (Obitel) 2016 Yearbook (Porto Alegre, Brazil: Editorial Sulina, 2016), 16.
34 Acosta-Alzuru, Carolina. "Telenovelas." http://telenovelas-carolina.blogspot.com/.
35 All the quotes from students are published on http://telenovelasfall2016.blogspot.com/, the class blog for Carolina Acosta-Alzuru's class on telenovelas at the University of Georgia. The blog—and those from previous years—make for fascinating reading because one can see the development of the students' knowledge and their increased identification with the telenovela they have chosen to follow in the course of the semester.
36 Jorge González, "Understanding Telenovelas as a Cultural Front," in Ilan Stavans, ed., *Telenovelas* (The Ilan Stavans Library of Latino Civilization, Santa Barbara, CA: Greenwood, 2010), 73–74.
37 Ana B. Uribe, *Mi México imaginado: Telenovelas, Televisión y Migrantes* (Colima, Mexico: El Colegio de la Frontera Norte, 2009), 233.
38 Maria Immacolata Vassallo de Lopes and Guillermo Orozco Gómez, eds., *Transnationalization of Television Fiction in Ibero-American Countries*, Ibero-American Observatory for Television Fiction (Obitel) 2012 Yearbook (Porto Alegre, Brazil: Editorial Sulina, 2012), 8.
39 Maria Immacolata Vassallo de Lopes and Guillermo Orozco Gómez, eds., *Transmedia Production Strategies in Television Fiction*, Ibero-American Observatory of Television Fiction (Obitel) 2014 Yearbook (Porto Alegre, Brazil: Editorial Sulina, 2014), 163.
40 Aguinaldo Silva, *Deu no Blogdo* (Rio de Janeiro: Blogbooks Editora, 2010), cited in Tania Cantrell Rosas-Moreno, *News and Novela in Brazilian Media: Fact, Fiction, and National Identity* (Lanham, MD: Lexington Books, 2014), 7.
41 Maria Immacolata Vassallo de Lopes and Guillermo Orozco Gómez, eds., *(Re)Invention of TV Fiction Genres and Formats*, Ibero-American Observatory for Television Fiction (Obitel) 2016 Yearbook (Porto Alegre, Brazil: Editorial Sulina, 2016), 82.
42 Maria Immacolata Vassallo de Lopes and Guillermo Orozco Gómez, eds., *Gender Relations in Television Fiction*, Ibero-American Observatory for Television Fiction (Obitel) 2013 Yearbook (Porto Alegre, Brazil: Editorial Sulina, 2013), 53.

Bibliography

Acosta-Alzuru, Carolina. "Telenovelas." (blog) http://telenovelas-carolina.blogspot.com/.
Acosta-Alzuru, Carolina. "Telenovelas, Culture & Society." (class blog) http://telenovelas fall2016.blogspot.com.
Álvarez, Valentina. *Lágrimas a pedido: así se escribe una telenovela*. Caracas, Venezuela: Editorial Alfa, 2007.
Andaló, Paula. "Love, Tears, Betrayal . . . and Health Messages." *Perspectives in Health Magazine*, 8, no. 2, 2003. www.populationmedia.org/wp-content/uploads/2008/03/paho-article-on-pmc-perspectives-in-health-magazine-1122003.pdf.

Bell-Villada, Gene H. *Conversations With Gabriel García Márquez*. Jackson, Mississippi: University Press of Mississippi, 2006.

Benavides, O. Hugo. *Drugs, Thugs, and Divas: Telenovelas and Narco-Dramas in Latin America*. Austin: University of Texas Press, 2008.

Bernal, Mauricio. "Museo Nacional Colombia reconoce con una exposición interés histórico las telenovelas locales." *El Periódico*, February 19, 2010. www.elperiodico.com/es/noticias/internacional/museo-nacional-colombia-reconoce-con-una-exposicion-interes-historico-las-telenovelas-locales-104815.

Brooks, Peter. *The Melodramatic Imagination: Balzac, Henry James, Melodrama, and the Mode of Excess*. New Haven and London: Yale University Press, 1976.

Cabrujas, José Ignacio. *y latinoamérica inventó la telenovela*. Caracas, Venezuela: Alfadil Ediciones, 2002.

Fuenzalida, Valerio. *Televisión y Cultura Cotidiana: La influencia social de la TV percibida desde la cultura cotidiana de la audiencia*. Santiago, Chile: Corporación de Promoción Universitaria, 1997.

Garvin, Glenn. "Fidel Castro is Dead: How Will History Remember Fidel Castro?" *Miami Herald*, November 16, 2016. www.miamiherald.com/news/nation-world/world/americas/fidel-castro-en/article117186483.html.

Hamburger, Esther. *Politics and Intimacy in Brazilian Telenovelas*. Unpublished dissertation, University of Chicago, 1999.

Joyce, Samantha Nogueira. *Brazilian Telenovelas and the Myth of Racial Democracy*. Lanham, MD: Lexington Books, 2012.

Lechner, Frank J., and John Boli, eds. *Globalization and Media*. West Sussex, England: Wiley Blackwell, fifth edition, 2015.

Martín-Barbero, Jesús. *De los medios a las mediaciones: Comunicación, cultura y hegemonía*. México, DF: Gustavo Gili, 1987.

Martín-Barbero, Jesús. *Communication, Culture and Hegemony: From the Media to Mediations*. Translated by Elizabeth Fox and Robert A. White. London: Sage, 1993.

Martín-Barbero, Jesús. *Oficio de cartógrafo: Travesías latinoamericans de la comunicación en la cultura*. Mexico, DF and Santiago, Chile: Fondo de Cultura Ecónomica, 2002.

Mazziotti, Nora. *Telenovela: industria y prácticas sociales, Enciclopedia Latinoamericana de Sociocultura y Comunicación*. Bogotá: Grupo Editorial Norma, 2006.

National Public Radio. "Episode 722: The New Telenovela." *Planet Money: NPR*, August 31, 2016.

Open Culture. "Gabriel García Márquez Describes the Cultural Merits of Soap Operas, and Even Wrote the Script for One." September 28, 2015. www.openculture.com/2015/09/gabriel-garcia-marquez-describes-the-cultural-merits-of-soap-operas.html.

Rincón, Omar. "Telenovela." *Avianca en revista*, December 2015.

Ríos, Diana L., and Mari Castañeda, eds. *Soap Operas and Telenovelas in a Digital Age: Global Industries and New Audiences*. New York: Peter Lang, 2011.

Rivero, Yeidy M. *Broadcasting Modernity: Cuban Commercial Television, 1950–1960*. Durham, NC: Duke University Press, 2015.

Rosas-Moreno, Tania Cantrell. *News and Novela in Brazilian Media: Fact, Fiction, and National Identity*. Lanham, MD: Lexington Books, 2014.

Singhal, Arvind, and Everett M. Rogers. *Entertainment-Education: A Communication Strategy for Social Change*. Mahway, NJ: Lawrence Erlbaum Associates, 1999.

Stavans, Ilan, ed. *Telenovelas*. The Ilan Stavans Library of Latino Civilization, Santa Barbara, CA: Greenwood, 2010.

Tufte, Thomas. *Living With the Rubbish Queen: Telenovelas, Culture and Modernity in Brazil.* Luton, England: University of Luton Press, 2000.

Uribe, Ana B. *Mi México imaginado: Telenovelas, televisión y migrantes.* Colima, Mexico: El Colegio de la Frontera Norte, 2009.

Vassallo de Lopes, Maria Immacolata, and Guillermo Orozco Gómez, eds. *Transnationalization of Television Fiction in Ibero-American Countries,* Ibero-American Observatory of Television Fiction (Obitel) 2012 Yearbook. Porto Alegre, Brazil: Editorial Sulina, 2012.

Vassallo de Lopes, Maria Immacolata, and Guillermo Orozco Gómez, eds. *Social Memory and Television in Ibero-American Countries,* Ibero-American Observatory of Television Fiction (Obitel) 2013 Yearbook. Porto Alegre, Brazil: Editorial Sulina, 2013.

Vassallo de Lopes, Maria Immacolata, and Guillermo Orozco Gómez, eds. *Transmedia Production Strategies in Television Fiction,* Ibero-American Observatory of Television Fiction (Obitel) 2014 Yearbook. Porto Alegre, Brazil: Editorial Sulina, 2014.

Vassallo de Lopes, Maria Immacolata, and Guillermo Orozco Gómez, eds. *(Re)Invention of TV Fiction Genres and Formats,* Ibero-American Observatory of Television Fiction (Obitel) 2016 Yearbook. Porto Alegre, Brazil: Editorial Sulina, 2016.

Vink, Nico. *Telenovela and Emancipation: A Study on TV and Social Change in Brazil.* Amsterdam: Royal Tropical Institute, 1988.

2

CHANGE AGENTS

Beyond the Melodrama

A friend of mine returned from Mexico, where she had been studying Spanish for six months. She reported that she had watched telenovela after telenovela to improve her command of the language, adding, "Telenovelas are sure the opiate for the masses. What a good way to keep people's minds off of Mexico's problems."

I found a strange echo of her words in those of Emilio Azcárraga Milmo, the Televisa television magnate known as "El Tigre" (The Tiger). Celebrating the runaway success of the Mexican telenovela *Los ricos también lloran* (The Rich Also Cry), he declared,

> Mexico is a country of a very screwed over humble class, who are never going to stop being screwed over. It's an obligation of television to bring entertainment to those people and take them away from their sad reality and difficult future.[1]

In other words, as my friend noted, "the opiate of the masses."

Yet since telenovelas began in the 1950s, they have offered a vehicle for social change, both deliberate and unconscious. Telenovelas offer models of patterns of behavior. They allow their viewers to identify with them and sometimes to firmly reject what they are seeing. They provide images of change, of possible social mobility. They show the viewers in the depth of the countryside what the big cities look like, and they offer city dwellers a sense of the countryside and its problems. They show small families and successful women. They put issues on the table that people don't generally talk about. They teach about history; they connect nations and consolidate identities.

And they also sometimes offer deliberate messages, intended to change behavior or to cause viewers to participate in society in a particular way. I was surprised to learn that the origin of these deliberate messages—despite the words of Emilio Azcárraga Milmo—was Mexico's Televisa.

Miguel Sabido, who was vice president for research at Televisa in the 1970s, invented the methodology of imparting prosocial values in a system known as entertainment-education.

"The key to Sabido's methodology is 'change,'" notes Samantha Nogueira Joyce.

> Characters may first be presented as having the opposite qualities and actions of what is being taught, but as time passes and the plot turns, they come to see the value of the program's underlying message such as safe sex, issues involving AIDS, abortion, family planning, domestic violence, racism and literacy, all in a nonthreatening and even enlightening manner.[2]

Sabido developed a series of telenovelas that incorporated prosocial messages. The first of these telenovelas was first aired in November 1975 and continued until December 10, 1976, in 280 half-hour episodes. *Ven conmigo* (Come with Me) promoted the Mexican literacy program. Silvia Derbez, a well-known telenovela star, plays Caridad, a middle-aged single schoolteacher in a rural area. The government is planning a literacy campaign and contracts Caridad to promote the campaign. The telenovela centers on a series of love stories involving Caridad's former fiancé, who abandoned her to marry a rich woman, and Carlos, an Education Ministry official who woos her, plus secondary love interests with problems of their own. The program was so successful that almost one million Mexicans enrolled in the state literacy program.

Arvind Singhal and Everett Rogers recount that Sabido had initially tried a more didactic approach with *Ven conmigo* than the melodramatic web of love stories. Indeed, the first episodes attempted to teach adults to read and write. Then the focus was switched to a dozen students enrolled in an adult literacy class, along with the accompanying love story. Citing a 1981 report from Televisa's Institute for Communication Research, Singhal and Rogers note that average ratings rose to 33 percent, higher than Televisa's other telenovelas at the time.[3]

After each episode, an epilogue provided both inspiration and practical information such as the address of the Education Ministry, where pamphlets about the literacy program could be obtained.

The popularity of the telenovela occasionally backfired; literacy students and those interested in the program caused Mexico City gridlock until well after midnight on one single day when 25,000 students converged on the address provided in the telenovela to pick up their literacy materials.

Sabido's second telenovela, *Acompáñame* (Accompany Me), which aired for nine months between August 1977 and April 1978, encouraged family planning and was said to have contributed to a decline in Mexican birthrate. The telenovela relates the story of three sisters and their respective marriages.

The Mexican government's national population council (CONAPO) reported that phone calls to the agency requesting family planning information zoomed from nothing to an average of 500 calls monthly. Many callers said they had been encouraged by watching the telenovelas.

Following up on a suggestion in *Acompáñame*, more than 2,000 women signed up as volunteers in the national family program. According to CONAPO, contraceptive sales rose 23 percent in one year, compared to a 7 percent increase the previous year. In addition, more than 560,000 women enrolled in family planning clinics, an increase of 33 percent from the previous year.

During the decade 1977 to 1986, Mexico experienced a 34 percent decline in its population growth rate. As a result, in May 1986, the United Nations Population Prize was awarded to Mexico as the most successful nation in the world in achieving population control.

Thomas Donnelly, then with the U.S. government agency USAID in Mexico, wrote,

> Throughout Mexico, wherever one travels, when people are asked where they heard about family planning, or what made them decide to practice family planning, the response is universally attributed to one of the soap operas that Televisa has done. . . . The Televisa family planning soap operas have made the single most powerful contribution to the Mexican population success story.

The third telenovela with an incorporated social message was *Vamos juntos* (Let's Go Together), aired between July 1979 and April 1980, which addressed responsible parenthood. The series was sponsored by the U.S. Department of Education and hosted by the well-known television hostess María Elena Salinas of U.S.-based Univision. *El Combate* (The Combat), the fourth in the series (1980), again focused on adult education. And the fifth telenovela, *Caminemos* (Let's Walk Together) (1980), promoted both family planning and sex education for adolescents, including the use of condoms. In a conservative Mexican society, with an equally conservative Roman Catholic Church, parents were not likely to talk to their children about such delicate subjects; the telenovela provided a way to approach the topic or for teens to learn on their own. A sixth telenovela, in 1981, *Nosotras las mujeres* (We the Women), aimed to provide role models to counter machismo and to make women aware of their important role in family and society. Later, *Los hijos de nadie* (Nobody's Children), made in conjunction with UNICEF in 1997, put the spotlight on homeless children, creating role models to change opinion and create awareness.[4]

The method of inserting messages into telenovela plots became very popular, adopted by both U.S. and international agencies, as well as Mexican television. In 2005, the Population Media Center, a non-governmental organization based in the United States, and the UNFPA, the United Nations Family Planning Agency, actually developed an 88-page guide entitled "Soap Operas for Social Change to Prevent HIV/AIDS: A Training Guide for Journalists and Media Personnel," edited by Kriss Barker and Miguel Sabido himself.

In that document, Sabido provides a user-friendly explanation of what his method is all about.

> [T]he most important element of entertainment-education is entertainment. Without entertainment, the program will have little or no audience—nor the emotional bonding by audience members with characters that leads to meaningful behaviorial change. The entertainment element should account for about 70 percent of the story. The methodology I created (which has become known as the "Sabido methodology") uses two of three subplots in a long-running serial drama to create entertainment—through changes in fortune, use of a range of human emotions, cliffhangers, compellingly well-written drama, strong acting, realistic productions, and the "appropriate" tone of the drama. The story can be boy-meets-girl or rags-to-riches (or whatever the producer and scriptwriters agree upon). The other 30 percent should be devoted to the "third plot" with the social content and the role models for behavior we are trying to teach/reinforce.[5]

The guide indicates that since the 1980s, the entertainment-education strategy has been used to convey health messages about family planning, HIV/AIDS, teenage pregnancy and other health-related issues in more than two hundred programs in fifty countries throughout the world. It also points out that the Sabido methodology does not just involve inserting a social message into a melodrama; there's serious social science research, focus groups, pretesting of pilot episodes, the establishment of advisory committees and technical review committees, monitoring and impact evaluation.[6]

Samantha Noguera Joyce observes,

> Sabido saw telenovelas as the perfect vehicle for social transformation due to several reasons. He believed that the emotional tone of the genre could be used to teach the audience certain social behaviors—adult literacy, family planning and to fight against poverty.
>
> One key aspect of his method is the prolonged exposure day after day for several months. . . . Sabido asserts that the format of the [telenovelas] as opposed to the soap operas, with a clearly defined beginning, middle, and end, provides the opportunity to tie in as well as to expand the needed infrastructure services (for example, a family planning clinic). Furthermore, the format makes it possible to connect the audience with infrastructure services in short epilogues at the end of every episode, in order to convey important information to the public. And finally, since the telenovela format is a reflection on what is good and bad in society, it is easy to add characters

for identification by the audience individuals and groups, so they can learn social behavior change without harming audience ratings. Telenovelas are after all a highly commercial enterprise by nature.[7]

Sabido, who began developing his methodology in the 1950s as a theatre director, said he got his inspiration from the 1967 Peruvian telenovela *Simplemente María* (Simply María), which tells the story of a peasant girl who comes from the Andean mountains to work as a maid. She ends up becoming literate and learning how to sew—eventually transforming into a high-end fashion designer. A throng of maids and lower-class women began to learn how to sew and to purchase sewing machines, so much that the Singer Sewing Company actually gave a gold sewing machine to the leading actress. The maids also started to ask their employers for the right to attend night school. Perhaps the social message was not intentional, but it worked: social mobility could be a reality if one studied and learned a trade.[8]

The telenovela ignited the public imagination, not only in Peru, but throughout Spanish-speaking Latin America. Long before the Internet, blogs and Twitter, thousands of fans wrote letters to their favorite characters. Vlado Radovich, the executive producer of *Simplemente María*, said that the letters were generally not sent to the television station, but to a barbershop shown by accident in one of the outdoor scenes. The network began to list the barbershop address (with the owner's permission) in the credits of each episode "so people would see the telenovela and know to send their letters to Yataco's place." The owner of the barbershop eventually opened up a chain of barbershops called "Simplemente María."[9]

Another influence leading to the inclusion of social messages in telenovelas may have been the long tradition of product placement in telenovelas. A leading actress is seen drinking a Coca-Cola; a handsome actor is riding in a Chevrolet; the rising star is using a certain brand of makeup. The practice of using certain products for a fee is common in both Latin America and the United States and is an additional financial resource to offset production costs. For example, in the last episodes of the Brazilian telenovela *Império*, a soda can with the name of a central character was thrown from a distance to distract the bad guy—a scene that was intensely commented upon on Twitter. It's not that different to use role models to entice viewers to use a specific product as to use the same role models to influence behavior.[10]

The Sabido methodology has percolated north. Telemundo, for example, entered into a partnership with the U.S. Census Bureau to promote the 2010 census in the telenovela *Más Sabe el Diablo* (The Devil Knows Best). The protagonist Pela Beltrán gets a census job, and the telenovela integrates information about the importance of the census while following Pela's daily life.[11]

It's yet another example of how Latin American telenovelas—whether it be their melodrama or their messages—filter from the periphery to the center, influencing the U.S. television industry and changing it. The influence also spreads from the largest countries with strong telenovela industries to other Latin American countries and beyond. The impact of the Sabido methodology gives a concrete way of noting that influence.

Even the smallest countries have been influenced by this methodology. Nicaragua, which has virtually no telenovela industry, developed an extremely popular series aimed at youth, *Sexto sentido* (Sixth Sense). A non-governmental organization called Puntos de Encuentro (Meeting Places) "not only succeeded in producing the first Nicaraguan telenovela . . . but it was a tremendous success," observes Thomas Tufte.[12]

The telenovela revolves around the lives of teenagers and preteens who face situations like family conflicts, first love, unwanted pregnancies and the pressure of friends to consume alcohol and drugs.[13]

According to the telenovela's website, "The idea for the series is to give youth tools with which to take control of their lives." Amy Bank, who created the telenovela along with Virginia Lacayo, the show's co-producer, was quoted as saying,

> Take control of your life. This means breaking taboos, questioning stereotypes, communicating, seeking support networks and problem solving individually and collectively—all of which the show does and encourages its viewers to do by addressing such complex issues as sexual orientation, rape, abortion and domestic violence in the context of a predominantly Catholic country that is the second poorest in the hemisphere. . . . For most Nicaraguans, television is their window to the world.[14]

With the exception of tallying up sales figures for telenovela distribution research, this type of window to the world—both the Sabido method and its social merchandising offshoots—may be the most quantitatively examined aspects of telenovelas. For example, the Inter-American Development Bank (IDB) did a case study on the impact of telenovelas on the divorce rate in Brazil. Divorce rates in Brazil, according to 2007 United Nations statistics, had increased from 3.30 per 100 marriages in 1984 to 17.7 in 2002, "a steeper trend than in comparable Latin American countries," according to the IDB.[15]

The report noted that telenovelas

> transmit new values and ideas to society. In addition to the fight for freedom, recurrent themes included criticisms of religious and traditional values, an appreciation of high standards of living and of "modern" lifestyles, female emancipation, adultery and criticisms of machismo.

The IDB performed content analysis on nine telenovelas from 1965 to 2004, and recorded variables for each of the main female characters, whether she was separated or divorced and whether she was faithful to her partner. The IDB found that while separation and divorce did not figure in the plots until the mid-1970s, an average of 20 percent of the main characters were divorced or separated in telenovelas between 1975 and 1984, when divorce was legalized in Brazil. Divorce was not seen as a negative trend, breaking up a family, but rather representing the woman's right to emancipation and not to be stuck with an abusive husband or an unsatisfactory relationship.[16]

At the annual Advisory Committee meeting of the David Rockefeller Center for Latin American Studies (where I work) in 2010, Sandra de Castro Buffington, then director of Hollywood, Health & Society at the Norman Lear Center, USC Annenberg, explained to a crowd of professors, students and wealthy donors how the power of the entertainment media can be used to improve the health and well-being of people worldwide.

She used as an example *Ladrón de corazones* (Thief of Hearts), a 2003 co-production between Telemundo and Argos Communication, which was affiliated at the time with Mexico's TV Azteca. The series, a mix of romance and narconovela, brings up the issue of breast cancer in a subplot. According to de Castro Buffington, viewers learned that radiation therapy is the best treatment following a lumpectomy, but that surgical removal of the breast is recommended in the case of early pregnancy. She added that a study found that identification with the telenovela characters led to viewers telling others about health topics (44%) and calling for information after hearing about a health topic in a telenovela (12%). Information seeking increased dramatically when an 800-number was given after a dramatic episode on cancer, she said. The same pattern was found with Telemundo's *Amarte Así*, which spotlighted diabetes.

Her presentation marked the first time I had ever heard about the deliberate inclusion of social messages in telenovelas, although I had long been intrigued by the power of telenovelas to get people to discuss and perhaps take action on sensitive subjects.

Although telenovelas continue to integrate the Sabido methodology of entertainment-education in Latin America and beyond, social merchandising—which invokes the broader concept of bringing up social issues that hopefully will lead to change—has become the predominant way of introducing these subjects. The most important difference between the entertainment-education method and so-called social merchandising is that the latter is conceived to make money, to be a commercial success, but to integrate socially relevant and often controversial themes in the process.

Chilean media scholar Valerio Fuenzalida talks about the experience of the 1980 telenovela *El milagro de vivir* (The Miracle of Living), which describes two parallel worlds of a high-class private health clinic and a scrappy working-class clinic, following the lives of doctors, nurses and patients. The writers showed the script to health professionals for revisions. They recommended that the telenovela emphasize self-responsibility and self-care, making the working-class clinic dignified and showing less of a "vertical" relationship between doctors and patients and health care workers. The story, in other words, had to be told through "psychological contact" and "a pact of interpretation" between the telenovela and its viewers.

"It's unrealistic to think of an audience that pays concentrated attention to learn from the telenovela like they would in a classroom," writes Fuenzalida. "Or that they would sit with a paper and pencil to jot down concepts, advice or recipes given without any prior warning in the course of the story."

Therefore, Fuenzalida observes, the focus has to be on story-telling that brings about "recognition, identification, projection." The social merchandising—the imparting of a social message—has to depend on viewers' emotional involvement in the narrative, stories that should in some way reflect their daily lives.[17]

The Ibero-American Observatory of Television Fiction (Obitel) considers the issue of social merchandising so important that it includes a section on the subject in each of its annual yearbooks.

Take, for example, the most recent 2016 yearbook, which takes a country-by-country look at the state of television fiction—particularly telenovelas—in 2015. Rather than specific action-oriented messages, telenovelas are daring to start conversations the public generally doesn't talk about. The Brazil report on socio-educative telenovelas airing in 2015 included three—*Império* (Empire), *Babilonia* (The Ambitious Woman) and *O Canto de Sereia* (The Siren's Song)— that addressed gender identity, gay relationships and homophobia. *Alto Astral* (Forever and Ever) took up the issue of prejudice against overweight people; racial intolerance was discussed in *Além do Tempo* (Time after Time), and violence against women in *A Regra do Jogo* (Rules of the Game); according to the Obitel report.[18]

The section in the report on Chile listed two telenovelas that touched on controversial themes: *Pituca sin Lucas* (Fancy Lady without Money), "classism, social inequality, social conventions"; and *Papá a la Deriva* (Dad Adrift), "parenthood, social classes," although Chileans at the same time were watching telenovelas from Mexico, Colombia and Brazil that treated social issues. Perhaps a bit ironically, the Mexico report listed a Chilean telenovela not mentioned in the Chile report as having strong social content: *Amores con trampa*, a Chilean telenovela that is on the ten most-watched list in Mexico, took up the issues of corruption, migration from the country to the city, and poverty.[19]

And in Mexico, *Antes muerta que Lichita* (Anything But Plain) focused on digital literacy and social responsibilty, helping viewers make the transition from analog to digital television; *Pasión y poder* (Passion and Power) examined political and corporate corruption, as well as the issue of social violence; *Que te perdone Díos, Yo no* (Let God Forgive You; I Won't), examined the issues of social violence, racial discrimination and addictions.

It wasn't that 2015 was an unusual year in terms of raising these controversial subjects. The 2014 Obitel Yearbook, which looked at telenovelas from 2013, found that social merchandising appeared in several fictional narratives. For instance, it pointed out that in Argentina—although productions with the highest ratings do not address social issues—telenovelas spurred debate on issues such as fertility treatments, hereditary diseases and environmental contamination connected to the fishing industry. In Brazil, the report said, subjects such as prejudice, social inclusion, adoption of children, women's rights, drug trafficking and same-sex relationships were present in the telenovelas. A popular telenovela in Uruguay, *Histórias de diván*, used its setting in a psychoanalysis practice to deal with issues such as addictions, discovery and acceptance of sexuality, and parent-child relations. The United States also had its share of controversial themes, the report pointed out, in particular the subject of immigration reform, which came up in formats on Univision, Telemundo and TV Azteca.

The report also mentioned—more along the lines of the Sabido methodology— a Mexican educational campaign was created with the slogan "Una Gota de Agua, una Gota de Vida" (A Drop of Water, A Drop of Life) to raise awareness about the importance of care for water. The insertion of these themes in telenovelas had some dramatic results, the report indicates. In Brazil, for example, the telenovela *Salve Jorge*, by addressing human trafficking, contributed to a 1,500 percent increase in the number of complaints against this type of crime, according to the Ministry of Justice. The telenovela was also a compelling experiment with its blend of fiction and reality, according to Obitel. In November 2012, about a month after the launching of the telenovela, the producers began to insert accounts of real-life experiences into the telenovela. The testimonies were also posted as videos on TV Globo's website. For example, João Borges recounts in a halting voice the story of his daughter, Simone, who went to Spain with the promise of a job. She was forced into prostitution and her handlers kept her passport and all her money. Some 15 other Brazilian women were in the same situation with her, the father says. Simone died in Spain in 1996, the same year she left Brazil. TV Globo was proactive in publicizing the plight of the victims of human trafficking through an interactive website known as Disque Salve (Dial Save), which was created in partnership with the NGO Viva Rio, to provide information and answer questions about trafficking and exploitation of people. Viva Rio actually operated Dial Save, training people for the web service and an additional call center. Coordinator Sandro Costa said the project recorded 456 cases in 22 weeks.[20]

A study on the impact of the telenovela observes:

> Therefore, it is clear that there is a transmedia ownership of the theme by the broadcaster, promoting its image as a company by linking social responsibility practices, besides increasing the visibility of their telenovela, guaranteeing an increase in audience.
>
> [T]he broadcaster . . . offered exclusive content viewing on its website, making supplementary materials to the plot available in digital environment, expanding the supply of the theme and extrapolating the television schedule.

Salve Jorge put a previously undiscussed and quite painful subject of human trafficking in the public eye with concrete results.[21]

Throughout Latin America, telenovelas dramatize controversial themes. Telenovelas provide models for different ways of life, as well as creating multiple layers in identity. All of this—sometimes inadvertently—constitutes social merchandising.

However, Brazil is the only country that has an official policy of incorporating this social content into telenovelas. This policy has often sparked concrete action, ranging from marches to organ transplant donations to changes in the law.

TV Globo's official social merchandising program started in the 1990s, although socially conscious programs were aired way before then. For example, *O Espigão* (The Skyscraper), a 1974 telenovela, raised issues about ecology and urban planning.

TV Globo is proud of its social content. On its website, it declares, "Globo's high-standard dramaturgy includes the dissemination of knowledge, the transmission of socio-cultural messages and the incentive for debate and social change."

The company won the Business in the Community Awards for Excellence in 2001, an international and prestigious social responsibility award in the Global Leadership Award category. Globo reports indicate that approximately 12,000 social content scenes have been inserted in its telenovelas since 1995.[22]

The themes are highly varied. In 1996, *O Rei do Gado* (The Cattle King) discussed agrarian reform; *Laços de Família* (Family Ties) in 2000 encouraged bone marrow donation, and the extremely popular 2001 telenovela *O Clone* (The Clone) shone the spotlight on the tragedy of drug use.

The 2003 *Mulheres Apaixonadas* (Women in Love) dealt with elder abuse, domestic violence and death by firearms. The telenovela actually contributed to the passage of three laws, one regarding senior citizens, one on disarmament and the third concerning violence against women. This is certainly one way of measuring concrete change through telenovelas.

Before the passing of the disarmament statute, some 20,000 people—including the entire cast of *Mulheres Apaixonadas*—took to the Copacabana waterfront in Rio de Janeiro to protest in favor of the legislation (in the telenovela, a character had been killed in the upper-class neighborhood of Leblon by a stray bullet). Actors wore T-shirts with the emblem "Brazil without Weapons." The Civilian Police Division of Weapons and Explosives Control organized a mobile station during the protest and collected weapons. The march was filmed and incorporated into the telenovela—reality and fiction mingling once again in the interests of social transformations.

The list of telenovelas incorporating these themes of social change goes on and on: the 2004 *Senhora do Destino* (Lady of Fate) examined adolescent pregnancy; *América* in 2005 dealt with the rights of the visually impaired; *Dua Caras* examined racial prejudice, while the 2007 *Páginas de la Vida* (Pages from Life) looked at Down syndrome.[23]

After the premiere of *Páginas de la Vida*, TV Globo's director Jayme Monjardim declared,

> It is impossible to do a telenovela nowadays without social merchandising. I believe this is intrinsic to the authors of this decade. I think they feel they

have the responsibility of always bringing, somehow, a discussion that can make a difference in changing our country and society.[24]

Testimony about how telenovelas contribute to social change ranges far and wide. In an unpublished 1999 thesis, Brazilian scholar Esther Hamburger notes,

> The widespread common-sense notion [is] that telenovelas influence various kinds of behavior changes—collective and individual, positive and negative. . . . *Body and Soul* was news because it was supposedly responsible for stimulating a rather positive behavior. Motivated by a heart transplant that saved the life of the female protagonist in the beginning of the story, *Veja* magazine interviewed the renowned cardiologist Dr. Zerbini, who confirmed that this telenovela had contributed to an increase in the number of organ donations, especially of heart donations. According to the medical doctor, the telenovela was more effective in persuading people to donate organs than any of the many advertising campaign physicians had tried.[25]

The actress in that telenovela, Danielle Pérez, was tragically murdered in a horrible case of life imitating art. Her mother, Gloria Pérez, a well-known Brazilian scriptwriter, wrote a telenovela about missing children afterwards, perhaps an outlet for her own grief and desire for justice. *Explode Coração* (Heart Explosion) depicts mothers demonstrating in front of the Candelária Church in downtown Rio de Janeiro, the site of a massacre of eight street children by police officers in 1993. The telenovela version of the mothers who search for their missing children aimed and actually did help to reunite some families. According to the Office of Public Safety, the percentage of children found during the broadcast period jumped from 55 percent to 80 percent. *Explode Coração* also makes a plug for non-governmental organizations (NGOs) such as Viva Cazuza in a scene in which the founder, a mother who had lost her pop musician son to AIDS, appears in the organization's playground in one of the telenovela scenes. The 2013 Obitel report remarks, "Considered one of the hallmarks of Brazilian telenovela, social merchandising is a communication strategy that consists of broadcasting social-educative messages embedded in fiction storylines."

As with the earlier Mexican productions developed by Miguel Sabido, international agencies have used the space of telenovelas to promote socially conscious agendas, for example, but sometimes both on- and offscreen. The United Nations Entity for Gender Equality and Empowerment of Women (UN Women) and the International Labour Organization (ILO) developed humanitarian and social campaigns with the actresses Taís Araújo and Malu Galli from the 2012 telenovela *Cheias de charme* (Sparkling Girls) in a campaign for maids' rights.[26]

Like many telenovelas, *Cheias de charme* is about class. It revolves around the story of three maids, three Marias: Maria da Penha, Maria Aparecida (Cida) and Maria do Rosario. Maria da Penha works in the house of a very famous singer, Cheyenne, who physically assaults her after the maid has accidentally burnt her dress while ironing. She goes to the police station to report her employer (something maids in most countries don't dare do). The three maids end up in jail for things they are not really guilty of and meet each other there. One day, on a lark, the three meet at Cheyenne's house while she is out. They dress up in her clothes and create a song, "Vida de Empreguete," which a friend films as a video clip that goes viral. The three form a trio, and soon their fame eclipses Cheyenne's. The story has more sophisticated overtones than *Simplemente María*, but it calls attention to maids' rights and employers' attitudes.

The Brazilian telenovelas have influence way beyond Brazil because they are exported to many other countries in Latin America and beyond. Thus, a telenovela promoting fair treatment of elders, for example, may be seen in Colombia, Argentina and farflung countries at the same time (the Globo website says that the most popular telenovelas have been exported to more than a hundred countries). Other Brazilian telenovelas have inspired remakes in which the Brazilian network sells rights to the script.

But why Brazil?

Samantha Nogueira Joyce may have a fairly succinct answer when she talks about *Duas Caras*, a telenovela dealing with race:

> Telenovelas in Brazil have been traditionally associated with their authors—intellectuals and members of the Brazilian Left—who for the most part were incorporated by TV Globo. The statement seems contradictory due to the capitalist nature of the genre and the socialist-based agenda of their writers, such as Aguinaldo Silva. What emerges from this contradictory scenario is an intellectual context nourished by the memory of oppression, a memory which cannot be understood without referring to the historical commitment of Latin American intellectuals to the people. Additionally, while memory and social consciousness are filtered by the mediation and constraints implied by the production of texts in a particular political and industrial context, leading the texts to bear the trace of a calculation, it also bears the trace of these social networks. It is in this context that we must understand entertainment-education (E-E) interventions, Social Merchandising (SM) and *Duas Caras*.[27]

Scriptwriters help shape history. Just as Valentín Pimstein, the Chilean emigrant in Mexico, could give shape to Miguel Sabido's ideas of education through entertainment, Brazilian writers living through the dictatorship, with a social consciousness forged by hardship, could see and interpret the world through that lens of necessary justice.

Upstairs, Downstairs

At a very elegant cocktail for Harvard Latin American alumni, I decided to chat with an alum from Mexico about telenovelas. "I loved them as a kid," he said with no apparent irony. "I watched *Los ricos también lloran* (The Rich Also Cry) every day with our maid."

Telenovelas are often a shared experience between classes; they are discussed in the kitchen, in the beauty parlor, in the nail salon and on the chauffeured ride to work or school.

Whether it's the maid who learns to sew or the trio of maids that becomes a singing sensation, whether it's a small-town working-class kid who makes it as a formidable drug trafficker or two families from different social classes who inhabit the same neighborhood, telenovelas are all about class.

Through these aspirational tales, telenovelas provide an important vehicle for potential social change—or at least an emerging enlightened way of seeing the world that might lead to social change. As we mentioned before in the Brazilian telenovelas and *Simplemente María*, the telenovelas show people in the lower class that they can move up, that they can have hope for a different future. María moves up through her hard work to become a trendy fashion designer. The three Marias in *Cheias de charme* reach success with their musical trio.

More often, the protagonist is able to move from one class to another through marriage, and telenovelas are often versions of the Cinderella story. And just as often, the character from the lower classes will move to the upper class by reclaiming his or her "real" status in frequent cases of mistaken identity. Thus, Alberto in *Derecho de nacer* (Right to Be Born) discovers that his mother is not his mother, that she rescued him from being killed at birth and raised him as her own. His biological mother belongs to one of the wealthiest families in Mexico, who had him out of wedlock as a teenager.

These archetypal stories of lower-to-upper class provide dreams (and sometimes models) of mobility. It is a powerful message to someone mired in poverty that hope is not impossible. That is why *Simplemente María* spurred thousands of maids to buy sewing machines.

In addition to inspiring the lower classes with dreams of hope, these telenovelas also offer a window onto the worlds of others. Upper-class people watch telenovelas too, and they see poor people portrayed with all their problems and dreams for a better life. Telenovelas humanize people of all classes (and, indeed, villains tend to be people of a higher-class status). Watching a telenovela means that you may see your maid or the person on the street in a different light, as people with stories and independent lives.

Unlike the use of birth control or the divorce rate, these types of attitudinal changes are hard to quantify.

"A significant part of the telenovelas' popularity lies in making the dream of rising in society come true: a dramatic narrative with social conflict, most often leading to social mobility for a principal character," observes telenovela scholar Thomas Tufte. He points out that telenovelas portray what is indeed the reality of Latin American society, sharp class divisions and social tensions, and sometimes actual social conflict. The telenovelas, he says, often stimulate social awareness—and social action. The viewer learns about family relations, gender characteristics and urban life, "thereby becoming a useful resource, enriching and often awareness raising and thought-provoking for the audience." Tufte points to many examples, ranging from the viewers' identification with the passionate emotions of a love-drama through admiration of female role models to the discussion of sensitive issues that take place in everyday life. He concludes by saying that the issues raised in telenovelas "reflect what are significant concerns for many people," and points out that viewers sometimes find the telenovelas more meaningful and pertinent to what they experience in their daily lives than the nightly news programs, which often do not reflect the audience's daily concerns.[28]

Class in Latin America is more entrenched than in the United States, although that is changing. The traditional rigid class system had a large, greatly dispossessed lower class, masses struggling to survive or on the verge of poverty, a small middle class, and a substantial elite class who could go to the universities and travel. In general, you could work hard all your life and never manage to rise to a higher class (although sometimes you might fall into a lower class because of migration or bad business judgment or the melodramatic flourish of being disinherited or switched at birth).

In the urban areas, the rich and poor lived in completely different neighborhoods; the poor went to public schools that barely educated them, if they could manage to go to school at all, and the rich went to elite private schools. There was no mixing of classes, and the only contacts between the classes were the maids, chauffeurs and the people one passed quickly on the street. In the rural areas, there may have been a little more contact with fieldhands and subsistence landowners, but it was pragmatic contact, not emotional contact. You ordered fieldhands around, just as slaves had been ordered around in a previous era; they might ask you for favors, but generally you were not involved in their lives.

I'm writing the previous paragraph in the past tense, although Latin America continues to remain very stratified, with a very small percentage of the population controlling the country's wealth. Today, it's not quite as distant a dream for a poor person to become middle class or wealthy. The reasons are at least threefold. First of all, there's the simple matter of economic development. According to the World Bank, the middle class in Latin America had grown 50 percent by the end of 2012. The World Bank Study found that one out of every three could be considered middle class; the region's poor are also the exact same proportion—30 percent of the population.[29]

And then there's the issue of immigration and the money immigrants send back home. This money—called remittances—is often used for families to build homes, provide for education or to set up a small business back home. The IDB says remittances are at a historical high. In 2015, Mexican immigrants sent $23.6 billion back home—about a third of the remittances in the region. Guatemala came next with $5.5 billion; Colombia received $4 billion. These remittances not only give the families who stayed behind economic support—they also give them a way to imagine a way into the middle class.[30]

Also inspiring an unfortunately realistic dream of class mobility is the drug trade. Whether as a low-level courier or a powerful drug lord, involvement in these illegal activities can rapidly move a person from one class to another. And just from general observation, I'd say that even if a person is not a drug trafficker or remotely involved with the trade, when people observe the ability to move from one class to another, it makes these dreams seem less remote. That factor probably accounts for the success of narconovelas, discussed in another chapter.

In addition to the proliferation of narconovelas, the emergence of a burgeoning middle class has meant more telenovelas with middle class, rather than rich, protagonists. The dream for a poor person now perhaps becomes moving into the middle class—because it seems more realistic—than to dream of mistaken identities or marrying the prince (of course, both kinds of dreams are still possible, which is why both types of telenovelas continue to be produced).

Two examples of these relatively recent middle-class-focused telenovelas are the 2012 *Avenida Brasil* in, obviously, Brazil, and Peru's *Al fondo hay sitio*. In *Avenida Brasil*, named after the long avenue in Rio joining its poorest neighborhoods with its richest, a very successful beauty salon owner decides to move from her poor working-class neighborhood to Ipanema, a ritzy neighborhood on the beach. Instead of the wealthy protagonist being a member of Brazil's elite, he is a rich soccer player. The story employs lots of the traditional telenovela schemes—secret identities, revenge and love—but the focus never shifts from the emerging middle class. The beauty parlor owner eventually returns to her own neighborhood because she enjoys the lifestyle there—but she does not give up her financial success and now middle-class habits.

"The subversive element of this novela is that it places a figure from the emerging middle class in the role formerly occupied by someone from the elite," *Avenida Brasil's* author João Carneiro told the *Financial Times*.

The telenovela, produced by TV Globo, was the first to be based almost entirely on characters from Brazil's strong emerging middle class. About 80 million people watched it during its final episode—more than watch the Super Bowl in the United States. Warnings about possible blackouts were issued by the national energy company because so many were using the grid at the same time.

Middle-class viewers loved the show because, in the words of the *Financial Times*, they "enjoyed having a mirror held up to them, while more affluent viewers revelled in this imagined glimpse of life lower down the pyramid." The newspaper report does not mention it, but poor viewers most likely found the series aspirational (and inspirational), being presented with a more realistic goal of reaching middle-class status and not runaway wealth.[31]

Peru's *Al fondo hay sitio* (There's Room at the Back) puts class front and center. The extremely popular series, which since its debut in 2009 has run four times as long as the average telenovela, centers around two families, the Gonzaleses and the Maldinis. The latter are the wealthiest family in the upper-middle-class neighborhood of the Lomas in Lima, and the Gonzaleses are an upwardly mobile family with peasant traditions from the mountainous province of Ayacucho, who were regarded as middle class in their hometown.

The Gonzaleses have inherited a half-built house in the neighborhood. Not all the neighbors are hostile; the Ferrand family befriends them. Of course, as any Romeo and Juliet telenovela would have it, one of the Maldini sons falls in love with a Gonzales daughter. Fernanda is sent to Boston to study, and Joel ends up in jail. In Boston, Fernanda falls in love with Mike, and they return to Lima together. A network of convoluting romances ensues, and Fernanda and Joel finally get married (but that's not the ending). But despite the plethora of love stories, vengeance plots and intrigues, the telenovela is situated squarely in the middle class: construction managers, lawyers, public relations executives and young professionals. The struggle is one between a wealthy family (but perhaps not that wealthy) and an upwardly mobile family, between the emerging and established classes, between people from the provinces and the city's upper middle class.

Even though the telenovela is still ongoing, there's already one undergraduate thesis on the series. Dahlia Anaís Belounis wrote the 2013 thesis, entitled "Al Fondo Hay Sitio: An Expression of Peruvian Cultural Identity," under the guidance of Guiliana Cassano, who just happens to be Peru's Obitel representative.

Belounis points out how some members of the Gonzales family, among them Doña Nelly and Reyna Pachas, are determined to achieve the Maldinis' status, and one of the ways they wish to do this is to employ maids and not have to go to the open-air market themselves.[32]

"*Al fondo hay sitio* portrays the life of this upwardly mobile class who from the 1990s until today is scaling all the economic stratas, but at the same time suffers a kind of rejection because of the prejudices and stereotypes of society," observes Belounis.

These telenovelas with a middle-class focus spark social transformation in a couple of ways: by increasing the images of social mobility and the possibility of escaping poverty and by giving the middle class a visual sense of belonging, of constructing its own identity.

Beyond the City

Another way in which telenovelas have fostered social change is by creating (or helping to create) national identities. Television came first to the big cities, both because that's where wealth was concentrated to buy the apparatus, but also because electricity and network signals were not readily available in the small towns and countryside. Images in telenovelas tended to reinforce city-centric viewpoints, taking place in large cities.

Although not everyone in Latin America may own a television, practically everyone has access to them, whether it's through watching at a neighbor's house, a local bar, a community center or streaming programs on ubiquitous cell phones.

But long after television permeated the rural areas of Latin America, people for the most part were seeing their protagonists in the capital cities, and city dwellers were not getting a chance to identify characters from different regions of their own countries. There are exceptions, of course; for instance, the 1976 *Escrava Isaura* (Figure 2.1) took viewers from coffee plantations near Rio de Janeiro to the areas surrounding Minas Gerais in the very tip of southeastern Brazil, with its mountains, valleys and extensive fertile lands. The viewers also get a glimpse of a freed slave community in the jungle. This is not São Paulo or Rio.

But more recently, the focus on regions has become commonplace. In Brazil, the 1996 *O Rei do Gado* (The Cattle King) centers on land reform, and takes the viewers to sugar plantations and rural areas. There's even a 1969 Colombian film, *El Candó*, that depicts the isolated mining region on Colombia's Pacific Coast.

However, it wasn't until much later that regionally focused telenovelas became a trend. By 1989, Colombia's RCN network had produced *Azucar* (Sugar), which

FIGURE 2.1 Edwin Luisi and Lucelia Santos in *Escrava Isaura*. *Escrava Isaura*, 1976, Produced by Rede Globo.

takes place in the verdant Cauca Valley in the southwest part of the country. It brings the viewer to the sugar plantations accompanied by the sounds of Afro-Colombian music. The 1994 Colombian telenovela *Café, con aroma de mujer* (Coffee, with the Scent of a Woman) (Figure 2.2) centered around the love of a poor coffee picker and the son of a rich coffee plantation owner. The series shows us about everything there is to do with coffee, from the lush fields where it is harvested to

FIGURE 2.2   Promotional Poster for *Café, con Aroma de Mujer*. *Café, con Aroma de Mujer*, 1993, Creator: Fernando Gaitán, Image: Margarita Rosa de Francisco and Guy Ecker.

International Coffee Association business in London. The heart of the action did not take place in Bogotá or even Medellín, but in the central coffee heartland. Yet, the links between the traditional coffee plantation and the Bogotá-based Cafeteros de Colombia (Colombian Coffee Growers Association) are clearly made: the coffee lands were not being shown to the exclusion of modernity; they were part of modernity and part of the Colombian identity. After the telenovela *Café* aired, the area became a tourist destination, and the Coffee Growers Association promoted a series of guesthouses on actual farms where visitors could stay and get a sense of the rural life. Also, when everyone all over the country is watching the same telenovelas, the regional telenovela allows people in the cities and other regions to recognize their fellow Colombians; it creates a sense of belonging. The issue of pride goes beyond a country's borders. For example, both *Café* and (to a lesser degree) *Azucar* were aired while Colombia was suffering the height of its drug war. Going through immigration in the United States or just about any other country, Colombians and those of us who lived in Colombia suffered stigma, bad jokes and sometimes embarrassing searches. *Café* helped change that external image and project a more positive and charming one. The Univision website, on the occasion of the telenovela's remake, recalls that although Juan Valdéz, the peasant in a typical hat, accompanied by his burro, had been institutionalized as a coffee icon since 1959, "the continental echo of the romance of Sebastián and 'La Gaviota' popularized the belief that coffee was a kind of Colombian gold, part of the national identity and pride."[33]

Café broadcast throughout Latin America. It was even remade in Mexico in a telenovela called *Destilando amor* (Distilling Love) in 2007. The coffee industry became the tequila industry, and the series starred Angélica Rivera, now Mexico's first lady. Like *Café*, it is a regional series, focusing on the agave fields of Jalisco, far from the nation's capital.

Bionovelas (telenovelas that center on biographical themes) also focus on the regional. For instance, the 2015 telenovela *Diomedes, el Cacique de la Junta*, which recounts the life of Diomedes Díaz, the vallenato star from Colombia's northern coast, evokes not only scenes from the tropical desert and nearby ocean, but gives another sense of regional identification through music.

"The telenovela has served to create a televisual 'national' in which the imagined community rallies around specific images of itself," writes Ana M. Lopez.

> Following in the footsteps of radio and cinema, television increasingly makes "living" the nation a tangible and daily possibility. In this mode, the telenovela has become a privileged site for the translation of cultural, geographic, and even political differences into the discourse of nationness.[34]

Telenovelas are projecting the nation, as Lopez observes. And the more they focus on different regions, sometimes quite underserved areas, the more they create a national bond, rather than one that is centered in the country's capital or major cities.

But why include these regional visions in a chapter on social transformations? They allow people from different regions of the country to see themselves, and to see themselves as citizens, as members of a country. Many of the telenovelas with panoramas of a region's beauty create a sense of pride. To be proud of one's country and one's nationality gives a greater sense of belonging and a greater sense of citizenship. And citizens are more prone to make social change, to care about their fellow countrymen and women.

Citizenship, Corruption and Other Timely Topics

Of course, another way of creating citizenship is to create a desire to band together to resolve problems. The first step toward that is talking about the problems. As we mentioned in Chapter 1, telenovelas manage to put on the table subjects that people don't generally talk about.

Obitel co-coordinator Maria Immacolata Vassallo de Lopes has written about the telenovela as a new form of citizenship:

> The [tele]novela is a unique example of how a television media system would be responsible for the emergence of a peculiar public space that in current years diversified and presented itself as a main alternative of personal realization, social inclusion and of power, that is, as a new form of citizenship.[35]

I'd asked a Peruvian friend, a reporter who has covered corruption and drug trafficking issues, about her favorite telenovela. She immediately came up with *O Bem-Amado* (The Well-Beloved), a 1973 Brazilian telenovela, made during a slight opening in the country's military dictatorship. The astonishing piece of work by theatre playwright Alfredo de Freitas Dias Gomes told the story of the fictional small town of Sucupira and its extremely corrupt mayor, Odorico Paraguaçu. He tries to build the city's first public cemetery, and the series is filled with political intrigue as the traditional Latin American political boss tries to make a profit for himself out of nearly everything. The problem is that no one in Sucupira dies. So the mayor tries to have someone killed. He even invites back Zeca Diabo, a well-known bandit, to the town in the hopes he will kill someone.

Dias Gomes explains in his autobiography how he used the telenovela to build a specific representation of the nation:

> In these stories, I always looked for inspiration in political facts, satirizing and criticizing the "system," in a period when censorship did not allow that. *O Bem-Amado* was a small window opened in the big wall of obscurantism built by the military regime. It does not mean that censors did not notice or did not mutilate the texts, but they had some difficulty doing that,

since they were never known for their intelligence. And when they acted, they made their stupidity evident. The novela was already half way through when they prohibited calling Odorico as "colonel." Later, they forbade calling Zeca Diabo as "captain."[36]

Tulane professor Mauro Porto points out how the telenovela provided a humorous satire of the "dictatorship and its megalomanic projects." When General Golbery do Couto e Silva resigned from the government because of disagreements with General-President João Batista de Figueiredo, he actually cited the telenovela, telling journalists, "Don't ask me anything. I have just left Sucupira."

"*O Bem Amado* represents an audacious and brave experiment on the part of TV," concludes Porto. Dias Gomes later wrote another political satire telenovela, *Roque Santeiro*, which was censored in 1975 and eventually broadcast after the dictatorship.[37]

Other scholars of telenovelas in Brazil have pointed to the political impact of *Vale Tudo* (Anything Goes), *Que Rei Sou Eu?* (What King Am I?) and *O Salvador da Pátria* (The Savior of the Country) in setting the stage for the country's first presidential election under the new democracy in 1989. By portraying issues of corruption and mismanagement of the political establishment, they enabled the rise of Fernando Collor de Mello, an obscure governor of a poor state. People yearned for an outsider. Night after night, they saw on their television screens portrayals that the political establishment could not and did not want to solve their problems. Collor campaigned with a platform to modernize and clean up corruption. He won.

In Mexico, a new media network named Argos—in competition with the powerful Televisa—broadcast Mexico's first telenovela dealing with corruption and political assassination, *Nada personal* (Nothing Personal). Mexico was still in shock over three high-profile real-life political assassinations, including the real-life assassinations of a popular Mexican presidential candidate, Luis Donaldo Colosio; a ruling party PRI leader, Francisco Ruiz Massieu, in 1994; and the killing of Cardinal Juan Jesús Posadas Ocampo in 1993.

An early scene in the telenovela shows a fictional Mexican police official, Commander Fernando Gomez, staring down at the body of his best friend, anti-corruption crusader Raul de los Reyes. De los Reyes had been gunned down on a Mexico City street just as he was about to be named Attorney General of the country, a post from which he could really make a difference.

Gomez looks sadly at the body of his friend. But he himself had overseen the entire assassination effort.

"It's nothing personal, brother," Gomez said. "Nothing personal."

The connections to the reality of daily news were often rather apparent in *Nada personal*. Mr. X, a politician who heads up a large drug-trafficking business, could be the double of former President Carlos Salinas de Gortari with his balding head and prominent ears. Gomez's officers torture people and plant evidence in a routine way, while the prosecutor takes great pleasure in persecuting witnesses to Gomez's crimes outside the courtroom.

In addition to being a thrilling detective story, the telenovela provided a vehicle to talk about the issue of corruption. "Society has had three years of not talking about anything else. People are totally convinced that they have been governed by gangsters," Carlos Monsiváis, a cultural critic, told the *Los Angeles Times*.[38]

And then there was the 1992 *Por estas calles* (On These Streets) in Venezuela. Like *Nada personal*, the telenovela broke with the format of the traditional love story to give a realistic view of the impact of corruption on Venezuelans' daily lives.

The telenovela, which tells the story of a corrupt ruler, also gives the viewer an inside look at crime-ridden slums and their problems. The intermittent water supply in poor neighborhoods, for instance, was brought to life when a romantic encounter was cut short by the news that the water was back on, leaving lovers scurrying to fill up barrels. When writing about melodrama, theorist Peter Brooks attributes its popularity to the fact that it insists on the dignity and popularity of the ordinary. *Por estas calles*, with its realistic detail to what happens in everyday life and the effects of political malfeasance, took this statement to a new height.

One viewer wrote, "All the problems of my neighborhood are there. . . . Now I read the newspaper every day to see whom the story is talking about." An unusual feature of *Por estas calles* was that it rapidly incorporated current news headlines into the story.[39]

An article in the magazine *Producto* observed,

> [*Estas calles*] became the communication phenomenon of the latest years: people speak like its characters, admire them, identify with them, suffer with their problems, relate [them] to daily events, and even use the telenovela as a center of information about what goes on in the nation.[40]

Subplots abounded, as with any telenovela, but almost all of the subplots were a form of societal critique. There was a doctor who provoked accidents in order to obtain kidneys to sell them on the organ black market. A police officer rented his gun to gang members in exchange for drugs.

Ibsen Martinez's series caused a furor and occasional admonitions from the Ministry of Communications, but the telenovela was allowed to stay on the air. Franklin Virgüez, one of the lead actors in *Por estas calles*, told an anecdote about encountering former President Carlos Andrés Pérez in New York in the mid-90s.

Pérez was dining with a Venezuelan priest when Virgüez walked into the restaurant with his wife. As the couple was leaving, the former president extended his hand firmly and commented, "You played in a telenovela that did a lot of harm to the country and to me personally." Virgüez recounted that the former president noted he was nervous and told him not to worry, that he had done a good job. Pérez bid farewell to the actor but returned almost immediately to comment that he watched the telenovela.

Carlos Andrés Pérez had been forced to resign from the presidency because of corruption charges on May 20, 1993.

What Pérez did not mention in the conversation was that the day after he resigned on national television, the fictional character Don Chepe—a composite of Pérez and former president Jaime Lusinchi—delivered a similar resignation speech on the telenovela.

Por estas calles is not just an old telenovela that talked about corruption from another era. In the chaos of today's Venezuela, where soap and toilet paper are difficult to obtain and political corruption is rampant, the telenovela is very present on the blogs and web, where it is enjoying an informal rerun. The themes of the telenovela, like shortages and corruption, are relevant today, but the series evokes nostalgia precisely because the show was allowed to stay on the air and evoked democratic discussion.

In today's Venezuela, the government tightly controls the media and the public often fears reprisals for criticizing the state. People look back to a time when they could talk freely. In 2015, four of the telenovela's actors—Carlota Sosa, Francis Romero, Aroldo Betancourt and Roberto Lamarca—got together to discuss the impact of the telenovela 23 years after its creation. The four actors agreed that they missed the freedom they enjoyed two decades ago to give voice to those without a voice.

"The telenovela helped Venezuelans be aware and to lose their fear about speaking out," said Roberto Lamarca.[41]

These telenovelas from Brazil, Mexico and Venezuela are just a sample of the genre that foments political awareness and takes on issues like corruption and inefficiency. Sometimes the critiques are woven into the plots in subtle ways; in other cases, the telenovelas focus on very specific issues.

But people are watching and identifying. As the comments about *Por estas calles* indicate, telenovelas live on in the historical memory and shape current attitudes toward politics. It is no coincidence that a Peruvian journalist attuned to issues of corruption remembers a Brazilian telenovela without prompting decades later.

Transformations

When I watch telenovelas, I'm looking to get absorbed in a torrid romance that seems nearly impossible or a compelling tale of someone who made it from rags to riches. I'm not looking to learn about society or change the way I think. Yet I remember watching *Café, con aroma de mujer* in my Bogotá living room and musing on how cut off I was from coffee country, even if I got more of a chance to travel as a journalist than most ordinary Colombians. I remember talking to my neighbors and how it shaped their sense of who they were as Colombians with a pride that had been virtually eclipsed by the violence of the drug wars.

I heard from Venezuelan friends about the power of *Por estas calles* to call for an end to corruption and for political action. I heard from Peruvian friends about how *Al fondo hay sitio* made them debate the issue of class.

Telenovelas are a way of transforming society, whether the change comes from an embedded message or simply a way of seeing the world differently. It's much easier, of course, to measure the fertility or divorce rate quantitatively and use focus groups and other instruments to relate the change to telenovelas. It's much easier. But perhaps it's not as profound.

As O. Hugo Benavides declares,

> Melodrama is far from a static or entirely escapist cultural practice . . . it has allowed for a more democratic form of visual representation but also a particular, distinct Latin American way in which to present itself to the continent and to the world.[42]

I couldn't agree more.

Notes

1 Don M. Coerver, Suzanne B. Pasztor and Robert Buffington, *Mexico: An Encyclopedia of Contemporary Culture and History* (Santa Barbara, CA: ABC-CLIO, 2004), 492.

2 Samantha Nogueira Joyce, *Brazilian Telenovelas and the Myth of Racial Democracy* (Lanham, MD: Lexington Books, 2012), 12.

3 Arvind Singhal and Everett Rogers, *Entertainment-Education: A Communication Strategy for Social Change* (Mahway, NJ: Lawrence Erdbaum Associates, 1999), 55.

4 Population Media Center, "History of Sabido Serial Dramas," www.populationmedia.org/product/sabido-history/. Also see Maria Immacolata Vassallo de Lopes and Guillermo Orozco Gómez, eds., *Quality in Television Fiction and Audiences' Transmedia Interactions*, Ibero-American Observatory for Television Fiction (Obitel) 2011 Yearbook (Rio de Janeiro, Brazil: Editorial Globo S.A., 2011), 177.

5 Kriss Barker and Miguel Sabido, *Soap Operas for Social Change to Prevent HIV/AIDS: A Training Guide for Journalists and Media Personnel* (South Burlington, VT, and New York: Population Media Center and the United Nations Family Planning Agency, 2005), 11.

6 Ibid., 32.

7 Samantha Nogueira Joyce, *Brazilian Telenovelas and the Myth of Racial Democracy* (Lanham, MD: Lexington Books, 2012), 92.

8 Population Media Center, "History of Sabido Serial Dramas," www.populationmedia.org/product/sabido-history/.

9 Arvind Singhal and Everett M. Rogers, *Entertainment-Education: A Communications Strategy for Social Change* (Mahwah, NJ: Lawrence Erlbaum Associates, 1999), 37.

10 Maria Immacolata Vassallo de Lopes and Guillermo Orozco Gómez, eds., *(Re)Invention of TV Fiction Genres and Formats*, Ibero-American Observatory for Television Fiction (Obitel) 2016 Yearbook (Porto Alegre, Brazil: Editorial Sulina, 2016), 136.

11 Brian Stelter, "U.S. Census Uses Telenovela to Reach Hispanics," *New York Times*, September 22, 2009, www.nytimes.com/2009/09/23/business/23telemundo.html.

12 Thomas Tufte, "Telenovelas, Culture and Social Change—From Polisemy, Pleasure and Resistance to Strategic Communication and Social Development," in Maria Immacolata Vassallo de Lopes, ed., *International Perspectives on Telenovelas* (São Paulo, Brazil: Edições Loyola, 2003), 11, www.portalcomunicacion.com/catunesco.

13 "Sexto Sentido." www.puntosdeencuentro.org/medios/tv-y-videos-tematicos/sexto-sentido/.

14 "Deep Dish: Waves of Change." http://deepdishwavesofchange.org/2010/04/28/sexto-sentido-telenovela-nicaraguense

15 Alberto Chong and Eliana La Ferrara, "Television and Divorce: Evidence from Brazilian Novelas," Working Paper #651, BR-N1020, Inter-American Development Bank, 2009, http://idbdocs.iadb.org/wsdocs/getdocument.aspx?docnum=1856109.

16 Alberto Chong and Eliana La Ferrara, "Television and Divorce: Evidence from Brazilian Novelas," Working Paper #651, BR-N1020, Inter-American Development Bank, 2009, http://idbdocs.iadb.org/wsdocs/getdocument.aspx?docnum=1856109.

17 Valerio Fuenzalida, *Televisión y Cultura Cotidiana: La influencia social de la TV percibida desde la cultura cotidiana de la audiencia* (Santiago, Chile: Corporación de Promoción Universitaria, 1997), 16. The translation is mine.

18 Maria Immacolata Vassallo de Lopes and Guillermo Orozco Gómez, eds., *(Re)Invention of TV Fiction Genres and Formats*, Ibero-American Observatory for Television Fiction (Obitel) 2016 Yearbook (Porto Alegre, Brazil: Editorial Sulina, 2016), 143.

19 Ibid., 189 and 294.

20 Maria Immacolata Vassallo de Lopes and Guillermo Orozco Gómez eds., *Transmedia Production Strategies in Television Fiction*, Ibero-American Observatory of Television Fiction (Obitel) 2014 Yearbook (Porto Alegre, Brazil: Editorial Sulina, 2014), 29.

21 Denise Avancini Alves and Maria Helena Weber, "Social Merchandising: Human Trafficking in Brazilian Soap Opera," *Advances in Journalism and Communication*, no. 3, 93, http://file.scirp.org/Html/3-2840075_61979.htm.

22 TV Globo, "Socio-Educational Action: Being Socially Responsible Is a Vocation," http://redeglobo.globo.com/Portal/institucional/foldereletronico/ingles/g_rs_merchandising_social.html.

23 Maria Immacolata Vassallo de Lopes, "Telenovela as a Communicative Resource," *Revista MATRIZes*, 3, no 1, 2009, 20–23.

24 Giuliana Regina Amaral Reginatio, "O Mercado social na TV Globo, O outro espetáculo do horario Nobre" (unpublished 2007 Master's Thesis, São Paulo, Faculdade Cásper Libano), 15, cited in Michele Mattelart and Armand Mattelart in *The Carnival of Images: Brazilian Television Fiction* (New York: Bergin and Garvey, 1990), 83.

25 Esther Hamburger, "Politics and Intimacy in Brazilian Telenovelas" (unpublished dissertation, University of Chicago, 1999), Introduction, 12.

26 Maria Immacolata Vassallo de Lopes and Guillermo Orozco Gómez, eds., *Gender Relations in Television Fiction*, Ibero-American Observatory for Television Fiction (Obitel) 2013 Yearbook (Porto Alegre, Brazil: Editorial Sulina, 2013), 29 and 34.

27 Samantha Nogueira Joyce, *Brazilian Telenovelas and the Myth of Racial Democracy* (Lanham, MD: Lexington Books, 2012), 87.

28 Thomas Tufte, "Telenovelas, Culture and Social Change—From Polisemy, Pleasure and Resistance to Strategic Communication and Social Development," in Maria Immacolata Vassallo de Lopes, ed., *International Perspectives on Telenovelas* (São Paulo, Brazil: Edicões Loyola, 2003), 4, www.portalcomunicacion.com/catunesco.

29 World Bank, "Latin America: Middle Class Hits Historic High," 2012, www.worldbank.org/en/news/feature/2012/11/13/crecimiento-clase-media-america-latina.

30 Inter-American Development Bank, "Record-Breaking Amount of Remittances Received in Latin American and the Caribbean," May 12, 2015, www.iadb.org/en/news/news-releases/2015-05-12/record-amount-of-remittances-to-region-in-2014,11158.html.

31 Joe Leahy, "A New Class of Soap: Brazil's Latest Telenovelas Reflect the Tastes and Hopes of a Rapidly Rising Middle Class," *Financial Times*, February 22, 2013, www.ft.com/content/d28b684e-7bbd-11e2-95b9-00144feabdc0.

32 Dahlia Anaís Belounis, "Al Fondo Hay Sitio: An Expression of Peruvian Cultural Identity" (unpublished thesis, Pontificia Universidad Católica del Perú, 2013), 78.

33 Univision, "Lo que nos hizo creer 'Café con aroma de mujer' de los colombianos (y del café)," www.univision.com/estilo-de-vida/cafe/que-nos-enseno-la-telenovela-cafe-con-aroma-de-mujer-de-los-colombianos-y-del-cafe. Translation is mine.
34 Ana M. Lopez, "Our Welcomed Guests: Telenovelas in Latin America," in Robert C. Allen, ed., *To Be Continued . . . Soap Operas Around the World* (London and New York: Routledge, 1995), 262.
35 Maria Immacolata Vassallo de Lopes, *Telenovela brasilera: uma narrative sobre a naçao*, Comunicação y Eduçacão, 26, 17–34, 2003 cited in Tania Cantrell Rosas-Moreno, *News and Novela in Brazilian Media: Fact, Fiction, and National Identity* (Lanham, MD: Lexington Books, 2014), 1. Translation is Cantrell's.
36 Alfredo de Freitas Dias Gomes, *Apenas um Subversivo*, Rio de Janeiro (Brazil: Editora Bertrand Brasil, 1998), 276, cited in Mauro P. Porto, *Media Power and Democratization in Brazil: TV Globo and the Dilemmas of Political Accountability*, Routledge Advances in Internationalizing Media Studies (London and New York: Routledge, 2012), 122. Translation is Porto's.
37 Ibid., 121.
38 Mary Beth Sheridan, "Corruption Makes for a TV Hit in Mexico," *Los Angeles Times*, December 14, 1996, http://articles.latimes.com/1996-12-14/news/mn-8886_1_tv-azteca.
39 "¿SERÍA POSIBLE? Así sería la novela 'Por estas calles' en la actualidad, según Franklin Virgüez," July 12, 2015, www.maduradas.com/seria-posible-asi-seria-la-novela-por-estas-calles-en-la-actualidad-segun-franklin-virguez/.
40 Tamara Slusnys, "Escribir en puntillas," *Producto*, December 27, 2016, www.producto.com.ve/pro/entrevista/escribir-en-puntillas.
41 Runrunes, "Vuelve 'Por estas calles' más vigente que nunca a 23 años de su transmisión," http://runrun.es/relax/224992/vuelve-por-estas-calles-mas-vigente-que-nunca-a-23-anos-de-su-transmision.html.
42 O. Hugo Benavides, *Drugs, Thugs, and Divas: Telenovelas and Narco-Dramas in Latin America* (Austin: University of Texas Press, 2008), 197.

Bibliography

Allen, Robert C., ed. *To Be Continued . . . Soap Operas Around the World*. London and New York: Routledge, 1995.
Avancini Alves, Denise, and Maria Helena Weber. "Social Merchandising: Human Trafficking in Brazilian Soap Opera." *Advances in Journalism and Communication*, no. 3. http://file.scirp.org/Html/3-2840075_61979.htm.
Barker, Kriss, and Miguel Sabido. *Soap Operas for Social Change to Prevent HIV/AIDS: A Training Guide for Journalists and Media Personnel*. South Burlington, VT, and New York: Population Media Center and the United Nations Family Planning Agency, 2005.
Belounis, Dahlia Anaís. *Al Fondo Hay Sitio: An Expression of Peruvian Cultural Identity*. Unpublished thesis, Pontificia Universidad Católica del Perú, 2013.
Benavides, O. Hugo. *Drugs, Thugs, and Divas*. Austin: University of Texas Press, 2008.
Chong, Alberto, and Eliana La Ferrara. "Television and Divorce: Evidence From Brazilian Novelas." Working Paper #651. Inter-American Development Bank, 2009. http://idbdocs.iadb.org/wsdocs/getdocument.aspx?docnum=1856109.
Coerver, Don M., Suzanne B. Pasztor, and Robert Buffington. *Mexico: An Encyclopedia of Contemporary Culture and History*. Santa Barbara, CA: ABC-Clio, 2004.
Fuenzalida, Valerio. *Televisión y Cultura Cotidiana: La influencia social de la TV percibida desde la cultura cotidiana de la audiencia*. Santiago, Chile: Corporación de Promoción Universitaria, 1997.

Hamburger, Esther. *Politics and Intimacy in Brazilian Telenovelas*. Unpublished dissertation, University of Chicago, 1999.

Inter-American Development Bank. "Record-Breaking Amount of Remittances Received in Latin American and the Caribbean." May 12, 2015. www.iadb.org/en/news/news-releases/2015-05-12/record-amount-of-remittances-to-region-in-2014,11158.html.

Joyce, Samantha Nogueira. *Brazilian Telenovelas and the Myth of Racial Democracy*. Lanham, MD: Lexington Books, 2012.

Leahy, Joe. "A New Class of Soap: Brazil's Latest Telenovelas Reflect the Tastes and Hopes of a Rapidly Rising Middle Class." *Financial Times*, February 22, 2013. www.ft.com/content/d28b684e-7bbd-11e2-95b9-00144feabdc0.

Matteart, Michele, and Armand Mattelart. *The Carnival of Images: Brazilian Television Fiction*. New York: Bergin and Garvey, 1990.

Population Media Center. "History of Sabido Serial Dramas." www.populationmedia.org/product/sabido-history/.

Porto, Mauro P. *Media Power and Democratization in Brazil: TV Globo and the Dilemmas of Political Accountability*. Routledge Advances in Internationalizing Media Studies. London and New York: Routledge, 2012.

Rosas-Moreno, Tania Cantrell. *News and Novela in Brazilian Media: Fact, Fiction, and National Identity*. Lanham, MD: Lexington Books, 2014.

Sheridan, Mary Beth. "Corruption Makes for a TV Hit in Mexico. *Los Angeles Times*, December 14, 1996. http://articles.latimes.com/1996-12-14/news/mn-8886_1_tv-azteca.

Singhal, Arvind, and Everett M. Rogers. *Entertainment-Education: A Communication Strategy for Social Change*. Mahway, NJ: Lawrence Erdbaum Associates, 1999.

Stelter, Brian. "U.S. Census Uses Telenovela to Reach Hispanics." *New York Times*, September 22, 2009. www.nytimes.com/2009/09/23/business/23telemundo.html.

Tufte, Thomas. "Telenovelas, Culture and Social Change—From Polisemy, Pleasure and Resistance to Strategic Communication and Social Development." in Maria Immacolata Vassallo de Lopes (ed.), *International Perspectives on Telenovelas*. São Paulo, Brazil: Edicões Loyola, 2003. www.portalcomunicacion.com/catunesco.

TV Globo. "Socio-Educational Action: Being Socially Responsible Is a Vocation." http://redeglobo.globo.com/Portal/institucional/foldereletronico/ingles/g_rs_merchandising_social.html.

Vassallo de Lopes, Maria Immacolata. "Telenovela as a Communicative Resource." *Revista MATRIZes*, 3, no. 1, 2009, 20–23.

Vassallo de Lopes, Maria Immacolata, and Guillermo Orozco Gómez, eds. *Quality in Television Fiction and audiences' transmedia interactions*. Ibero-American Observatory of Television Fiction (Obitel) 2011 Yearbook. Rio de Janeiro, Brazil: Editorial Globo S.A., 2011.

Vassallo de Lopes, Maria Immacolata, and Guillermo Orozco Gómez, eds. *Social Memory and Television in Ibero-American Countries*, Ibero-American Observatory of Television Fiction (Obitel) 2013 Yearbook. Porto Alegre, Brazil: Editorial Sulina, 2013.

Vassallo de Lopes, Maria Immacolata, and Guillermo Orozco Gómez, eds. *Transmedia Production Strategies in Television Fiction*, Ibero-American Observatory of Television Fiction (Obitel) 2014 Yearbook. Porto Alegre, Brazil: Editorial Sulina, 2014.

Vassallo de Lopes, Maria Immacolata, and Guillermo Orozco Gómez, eds. *(Re)Invention of TV Fiction Genres and Formats*, Ibero-American Observatory of Television Fiction (Obitel) 2016 Yearbook. Porto Alegre, Brazil: Editorial Sulina, 2016.

World Bank. "Latin America: Middle Class Hits Historic High." 2012. www.worldbank.org/en/news/feature/2012/11/13/crecimiento-clase-media-america-latina.

3

BEYOND BETTY

Gender and Sexuality

Betty came bouncing into my living room and stayed for more than three hundred nights. Betty—more formally known as Beatriz Aurora Pinzón Solano—captivated me with her raucous laugh, her braces and her thick-framed glasses, her awkward demeanor and, yes, her financial wizardry. The Colombian telenovela *Yo soy Betty la fea* (I am Betty, the Ugly One) (Figure 3.1) was the one show I couldn't miss. I was not alone: more than 80 million people throughout Latin America and the United States watched the program, and it was a topic of conversation in myriad chatrooms, websites, newspaper columns and just around the watercooler in the office.

And Betty came into my life again a few years later as *Ugly Betty*, a U.S. adaptation starring America Ferrera. Even though I had watched the original, the adaptation with its awkward, slightly overweight Latina protagonist became the one show I couldn't give up.[1]

It seemed natural that I should choose the Betty theme as the focus of a chapter on gender. I was surprised when I received a bit of pushback from the experts. "It's been written about so much," they said. So I thought about it quite a bit. After all, I could focus on telenovelas featuring the Peruvian female taxi driver or the seamstress, the Mexican drug lord, the middle-aged married woman who took a lover, the femme fatale, the prostitute with the heart of gold. I could focus on how the themes of abortion, divorce, birth control, abuse and rape all emerged in telenovelas long before they were comfortable topics in Latin society. Or I could focus on the first lesbian couple to adopt a child in a telenovela or the first kiss between two women.

Don't worry; I will get to all of them. But I decided to start with Betty because the series can give us some insights into how gender plays out in many telenovelas.

FIGURE 3.1   Ana María Orozco as "Betty, la fea." *Yo soy Betty, la fea,* 1999, Produced by María del Pilar Fernández, Ana María Orozco and Adriana Franco.

But first the story for those of you who haven't seen the program.

Betty, a brilliant economist with a master's in finance, applies for a secretarial job at EcoModa, a ritzy fashion house in Bogotá. Her looks have kept her back; her voice is shreeky shrill and she has trouble asserting herself. At EcoModa, she immediately develops a strong group of friends dubbed by the company's star designer Hugo Lombardi as the *cuartel de las feas*—"the Ugly Women's Club." Like her, the other six members of this group are outsiders: an Afro-Colombian, an overweight woman who has a problem with compulsive eating, a short divorceé, a tall giraffe-like spinster, an older woman and a hypersexualized flirt who often uses her body to get ahead.

Fernando Gaitán, the show's creator and screenwriter, told the press that Betty and her friends appeal to the average viewer, "Only one woman out of 10 is considered beautiful and most of them suffer because they don't comply with the stereotypes of the market."[2]

Betty's friends respect her loyalty, honesty and intelligence, and with their moral support, she manages to climb the company's ranks. She also manages to fall in love with her boss, Armando Mendoza, the son of EcoModa's owner.

Her feelings are not reciprocated—at least not at first. Over and over again, Betty bails him out from his gross mishandling of the company. Armando recognizes her talent, but is so ashamed of her looks that he once insisted she hide in his car trunk when he went to an important business appointment.

Nevertheless, aware that Betty knows all the company's inner secrets, Mendoza decides to seduce her to ensure her loyalty. Even then, he confesses to his best friend, Mario, that he still considers her "a little monstrosity."

But then he finds himself falling in love despite his own attitude.

Betty, however, discovers letters from Mario that reveal Armando was manipulating her. She decides to quit, but not before revealing the company's mismanagement and financial disarray. Her friend Catalina aids Betty in finding a temporary job working at the Cartagena beauty pageant. Bit by bit, Catalina helps her buy new clothes, go to a hair stylist and to get new, more attractive eyeglasses—a slow and respectful makeover. Betty is courted by a handsome and talented French photographer, Michel, who admires her intelligence and humor, as well as her emerging good looks.

With her new fashionable wardrobe and improved looks, she ends up back at EcoModa—this time running the company. When Betty arrives, Armando has just returned to the company after a leave "to think things over," but he is no longer the boss. Betty dumps Michel and forgives Armando, marrying him and presumably living happily ever after.

For days, the viewers had watched her makeover and wondered: Armando or Michel (or, perhaps, no one; but this is a telenovela, after all). Many Colombians (and others) loved the ending—the heroine gets her man, after all. She is now an attractive businesswoman with fashionable glasses, stylish clothes and long hair, but thankfully she definitely does not look like a sultry fashion model. And she is the head of a successful company that she managed to save through her financial acumen. The story ends with the birth of the couple's daughter, who looks remarkably like Betty as an infant.

I personally hated the ending—and so did many of my friends and pundits in the press. The telenovela had stressed Betty's talents and spunk all along, and now it was returning to her looks and marital status (her talents, while acknowledged, were very much not emphasized as the telenovela drew to an end).

Florence Graves, a Colombian feminist writer originally from France, charged that Betty's makeover sends the wrong message by suggesting that women only become successful through their appearance. "[I]t's a lost opportunity to talk about different kinds of romantic relationships between women and men, based on different things than looks," she said.[3]

She added that the show had begun to illustrate the strength of "hard-working Colombian women and not those models that always appear on the evening news."

Yeidy M. Rivero, a professor from the University of Michigan, recalls that she got hooked on *Yo soy Betty, la fea* when Clemencia Rodríguez, a Colombian friend and television scholar, expressed her enthusiasm for the telenovela, which was also being broadcast at the same time on the U.S. Spanish-language Telemundo. "Her excitement for this show was so contagious that I decided to tune in. . . . Needless to say, like my friend and millions of viewers across the Americas, I was hooked. I cried with and for Beatriz. I laughed with her funny friends (El cuartel de las feas [The Ugly Woman Club]) and like some fans, I was quite disappointed by the traditional telenovela marriage ending."[4]

In an academic article, Rivero points out that by the end of the telenovela both Betty and the *cuartel de las feas* have been made over into attractive women. "In the rather simplistic rhetoric of working-class empowerment (i.e. anyone can 'make it'), Beatriz's hard work and intelligence allowed her to become the company's president. However, this success in the workplace came with a price; she had to alter her physical appearance."[5]

Journalist Sandra Hernandez has harsher words, "The premise was stunning: a woman whose appeal is her intelligence, humanity and humor struggles to be seen, heard and, ultimately, adored. . . . And then, just in the nick of time, Betty sheds her ugly duckling image and transforms herself into a beautiful executive who struggles with the realization that her lover isn't a prince."

Hernandez points out that in the traditional happy-ending style, Betty overlooks Armando's faults and decides to marry him. With a certain not-very-veiled tone of outrage, Hernandez says that even if Gaitán wanted to convey that Betty could get ahead by hard work and sheer intelligence, the subtext tells us something else. Betty, whom Hernandez describes as an "antiheroine," is smart enough to save the company, but not enough to recognize Mendoza for "the lying, cheating louse that he is." She charges that Gaitán is putting forth a stereotyped message, that women cannot find true happiness by themselves, but need a man to help them accomplish their dreams.[6]

Michele Hilmes, writing in an anthology on the many versions of the Betty telenovela throughout the world, calls the story a "mixture of age-old myth and postmodern playfulness."[7]

She has no problem with the ending, describing Betty as "a nice girl with big ambition, the ugly duckling who not only married some species of prince, but won recognition for her abilities and talents as well."[8]

The debate about the Betty ending got me thinking. My original reaction had been strongly against the ending (and kind of still is), but it made me think of the tensions one finds in many telenovelas, new and old.

There's an inbuilt duality even in the weepiest of telenovelas. First of all, the protagonist is most often a woman, which means that women are seeing themselves on the screen. That's a feat in itself. It's the reason that activists have insisted over the years in getting more women, people of color, and people of diverse sex orientations on the big and little screens.

As we mentioned in the introduction, unlike soap operas, telenovelas attract both men and women; it's not quite a 50-50 split, but almost, but for at least half the audience, it's a chance to identify with the women who form the center of a program.

But beyond that, women in telenovelas make things happen—the concept academics call "agency." They (most often) are not just victims. Their agency may be in climbing their way out of poverty or providing for a family or engaging in an unusual profession or simply taking certain steps to ensure themselves of engaging with the person they consider Mr. Right.

The reason television viewers may have reacted so strongly in favor or against the ending of "Betty" is that the program makes the duality quite transparent. On the one hand, Betty is a financial whiz, a capable genius who can strategize the rescue of a mismanaged company; she is strong enough to reject a suitor who has manipulated her and to start a new professional and love life. She makes the decision to have a beauty makeover. But on the other hand, she sees success as achieving superficial beauty and marrying the man of her dreams, who happens to be the same man who previously manipulated and abused her.

The major complaint about this duality is that Betty started out by being a strong and unusual woman, albeit ugly, aided by a group of strong and unusual women, also deemed ugly, and that we end up with the "same old Cinderella story."

The frequency with which the Cinderella story was mentioned sent me scrambling back to the original fairy tale. There I found the same kind of tension, the same kind of duality found in many telenovelas. It's true that Cinderella's life is transformed when the glass slipper fits, the prince recognizes her for who she is, and they get married and live happily ever after.

However, it's Cinderella who decides that she wants to go to the ball; it's Cinderella who patiently sorts out lentils from the ashes to meet her stepsister's demands in order to attend the ball; it's Cinderella who gets cleaned up and makes a point of having the prince try the slipper on her foot. She is not merely a passive victim.

And, at least in the Disney version, she has some female backing in the form of the fairy godmother (not unlike Catalina in "Betty") who assists her in her quest to get to the ball.

I was surprised to find that there is no fairy godmother in the Grimm Brothers' version of the tale. Instead, enchanted birds by a tree at her mother's gravesite provide her with her gold-and-silver dress and slippers. Aschenputtel, Cinderella's name in this fairy tale, is actually responsible for creating the tree. When her father goes away on a business trip, he asks his daughter and two stepdaughters what they would like. The stepdaughters ask for gold and pearls; the Cinderella figure asks for a twig that she plants on her mother's gravesite and waters with her tears.

I found a funny but astute comment on a website while I was researching the Cinderella stories: "Aschenputtel is clearly powerful as hell, so why she wants to marry some dude who chases her into a pigeon coop is beyond me," writes J.R. Thorpe, referring to Aschenputtel/Cinderella taking flight into a chicken coop after the ball—with the prince in hot pursuit. I don't think it's coincidental that Thorpe's remarks echo the debate about the end of the telenovela.[9]

When one goes further back, to the 1697 story on which the Grimms based their fairytale, *Cinderella, or the Little Glass Slipper* by Charles Perrault, one finds the duality actually spelled out in the author's stated morals at the end of the tale:

"The first moral of the story is that beauty is a treasure, but graciousness is price-less. Without it, nothing is possible; with it, one can do anything," writes Perrault, stressing the theme of empowerment.

However, Perrault's second moral states, "[I]t is a great advantage to have intel-ligence, courage, good breeding, and common sense. These, and similar talents, come only from heaven, and it is good to have them. However, even these may fail to bring you success, without the blessing of a godfather or a godmother," thus putting an emphasis on fate or passivity, waiting for the fairy godmother (or indeed, the charming prince).[10]

Telenovelas tap into the Cinderella archetype, but—consciously or unconsciously—also reflect the tensions of the original tales. What Betty does is to underline those tensions; her figure is clearly an alternative one, and the ending seems to under-mine that status in a more obvious way than in more traditional telenovelas.

The tensions seem appropriate for a continent that is rapidly modernizing, shifting from an agrarian society to an industrial one, shifting from the country-side to the large, sprawling cities. Innate contradictions have long existed: single mothers are heads of households throughout Latin America, and yet machismo—male dominance—rules; women are presidents (the first was Isabel Perón in Argentina in 1974), senators, heads of companies, lawyers, architects, doctors and drug lords, yet the prevalent stereotype still is to a large extent wife and mother. In traditional Latin American cultural terms, the role of woman is often separated into those of "Mary-figure" and "whore," a dichotomy that is threatened by the new roles of women in contemporary society. Telenovelas help women—and all viewers—understand and identify with a multiplicity of roles. The duality doesn't disappear; it just gets mitigated, as it did in *Betty la fea*.

The telenovela has translated well to other cultures in part because of its famil-iar and almost universal riff on the Cinderella story and in part because women throughout the world are dealing with their own marginality, facing the duality of being their own agents and being subject to the fatalistic will of others—"someday my prince will come."

In the U.S. version, *Ugly Betty*—a telenovela-comedy hybrid—an immigrant woman is the person on the margins, and again she is trying to blend a profes-sional life with her family duties and eventual love interests.

"[Betty's] take on female aspiration and desire, renew the brand and reaffirm the universal—timeless, possibly—story centring on a heroine, on a young woman suffering a prolonged ordeal before her vindication and triumph," observes Marina Warner.[11]

This archetypal story plays out in many countries, based on the Colombian version. The Russian Katya in *Ne Rodis' Krasivoy* and the German Lisa in *Verliebt in Berlin* are professional women who eventually end up marrying their bosses after a beauty makeover, while in the version in Spain, Bea, the Betty character, gets no makeover, but nevertheless wins her boss's love.

Janet McCabe notes how we are seduced into the feminine ideal:

> Any casual comparison of the after images of the different Betties indicate
> similar accepted attitudes and values as to what the correct female body
> should look like. Following the removal of what offends, of anything that
> troubles the perfect female body as an object of desire—braces, glasses, those
> few extra pounds—the heroine emerges as the feminine ideal. Always cul-
> turally specific with deeply entrenched ideology internalized, the images of
> Betty as beautiful swan are compelling enough to entangle us psychically
> and from which we are not entirely able to free ourselves.[12]

Although McCabe does not directly address the tension permeating telenovelas
(and their archetypal ancestors, the fairy tale), she implies it with her statement that
"we are not entirely able to free ourselves." There is another attitude, that of agency,
that is expressed in the telenovela, but we get too enmeshed in the passive beautiful
swan tale to be able to free ourselves and honor that aspect of the female experience.

By emphasizing the relationship of the telenovela to the archetypal fairy tale,
I don't mean to imply that the telenovelas are not grounded in reality. They draw
much of their strength from superimposing the reality of everyday life onto the
archetypal framework.

Scriptwriter Fernando Gaitán has said on several occasions that he drew his
inspirations from the conversations of the secretaries he would overhear at the
television station RCN, where he was working. Yeidy Rivero relates the Betty
story to another type of daily life, the grittiest of telenovelas, the narconovela *Sin
tetas no hay paraíso* (Without tits, there is no paradise).

> Even though at first glance, women's painful struggles with their bodies
> seem to be the central theme of these two hits, what connects *Betty la
> fea* and *Sin tetas no hay paraíso* is more than beauty and ugliness. In these
> two stories, the woman's rejection of her body becomes an instrument for
> exploring class stratification and poverty, societal and political corruption,
> and violence—physical and psychological. This thematic richness that per-
> meates many Colombian telenovelas and series is most likely facilitating
> global adaptations of Colombian formats.[13]

And in this exploration, particularly of class stratification, we might see further
shades of Cinderella in this telenovela—and many others. Gender is intimately
linked to class. Cinderella manages to rise above her class of origin (and remember she's originally from a well-off family, although not a princess) after she has
fallen into the position of kitchen maid after her father remarries. In traditional
Latin American society, social mobility is often through marriage, rather than hard
work. Betty seems to be doing otherwise for much of the telenovela, but as we
shall see, Betty is not alone.

In Latin America, it's not uncommon to have this downward shift in class status, just like Cinderella. The exodus of rural Latin Americans to the big cities, whether because of job or educational opportunities or fear of violence in the countryside, at least initially produces a drop in class status. People who had their own farms and animals, people who were leaders or at least recognized citizens of a community, become anonymous residents of slums, buy their food in supermarkets or city plazas instead of growing their own food, and scrape by for a living. Some manage to attain a situation of stability or even prosperity through marriage or hard work or education or sheer luck; the question is one of adapting to the modernized life.

Betty is working class or perhaps lower middle class, and her "ugly" mannerisms reflect that status. The tension in the telenovela is how she is going to rise above that status.

Ugly Betty, the U.S. version, makes the issue of class and gender even more apparent. When Betty shows up for her job interview at the Meade fashion magazine, she is asked by the receptionist in very slow and enunciated tones whether she is delivering something. Betty is wearing a Mexican poncho, and the receptionist can only perceive her as a messenger, not a colleague. Her looks define her class.

Oscar Benavides notes,

> This particular process of westernization is obvious to any Latin American who has suffered social oppression, as is the case for most of the continent's population. The struggle between beauty and ugliness is incorporated not only in the ever-present melodramatic conflict between good and evil but also in the "modern" struggle between the global west and the local nonwest. The successful characters represent a modernized, developed world toward which the ugly locals, or premodern Latin natives, strive. The native/ugly women are not "at home" in the modern world of office and finance, which is what makes Betty powerful.[14]

Betty evokes the duality of the Cinderella story—the passivity and the agency; she shows us how class threads its way through any woman's story and how women cope in the face of an oft-confusing modernity. We identify with her. She makes us laugh and she makes us cry. And she gives us new ways of understanding the roles of women in telenovelas.

A Multitude of Roles

Long before Betty—ever since the beginning of telenovelas as a uniquely Latin American genre—women have been front and center of the genre.

The first telenovela produced in Mexico was the 1958 *Senda prohibida* (The Forbidden Path), sponsored by Colgate-Palmolive, the 2016 Obitel report recollects. The series was actually written by a woman, Fernanda Villeli (whose real name was María Orfelia Villenave Garza), a pioneer in the field who during her 40-year career would write dozens of telenovelas. She relates the saga of Nora, a young, ambitious woman from a poor countryside town. Nora falls in love with a rich lawyer, who is her boss and happens to be married. (No copy of this film exists, so I've had to rely on the Ibero-American Observatory of Television Fiction [Obitel] 2016 report and a few film clips on YouTube.) Some versions say that she did not fall in love, but saw a relationship with Federico as a key to getting ahead. In any case, he showers the young woman with luxurious gifts and decides to leave Irene, his stay-at-home wife. Although married men often had mistresses, known as a *casa chica* or "little house," Federico actually breaks the "rules" by moving out with Nora. When he loses his fortune, Nora doesn't support him so he returns to his wife. "Reaffirmation of bourgeosie values," the Obitel report asserts, "but at the same time puts on the table the middle-class fear of all these young women moving in from the countryside."[15]

Looking at the plot of *Senda prohibida* from the point of view of gender, I find it extraordinary for its day and age. Nora goes from a little town to work as a secretary, a job in the formal workforce. She does not go to sell tacos on the street or to work as a maid. Being a secretary is an upwardly mobile job (although perhaps not in the way Nora eventually uses it), one which perhaps represents the shift from the countryside to the city as a positive outcome of modernization. Even in the United States in 1958, women made up only a third of the workforce; in 2016, women make up only 45 percent of the workforce in Mexico.[16]

Thus, while the Obitel analysis is undoubtedly accurate that the telenovela reflects the middle-class fear of young women coming in from the countryside, it also represents "agency" or an active achievement on Nora's part. One of the reasons I wrote at length about the Betty story and its relationship to a more nuanced interpretation to Cinderella is because we see the tension between agency and fate or passivity going back to the beginning of telenovelas.

Certainly we can see it here. Nora's achievements and also her downfall come about because of her relationship with her boss. But in a sense, her boss's downfall happens because of his infatuation with Nora; it takes another woman—the stay-at-home wife—to rescue Federico.

The moral of the story might not have been one favorable to a feminist viewpoint (but then many feminists thought Betty let them down in that respect too). However, the telenovela presents gender roles in a way that can be talked about as viewers watch night after night.

The next Mexican telenovela, also in 1958, was also one that pivoted around gender roles, this time involving an emasculated male lead. In *Gutierritos*—also written by a woman, Estela Calderón—a man is browbeaten by his stay-at-home wife Rosa because he does not provide her with the lifestyle she yearns for. In the office environment, he and his coworkers are surrounded by secretaries with short skirts (at a time, as mentioned earlier, women do not form a large part of the formal workforce). And his boss finally hires a young woman named Elena, who, unlike the other secretaries, is timid, quiet and somewhat insecure.

Gutierritos adores her, but is too timid to speak his love. Instead, he spends his time writing a diary, which a writer friend encourages him to publish under a pseudonym. The book makes lots of money, and his wife Rosa finally accepts him.

Watching this 1958 telenovela—which was so popular it was remade in 1966—I was struck by the inversion of gender roles. Gutierritos—whose real name is Ángel Gutiérrez—actually sobs as he is harangued by his wife. Although crying is quite common in telenovelas, men don't cry nearly as often—unless perhaps over tequila or beer in the company of equally inebriated men, what might be called the masculinity of *despecho*, melodramatic heartbreak. But men merely crying by themselves or with a best friend is so rarely seen in telenovelas that in 2009, more than 50 years later after *Gutierritos*, Colombia's Caracol broadcast a telenovela called *Los hombres también lloran* (Men Also Cry).[17]

But cry Gutierritos does, and in the process, he manages to escape both his low-level office position and his henpecking wife. It's a tale that—like many telenovelas—makes us think about gender and class. It's also a telenovela that can be seen as reflecting on the process of modernization. The scenes in the office, the secretaries filing out in their short skirts, for example, seem almost factory-like. Yet Gutierritos's success—although anonymous—is achieved through the pre-industrial trade of writing, a throwback to tradition.

Another telenovela that inverts the feminine and masculine roles (and where men also cry) is *Pedro el escamoso* (Pedro the Show-Off), which aired in Colombia from 2001 to 2003. Like Nora in the earlier Mexican telenovela, Pedro leaves his countryside town for the big city, not so much to find a better life, but to escape the trouble he has gotten into by being too much of a womanizer. He goes to work as a chauffeur for an upper-class businessman and falls in love with his boss's secretary Paula, who, of course, is in love with her boss. But, like Gutierritos, he suffers in silence. Again, modernization rears its head. In the countryside, with its traditional machismo values, perhaps Pedro felt comfortable being a womanizer. Now in the big city, and with a more rigid modernized structure, he feels he must bear his love in silence.

Darío Armando García, better known as "Dago," who co-wrote the script with Luis Felipe Salamanca, said,

> Everything that, generally, men would do in a telenovela, women would do in this one. Here, women manipulated, here women lied, here women played around with other men, and everything that women did in this telenovela, men [did] in the traditional ones. Then, here Pedro suffered, Pedro was the victim, Pedro was faithful and a lot of other things, then by reversing the roles, we made a classic telenovela.[18]

Telenovelas are fun and addictive entertainment, but they also help the viewers interpret their complex worlds. I've included these two male-underdog telenovelas from two very different periods precisely because they help us see how female roles are generally portrayed. In these two telenovelas, one can also see the duality between the things these men can control and change and the passivity of being subject to a fate that may turn out either well or badly but is largely out of one's control.

Whether the protagonists are men or women, they provide mirrors for gender roles. In part, this is because of the very nature of the viewing experience, night after night, in a ritual form, at a certain time, often in the company of family and friends, and then later discussed at the watercooler or the sewing circle or, more recently, on Facebook, Twitter and the web.

Reginald Clifford described this process nicely:

> Telenovelas usually engage people in the intimacy of their home, the site where Silverstone [Silverstone, Roger, 1994, *Television and Everyday Life*. London: Routledge] suggests that one community forms to view another; it is the site of conflicts, rituals, and sharing in dimensions that are gendered, generational and class-oriented. It is, as [TV Azteca's] Veronica Vásquez states, "life itself." It is a site where the emotions of everyday life are internalized and externalized. Respondents frequently assert that a telenovela, particularly one with tones of realism, provides a measure for broaching a subject that families enjoy discussing but may find difficult to raise. A son or daughter may want to probe the parental limits placed on certain subjects such as sex, parental control, drugs, or sexuality but does not want to be perceived as being active in transgressing them. Conversely, a parent may want to probe the world of their children without appearing inquisitorial or nosey.[19]

Simplemente María: Not So Simple

That process of interaction between the telenovela and the viewer appeals to the multitude of roles of strong women, in which in the tension between agency and passivity, agency wins out.

One of the first and most iconic roles dates back to 1969. *Simplemente María* (Simply María), a Peruvian telenovela, tells the story of a young woman who leaves her beloved village in the Andes mountains to work as a maid for a wealthy family and eventually becomes a successful seamstress and fashion designer. We've already looked at this telenovela in terms of social change, but what can it tell us in terms of gender?

The telenovela starts with María Ramos in her village, blessing her brothers and sisters as she departs for the big city. She is shown guiding a donkey—a rather blatant symbol of village life and the pre-industrial past. We then see a monstrous train—a huge hulk blasting toward the city—again, a rather blatant symbol of progress and industrialization, powerful and threatening at the same time.

María ends up in the big city with no one to meet her and nowhere to go. Using her wits, she calls upon the head of the train station to ask where a friend of hers lives in the city.

He retorts that he has no idea, that he only knows the people who work for him, fuming at her to explain why she expects him to know where everyone lives. She simply replies, without a touch of aggressivity, that in her town, the station-master knows where everyone lives. Her small-town, innocent vision becomes apparent to the stationmaster. Taking pity on her, he helps her by looking through the classified ads for the illiterate young woman to identify a possible job, and he calls the prospective employer.

One thing leads to another. She gets the job but is seduced by Roberto, a medical student whom she meets on her first outing to the city. She finds out she is pregnant; he promises to marry her, but then abandons her.

She moves into a working-class neighborhood, has her child, works as a maid during the day and begins adult literacy classes with a teacher by the name of Esteban at night. Esteban's mother teaches her to sew. María goes to work in a local dress shop to support herself and her child. Eventually, she becomes a popular fashion designer and moves to Paris to found a high-end clothing boutique. After 20 years of friendship and courtship, she marries Esteban, who has given her emotional support and encouragement over the years. The telenovela goes on for more than four hundred episodes, with her son (played by the same actor as the deceptive medical student) falling in love and marrying the niece of her former lover.

Again we have the naïve young woman coming into the big city from the countryside, managing to find success and love. In essence, María becomes prosperous because she has managed to dominate the most industrial of products— the sewing machine, which has replaced handwork. The telenovela has enjoyed several remakes in many different countries, perhaps because it hits this chord that women can make a difference in their own lives, that they have "agency." The telenovela, based on a story by Argentine writer Celia Alcántara (a 1967 Argentine version of *Simplemente María* with Irma Roy actually predates the runaway successful Peruvian series), was first remade under that title (with an "s" added— *Simplesmente Maria* for the Portuguese) in Brazil in 1970, then in Venezuela in 1972, then in Mexico in 1989 and again in 2015. But many other telenovelas— one could even argue that Betty has a tinge of the themes of the telenovela—have used a variation of the plot to create their own shows.

"*Simplemente Maria* is the founding myth," says Venezuelan telenovela writer Alberto Barrera Tyszka, quoted in a popular anthology on telenovelas. "For many years, telenovelas were nothing but variations on its plots and themes."[20]

María is the epitome of the self-made woman. The telenovela had a major impact: both literacy classes and sewing machines spiralled in popularity. The Singer Corporation even gave the actor who plays María, Saby Kamalich, a gold Singer sewing machine in appreciation.

In a talk to the 1994 annual meeting of the American Public Health Association (APHA), Arvind Singhal and Everett M. Rogers presented their work on the telenovela in a paper entitled "Simplemente Maria and Formation of the Entertainment-Education Strategy," showing how María empowered women through her example. The telenovela also led to the realization on the part of scriptwriters and those who work in social services that telenovelas could be used to effect social change, as we discussed in the previous chapter.[21]

While social change can come about by deliberately inserting messages into telenovelas, it also happens through the provision of different types of role models—what it means to be a woman and what it means to be a man. As in *Gutierritos* and *Pedro el escamoso*, there's a lot being said in *Simplemente María* about men too. The hero of the story is not the wealthy man—the medical student—but the long-suffering teacher, Esteban, who eventually after 20 years gets to marry María. But in the meantime, he is kind, gentle, helpful, supportive of her and her son—the kind of role model that might be more usual in today's society.

These four early telenovelas illustrate gender roles that are far from the passive victims of fate and machismo while incorporating enough of those elements to create an inherent dramatic tension. The tension continues in later novelas (again, including Betty). Just to mention a few, there's the 1994 *Café, con aroma de mujer* in which the protagonist Teresa Suárez, "Gaviota," and her mother labor as agricultural migrant workers throughout Colombia, always arriving in October to the large Casablanca coffee plantation. The wealthy owner finds them permanent work, and when he dies, his grandson Sebastián comes back to the plantation and falls in love with Gaviota, who helps him overcome his fear of women—the first romantic experience for both of them.

Gaviota and Sebastián say farewell and agree to meet in a year in Casablanca. He returns to his studies in Europe. She soon finds out she is pregnant and she obtains what she thinks is a job as a model in Europe. Instead, she is lured into prostitution. Men don't seem to want a pregnant prostitute though, so she does not actually exercise the profession. Eventually, however, she does miscarry her child. Sebastián goes to Casablanca, but he does not find her but hears the rumors about her prostitution and has decided Gaviota has abandoned him. He decides to marry his childhood friend, Lucía, even though they both know it will be a sexless marriage. Gaviota arrives in Casablanca the morning after Sebastián's marriage to Lucía. Her hopes dashed, she assumes a new identity and returns to Colombia. Gaviota settles down in Bogotá, but she feels very much out of place in the large chaotic city and returns to coffee country, where she climbs her way to a position as a top executive for a coffee export business. Sebastián returns also, and is intent on finding her. Lucía and her allies plot to prevent that encounter, but the two find each other and eventually are married.

Perhaps the Betty comparison isn't fair here since Fernando Gaitán authored both scripts, but it is another example of a woman who gets to the top through her own wiles and achievements. From the very beginning, Gaviota has established herself as someone who is interested in rising to the top. In the first episode, she is talking to the plantation caretaker about the rickety state of a table. He observes that she is a bit old (she's 18 at the time) to be concerning herself with homework. "I don't want to be picking coffee my whole life," she replies. "Being good at reading and writing will get me further than just picking coffee."

She gets to the top through her own efforts, although it certainly is not a detriment that she is beautiful. However, unlike most other telenovelas, she does not achieve success by moving away from the rural countryside to the big city; indeed, she abandons the big city—or the two big cities, Paris and Bogotá—to return to her roots in the Colombian countryside.

In terms of holding up a mirror to identity, the series confirmed to viewers that the nation's women are not confined to the urban life—not even for progress. Women, men and children watch and discuss these telenovelas—whether in living rooms, offices or the ubiquitous telenovela chatrooms, and women have an opportunity to identify with strong women protagonists.

"The ubiquity of telenovelas showed the cultural genre as one of the most important symbolic forms used in everyday cultural life," writes Jorge González.

> The detailed observation of households viewing telenovelas was the most important time when the whole family was together. In spite of the normal prejudices held toward telenovelas, we found complex reactions. At times people surrender to the intrigue and the plot and at others experience forms of critical distancing. We also found that many women who normally invest their lifetime in serving others treat watching a telenovela as a time that is sacred, untouchable and not negotiable. Moreover, they compared characters in the telenovela with themselves in terms of emotional attitudes, dressing styles or manners. In effect, there are a number of processes of appropriation, social use, consumption, interpretation and shared meaning going far beyond the simplistic statements about this genre.[22]

A very different type of identification and controversy took place with the role of the strong woman in *Mirada de mujer* (Gaze of a Woman), a 1997 TV Azteca Mexican production (Figure 3.2). This time there is also a difference: the protagonist is in her 50s. Her husband, a well-known lawyer, is having an affair with a younger woman, and María Inés is supposed to—like a traditional good Latin American wife—just turn her eyes the other way. After 27 years of marriage, her husband abandons her. She gazes into the mirror and sees that she has a good life with lovely children and a wealthy lifestyle, but devoid of passion.

She finds Alejandro, a writer who is 20 years younger than she, and starts an affair. Her three adult children blame her for the breakup of the marriage, but later come to terms with the change in their mother's life.

For the most part, when telenovelas overtly or in an unconscious manner stress women's power in decision-making, it is through her success in work and

FIGURE 3.2 Still from *Mirada de mujer*. *Mirada de mujer*, 1997, Produced by Epigmenio Ibarra and Carlos Payán, Image: Margarita Gralia and Carlos Torres Torrija.

her wiles in getting her Prince Charming. The role of wife is often questioned: women in loveless relations; women married to the wrong man before they can eventually wed Prince Charming; the woman who endures affairs and get her revenge.

A Mirror for Society

But *Mirada de mujer* takes on the subject of matrimonial unhappiness with a special kind of determination that women can find happiness outside the home—and not just at work. Of course, María Inés's husband is also having an affair; the telenovela calls into question the double standard. It is actually he who abandons the marriage, but the children blame their mother.

The telenovela takes on myriad taboo subjects: breast cancer, interracial relationships, infidelity, divorce and rape. But it keeps coming back to the question of agency, a woman's right to take control over her own life. It also recognizes women as sexual human beings—beyond being the passive recipients of the desire of men.

Although it appeared to be completely successful in projecting taboo subjects, the principal actress, Angélica Aragón, confessed at a director's panel at a conference in Australia on telenovelas and soap operas that a scene had been altered because of viewer pressure. When the protagonist's elder daughter in the telenovela becomes pregnant, she decides to opt for an abortion—surely the epitome of taking control over one's own life. Viewers were furious, so the producers chose to let her miscarry instead. Aragón emphasized in the panel, however, that despite the outcome of the abortion scene, the telenovela had the immense power to structure social expectations. In her role as an independent woman, she said, she was able to provide a model for her viewers.

Telenovela producer Epigmenio Ibarra said in interviews with newspaper reporters that he understood the telenovela's power: "[It] was envisioned as a mirror of society; . . . to talk of the disintegration of the family is not to foster disintegration, but to encourage discussion of the causes of disintegration. We hoped to initiate debate with the telenovela, to provoke polemic reflections."[23]

It's easy at first look to view *Mirada de mujer* (Figure 3.3) as a completely different type of telenovela, with a vision of gender that's quite apart from Betty or Pedro or Gutierritos or María or Gaviota. María Inés is an upper-class woman who does not come from the countryside or find herself pregnant by the wrong man; she's not in economic straits and hasn't been lured into the sex trade. She's attractive, but older than most telenovela protagonists . . . a middle-aged star. She's not caught up in the conflict between the old agricultural ways and the emerging industrial (or even post-industrial) society.

Or maybe she is.

Her marriage represents an example of the traditional patriarchal society in which her husband puts the bread on the table and she has the children and lives a tranquil, well-respected and economically plentiful life with an elegant house, ample servants, a late-model car, fashionable clothes and limitless credit cards— but her life has no passion. These are the old ways, even if the telenovela never explicitly says so.

FIGURE 3.3 Angélica Aragón in *Mirada de mujer*, 1997, Produced by Epigmenio Ibarra and Carlos Payán.

Her decision to have an affair with a much younger man seems to reflect women's liberation—although the telenovela never uses that term—and a more modern way of seeing women's role in society. If the tension between romantic fatalism/passivity and self-made women/agency is a theme in most telenovelas, *Mirada de mujer* expresses it as a continuum. María Inés goes from being the passive housewife to the woman who takes control of her own life and desires.

Most telenovela protagonists are border crossers, whether the border is the one between the country and the city or the class borders between poverty and wealth. But María Inés is also a border crosser: she is crossing the border of aging and independence. Her lover (like María's supportive schoolteacher or Gutierritos, who finds his redemption through the pen) is a writer who is supportive of her. He defends his own emotions and validates hers.

Martin Ponti calls telenovelas "dramas of identity, framed in a love story." I'd agree: these dramas of identity playing out the tension between agency and passivity provide a view of the world that allows women—and men—and hold up a mirror to their roles in a changing society.[24]

Esther Hamburger, an academic from Brazil who has written extensively about telenovelas, almost seems to be writing about *Mirada de mujer* when she discusses the 1979 Brazilian telenovela *Malu Mulher* (Malu, a Woman).

> Issues related to the role of women in society, in the family and at work constituted a privileged source of so-called "provocative" topics in telenovelas. The word feminism, however, was barely mentioned, and even though some series, such as "Malu Mulher" (Malu, a Woman) were successful because they had an undeniable feminist flavor, gender and family conflict were rather framed in terms of personal situations and conflicts. Perhaps this trajectory of liberation was possible because feminist issues were presented in a diluted and de-politicized framework, in a television program that was considered as female.[25]

What Hamburger calls a "diluted" and "de-politicized framework" is precisely the way in which telenovelas gain their power. They are not pamphlets, they are not advocates, and yet women can identify with the different roles, helped along with melodramatic stories of love and success.

The success of these stories is not only in the watching; it is in the creation of community and identity—virtual or otherwise. In other words, people get hooked on telenovelas and it influences the way they act. Since many Latin Americans watch telenovelas as young children, they often get to hear and talk about sexuality through these programs. A Puerto Rican colleague, who grew up in Boston, recalls hearing about "assault" in a telenovela (she doesn't remember which one) when she was nine or ten. She went running to her mother in the kitchen and asked about the word. She remembers that her mother seemed relieved, not angry, to have the topic broached by her daughter. An Ecuadoran friend from Quito similarly remembers learning about rape when she was 15 (although she understood it only as violence against women) by watching the 1983 Venezuelan telenovela *Leonela*, which tells of a young woman who is raped by a drunken wedding guest. Leonela becomes pregnant and falls into disgrace with high society; she eventually—after many twists and turns—ends up marrying the rapist. Another Puerto Rican friend also recalls learning about rape from *Leonela*, but adds in indignation, "How on earth could she fall in love with her rapist! What a bad message!"

What I felt startling was that all three women—without knowing what our conversation would be about—dredged up specific memories from decades ago about the impact of a telenovela on their sexual knowledge. In all three cases, the memories elicited an emotional response, especially in the case of the second Puerto Rican woman, who has a teenage daughter (who happens to be hooked on *Jane the Virgin*, a U.S. telenovela-dramatic series hybrid based on the 2002 Venezuelan telenovela *Juana la vírgin*).

Telenovelas touch upon themes that viewers are often not exposed to in daily life. For example, telenovelas portrayed divorce way before 1977, when the Brazilian Congress legalized divorce.

The 2015 Obitel report notes some of the controversial themes treated by telenovelas in the previous year: "family relations; ambition; homoaffective relations between men; gender identity; homophobia; child adoption; rape; homoaffective relations between women; heart transplant; alcoholism; Parkinson's disease."[26]

The knowledge sometimes leads to action. For example, the Inter-American Development Bank, in a 2008 study on Globo TV in Brazil, found that plots that depicted women's professional life and independence, as well as reproductive technologies (*Barriga de Aluguel* [Belly Rent], 1990, and *O Clone* [The Clone], 2001) influenced "a modern style of life" and "feminine emancipation." The study suggested that telenovelas also influenced divorce rates. When the woman protagonist of a novela was divorced or single, the divorce rate increased, on average, 0.1 percent.[27]

Women are influenced by telenovelas by seeing themselves as protagonists, by learning about topics that shape their lives such as sexual violence, divorce and reproductive rights, and by acting on that knowledge—whether through unconscious patterning or conscious activism.

Benavides, in discussing *Xica da Silva*, a Brazilian telenovela, sums it up:

> It is telling that in most soap operas women more than men are central protagonists, which, to some degree, expresses something that (male) social scientists might have been slow to understand: the women (elite or not) have (and have had) much more agency than anyone would want to admit.[28]

Notes

1   Mimi Whitefield, "New Formulas Keep Spanish-language Soap Operas Rolling in the Dough," *The Miami Herald*, November 20, 2000.
2   Margarita Martínez, "Betty 'The Ugly' Reveals a Truth About Beauty," April 2, 2001, http://womensenews.org/2001/04/betty-the-ugly-reveals-truth-about-beauty/.

3 Ibid.

4 Yeidy M. Rivero, "Our *Betty*: The Legacy of *Yo soy Betty, la fea*'s Success in Colombia," in Janet McCabe and Kim Akass, eds., *TV's Betty Goes Global: From Telenovela to International Brand* (I.B. Tauris & Co. Ltd., New York, 2013), 45.

5 Yeidy M. Rivero, "The Performance and Reception of Televisual 'Ugliness' in *Yo soy Betty la fea*," *Feminist Media Studies*, 3–1, 65–81, 2003.

6 Sandra Hernandez, "The Ugly Truth About 'Betty la Fea': A Telenovela Heroine for Our Times Betrays Her Feminist Fans," June 1, 2001, www.salon.com/2001/06/01/betty_2/.

7 Michele Hilmes, "The Whole World's Unlikely Heroine: Ugly Betty as Transnational Phenomenon," in Janet McCabe and Kim Akass, eds., *TV's Betty Goes Global: From Telenovela to International Brand* (I.B. Tauris & Co. Ltd., New York, 2013), 26.

8 Ibid., 33.

9 JR Thorpe, "9 Things About the Original Brothers Grimm Cinderella Story That Are Nothing Like the Disney Version," January 29, 2015, www.bustle.com/articles/61053-9-things-about-the-original-brothers-grimm-cinderella-story-that-are-nothing-like-the-disney-version.

10 Charles Perrault, "Cendrillon, ou la petite pantoufle de verre," *Histoires ou contes du temps passé, avec des moralités: Contes de ma mère l'Oye* (Paris, 1697) in Andrew Lang, ed., *The Blue Fairy Book* (London: Longmans, Green, and Co., 1889), 64–71.

11 Marina Warner, *From the Beast to the Blonde: On Fairy Tales and Their Tellers* (London: Vintage, 1995), quoted in Michele Hilmes, "The Whole World's Unlikely Heroine: Ugly Betty as Transnational Phenomenon," Janet McCabe and Kim Akass, eds., *TV's Betty Goes Global: From Telenovela to International Brand* (New York: I.B. Tauris & Co. Ltd., 2013), 26.

12 Janet McCabe, "Introduction: 'Oh Betty You Really Are Beautiful,'" Janet McCabe and Kim Akass, eds., *TV's Betty Goes Global: From Telenovela to International Brand* (New York: I.B. Tauris & Co. Ltd., 2013), 20.

13 Yeidy M. Rivero, "Our *Betty*: The Legacy of *Yo soy Betty, la fea*'s Success in Colombia," in Janet McCabe and Kim Akass, eds., *TV's Betty Goes Global: From Telenovela to International Brand* (New York: I.B. Tauris & Co. Ltd., 2013), 45. Rivero mentions that Gaitán based his *cuartel de las feas* on the secretaries at RCN; I'd heard this story repeatedly in Colombia in local press and television interviews. I especially like the anecdote because it grounds Betty's fairy-tale quality in everyday life. In a sense, that's what narconovelas do too. They tell this rather fabulous rags-to-riches story, which rather than being a fairy tale, is based on the gritty daily reality of newspaper headlines. For more on narconovelas, see the chapter on the subject in this book.

14 O. Hugo Benavides, *Drugs, Thugs, and Divas: Telenovelas and Narco-Dramas in Latin America* (Austin: University of Texas Press, 2008), 58.

15 Maria Immacolata Vassallo de Lopes and Guillermo Orozco Gómez, eds., *(Re)Invention of TV Fiction Genres and Formats*, Ibero-American Observatory for Television Fiction (Obitel) 2016 Yearbook (Porto Alegre, Brazil: Editorial Sulina, 2016), 302.

16 Marlene A. Lee and Mark Mather, "U.S. Labor Force Trends," *Population Bulletin*, 63, no. 2 (Population Reference Bureau, Washington, DC, June 2008), 5.

17 http://telenovelasfall09.blogspot.com/2009/10/men-cry-too.html. The blog is run by Professor Carolina Acosta-Alzuru in the context of her University of Georgia class, "Telenovelas, Culture and Society." The students each follow a particular telenovela and write about it in the blog. For more on this class, see Chapter 1 of this book.

18 Jaime S. Gómez, "Telenovelas from Rio Grande to the Andes: The Construction of Latin American and Latino Identities Through Media Production Creative Process," in Diana L. Ríos and Mari Castañeda, eds., *Soap Operas and Telenovelas in a Digital Age: Global Industries and New Audiences* (New York: Peter Lang, 2011), 28.

19 Reginald Clifford, "Engaging the Audience: The Social Imagery of the Novel," in Ilan Stavans, ed., *Telenovelas* (The Ilan Stavans Library of Latino Civilization, Santa Barbara, CA: Greenwood, 2010), 94.

20 Ibsen Martínez, "Romancing the Globe," in Ilan Stavans, ed., *Telenovelas* (The Ilan Stavans Library of Latino Civilization, Santa Barbara, CA: Greenwood, 2010), 62.

21 Arvind Singhal and Everett M. Rogers, "Simplemente Maria and Formation of the Entertainment-Education Strategy," [Unpublished] 1994. Presented at the 122nd Annual Meeting of the American Public Health Association [APHA], Washington, DC, October 30–November 2, 1994. Also see Arvind Singhal, Rafael Obregón and Everett M. Rogers, "Reconstructing the Story of *Simplemente María*, the Most Popular *telenovela* in Latin America of All Time" (Gazette, University of Texas at El Paso 54, 1–15, 1994), http://utminers.utep.edu/asinghal/Articles%20and%20Chapters/singhal_obr egon_rogers.pdf. I discovered the second article long after the first and found that the University of Texas article illuminates some of the thinking of the unpublished paper, which was presented to a specialized audience. For more on telenovelas and social change, see the chapter on social change in this book.

22 Jorge González, "Understanding Telenovelas as a Cultural Front: A Complex Analysis of a Complex Reality," in Ilan Stavans, ed., *Telenovelas* (The Ilan Stavans Library of Latino Civilization, Santa Barbara, CA: Greenwood, 2010), 74.

23 *Reforma*, 1997, 9E, quoted in Ilan Stavans, ed., *Telenovelas* (The Ilan Stavans Library of Latino Civilization, Santa Barbara, CA: Greenwood, 2010, Santa Barbara, California), 55.

24 Martin Ponti, "Globo vs. Sistema Brasileiro de Televisão (SBT)" in Diana L. Ríos and Mari Castañeda, eds., *Soap Operas and Telenovelas in a Digital Age: Global Industries and New Audiences* (New York: Peter Lang, 2011), 221.

25 Esther Hamburger, "Politics and Intimacy in Brazilian Telenovelas," Chapter 4 (unpublished dissertation, University of Chicago, 1999), 168. Professor Hamburger was a 2015–16 Peggy Rockefeller Visiting Scholar at the David Rockefeller Center for Latin American Studies, and we spent much time discussing telenovelas. She generously shared her thesis with me.

26 Maria Immacolata Vassallo de Lopes and Guillermo Orozco Gómez, eds., *Gender Relations in Television Fiction*, Ibero-American Observatory for Television Fiction (Obitel) 2013 Yearbook (Porto Alegre, Brazil: Editorial Sulina, 2015), 120.

27 Alberto Chong and Eliana La Ferrara, "Television and Divorce: Evidence from Brazilian Novelas," Working Paper #651, BR–N1020, Inter-American Development Bank, 2009, http://idbdocs.iadb.org/wsdocs/getdocument.aspx?docnum=1856109.

28 O. Hugo Benavides, "Seeing Xica and the Melodramatic Unveiling of Colonial Desire," in *Drugs, Thugs, and Divas: Telenovelas and Narco-Dramas in Latin America* (Austin: University of Texas Press, 2008), 32.

Bibliography

Benavides, O. Hugo. *Drugs, Thugs, and Divas: Telenovelas and Narco-Dramas in Latin America.* Austin: University of Texas Press, 2008.

Chong, Alberto, and Eliana La Ferrara. "Television and Divorce: Evidence From Brazilian Novelas." Working Paper #651. Inter-American Development Bank, 2009. http://idbdocs.iadb.org/wsdocs/getdocument.aspx?docnum=1856109.

Hamburger, Esther. *Politics and Intimacy in Brazilian Telenovelas.* Unpublished dissertation, University of Chicago, 1999.

Hernandez, Sandra. "The Ugly Truth About 'Betty la Fea': A Telenovela Heroine for our Times Betrays Her Feminist Fans." June 1, 2001. www.salon.com/2001/06/01/betty_2/.

Martínez, Margarita. "Betty 'The Ugly' Reveals a Truth About Beauty." April 2, 2001. http://womensenews.org/2001/04/betty-the-ugly-reveals-truth-about-beauty/.

McCabe, Janet, and Kim Akass, eds. *TV's Betty Goes Global: From Telenovela to International Brand.* New York: I.B. Tauris & Co. Ltd., 2013.

Perrault, Charles. "Cendrillon, ou la petite pantoufle de verre." *Histoires ou contes du temps passé, avec des moralités: Contes de ma mère l'Oye.* Paris, 1697, in Andrew Lang (ed), *The Blue Fairy Book.* London: Longmans, Green, and Co., ca. 1889.

Ríos, Diana L., and Mari Castañeda, eds. *Soap Operas and Telenovelas in a Digital Age: Global Industries and New Audiences.* New York: Peter Lang, 2011.

Rivero, Yeidy M. "The Performance and Reception of Televisual 'Ugliness' in *Yo soy Betty la fea.*" *Feminist Media Studies,* 3–1, 2003, 65–81.

Singhal, Arvind, and Everett M. Rogers. "Simplemente Maria and formation of the Entertainment-Education Strategy." Unpublished presentation, presented at the 122nd Annual Meeting of the American Public Health Association [APHA], Washington, DC, October 30-November 2, 1994.

Stavans, Ilan, ed. *Telenovelas.* The Ilan Stavans Library of Latino Civilization, Santa Barbara, CA: Greenwood, 2010.

Thorpe, JR. "9 Things About the Original Brothers Grimm Cinderella Story That Are Nothing Like the Disney Version." January 29, 2015. www.bustle.com/articles/61053-9-things-about-the-original-brothers-grimm-cinderella-story-that-are-nothing-like-the-disney-version.

Vassallo de Lopes, Maria Immacolata, and Guillermo Orozco Gómez, eds. *Gender Relations in Television Fiction,* Ibero-American Observatory of Television Fiction (Obitel) 2015 Yearbook. Porto Alegre, Brazil: Editorial Sulina, 2015.

Vassallo de Lopes, Maria Immacolata, and Guillermo Orozco Gómez, eds. *(Re)Invention of TV Fiction Genres and Formats,* Ibero-American Observatory ofr Television Fiction (Obitel) 2016 Yearbook. Porto Alegre, Brazil: Editorial Sulina, 2016.

Whitefield, Mimi. "New Formulas Keep Spanish-language Soap Operas Rolling in the Dough." *The Miami Herald,* November 20, 2000.

4

GAY LOVE, GAY KISSES

Most telenovelas focus on heterosexual love and desire. The images of gays in early telenovelas (when they were even present) were all too often only in the context of a clownish figure or an empathetic hairdresser. If telenovelas project opportunities for shaping identification, there was little for a gay person to identify with. Nevertheless, gay sexuality has been finding its way into telenovelas for many years. If we choose to measure increased portrayals of gay sexuality in telenovelas by its physical expressions, we might take a look at the very basic subject of kisses—not the peck on the cheek Latin Americans are so fond of, but the long, lingering type associated with romance—be it heterosexual or gay.

So when was the first portrayal of a passionate kiss between two women in a telenovela?

It was more than 30 years ago, in the 1988 Colombian telenovela *Los pecados de Inés de Hinojosa* (The Sins of Inés de Hinojosa). The well-known actresses Amparo Grisales and Margarita Rosa de Francisco portrayed the forbidden 16th-century love between two women.

A married woman with a violent and unfaithful husband finds love with his niece, who has been raped by her uncle. In addition to the first gay kiss between two women, the telenovela also broaches the subject of incest.

Both actresses were known as heterosexuals—Amparo Grisales, who plays the lead role, was dating famed Colombian singer Carlos Vives at the time. And putting the romantic love in a historical framework makes it more audience-friendly in a conservative society. In a massive celebration of 60 years of television in Colombia, the show, produced by R.T.I. television, was chosen as one of the most important in the history of the country's broadcast industry.[1]

So when, then, was the first passionate kiss between two men?

In 2010, in the Argentine telenovela *Botineras*, Manuel Riveiro, known as *Flaco* or Skinny, and Gonzalo Roldán, known as Lalo, kiss each other passionately in the locker room. The scene is unusual not only because two men kiss each other (and the telenovela ratings shot way up!), but because they are traditionally masculine soccer players.

Botineras, whose title has been translated (non-literally) as "Love for the Game," revolves around soccer players and their various love interests who become embroiled in a murder mystery. The program, broadcast on Argentine network Telefe, started off as a sports comedy and evolved into a police drama. Although the two men are not the protagonists, their relationship drew considerable attention at a time when Argentina was debating its same-sex marriage law.

In *Out in the Periphery*, a comparative study of gay rights in Latin America, Bard political science professor Omar Encarnación observes that the telenovela was "the most talked-about support" for marriage equality in Argentina. The subplot about Flaco and Lalo, according to Encarnación, was co-written with gay rights activists.[2]

Flaco decides to out himself before the media outs him. When he is asked by the media about his views on gay marriage, he replies that "It is natural to be respectful, and what alters the natural order is, it seems to me, to deny the rights to those who are the same." A straight teammate supports the statement, adding, "We are part of a community . . . we are all equal."

In an e-mail, Encarnación explains,

> [*Botineras* aimed] to promote same-sex marriage, and in particular to convey the message that gay people's desire for marriage stemmed from the same reasons that straight people want marriage: love, companionship, etc. This message was woven through the story line about a football player that comes out to his team mates and reveals that he intends to marry his partner. . . . The relevance of all of this, is that the story line is meant to challenge that gay people simply want marriage because all they care about is equal treatment under the law. The soap also featured the first gay kiss in Argentine television and, as such, it is widely acknowledged to have impacted public opinion right before the final congressional vote on same-sex marriage.
>
> Finally, the story line challenged stereotypes about homosexual men by delving into homosexuality in the world of sports.[3]

So, unlike *Los pecados de Inés de Hinojosa*, which is set in a distant past, *Botineras* is both contemporary and newsworthy. Gay marriage became legal in Argentina in July 2010.

Three years after Argentina legalized same-sex marriage, *Farsantes* (The Bluffers), a 2013 Argentine telenovela, also offered viewers a passionate kiss, this time between the two main protagonists. Two lawyers, Guillermo Graziani and Pedro Beggio fall in love with each other.

In the first episode, Guillermo invites Pedro to become a member of his law firm. The two become fast friends and inseparable colleagues, always talking on the phone late at night about work-related topics. One morning, the conversation turns personal when Pedro expresses his doubts about marrying his girlfriend Camila. The two men hug strongly—a mix of erotic desire and fraternal compassion.

About 30 episodes into the series, Pedro feels quite sick and his friend takes care of him, sitting with him as he sleeps. When he wakes up, he slowly leans toward Guillermo and kisses him on the lips. The two look tenderly at each other.

However, their love eventually leads to Pedro's death. Camila, overtaken by jealousy, stabs and kills him. Viewers were outraged, and the show's ratings plunged. One viewer, who identified herself as Soledad, wrote:

> The scriptwriters killed one of the most loved characters of Argentine fiction ... without any kind of consideration or responsibility. ... We do not know if Argentina will be more tolerant and less discriminatory. ... What we do know is that the story between Guillermo and Pedro was a love story because it will always live in our hearts.

Another viewer, who identified herself as Sandra, wrote, "We have our place where Guille and Pedro live and are happy, away from pain and human misery."[4]

Carlos Gustavo Halaburda, an Argentine graduate student at the University of British Columbia, relates how a group of fans "hung large signs with the picture of the two men kissing each other in front of the doors of Pol-ka TV studio in Buenos Aires city. The sign read 'No todas las historias de amor terminan mal. Pedro y Guillermo hasta el final' (Not all love stories have a tragic end; we demand a happy ending for Pedro and Guillermo)."[5]

And the viewers actually got their way! (Sort of; no spoilers here.)

A few months later, fans in Brazil would demand "the kiss" in *Amor à Vida* (Love of Life) (Figure 4.1), a 2013 Globo prime-time telenovela. The couple's Twitter supporters—more than 600,000 of them, in fact—encouraged them with "Kiss him, Felix!" (#beijafelix) and also "gay kiss" (#beijogay). The BBC reported that more than 3,200 comments on the story were posted on its Brazil Facebook page, many of them welcoming the kiss. The supporters called the kiss "overdue" and a "taboo-breaker," while critics charged that the telenovela would encourage children to be gay or objected on religious grounds.[6]

On January 31, 2014, protagonists Felix and Niko kiss deeply on the mouth, and according to the Spanish news agency EFE, the kiss made the front pages of all Brazilian morning papers and was one of the ten subjects most tweeted about in the world on Twitter.

FIGURE 4.1 *Amor à Vida,* 2013, Creator: Walcyr Carrasco, Image: Paolla Oliveira, Mateus Solano.

"How are we supposed to assume this broadcast?" asks the 2015 report by the Ibero-American Observatory of Television Fiction (Obitel).

> Is that a sign of opening up, or is it a daring act of TV fiction narrative towards sexual diversity? Does it mean, perhaps, that from now on we can overcome the censorship and the taboo of speaking about sexual diversity in the Ibero-American telenovelas without resorting to labels, clichés or discriminating stereotypes? The question hangs in the air, but the kiss scene

remains an image as a natural affective interaction in a love relationship between two men.[7]

#BeijaFélixeNiko had been a major trending topic on Twitter for months. The protagonists had had a long and steamy relationship, but unlike in heterosexual relationships, much was left up to the viewer's imagination. Their "passionate peck" was long awaited. The kiss takes place at the end of the final episode, after which Felix and Niko "go on to live together and raise a family," according to a Brazilian news site.[8]

However, even though gay characters have been seen in telenovelas since the 1970s, these expressions of sexuality are few and far between. Sexuality is generally not projected as an open part of the perception of what it means to be gay. In 2005, also in the last episode of a prime-time telenovela, the director had filmed a scene of two male characters kissing, but television management censored it at the last moment. In 2011, *Insensato Coração* (Irrational Heart) was scheduled to have a gay kiss, but after extensive consultations through web forums, it was decided the public was not ready. That same year, Globo even censored a scene in an episode of the U.S. animated series *The Simpsons* because it showed Homer Simpson kissing another male character, the bartender Moe—even though both are straight. The network argued that the show aired on Friday mornings and could be watched by children.

Edson Pimental, the executive director of TV Globo, told author Fréderic Martel at the time about the *Insensato Coração* incident, "We make mainstream television; we're not there simply to provoke."[9]

Thus after such experiences with censorship and self-censorship, the kiss between Felix and Niko was celebrated as a victory both for gay rights and for freedom of expression.

"People gathered in front of the television in angst, and celebrated the kiss as if it was the World Cup," Brazil's first openly gay congressman Jean Wyllys told BBC Trending in an interview. Wyllys was not a disinterested viewer; he had helped start the hashtag campaign to try to prevent another censorship of a kiss, as in 2005.[10]

Not all politicians agreed with the gay activists. One congressman, Jairo Bolsonaro, called the kiss "a milestone in society's perversion."

A milestone it was, although not necessarily of the type Bolsonaro had in mind.

Despite the abundance of fairly progressive portrayals of gays in Brazilian telenovelas, the sensuous and sometimes steamy kisses between heterosexual partners were simply absent or discreetly implied in gay relationships.

Lesbians were quicker than gay men to enjoy the first same-sex kiss in a Brazilian telenovela, although certainly not as early as the Colombian kiss. The 2004 TV Globo *Senhora do Destino* (Master of Destiny), however, took place in contemporary Brazil, not in a piece of historical fiction. Jenifer and Eleanora, a lesbian couple in their mid-20s, managed to exchange a passionate, although somewhat short of steamy, kiss and are later shown (again discreetly) naked in bed, presumably after making love.

The story also has a traditional happy ending: like Niko and Felix almost ten years later, Jenifer and Eleanora were married through a "lawful agreement" and adopt a son.

"This was a watershed moment within the genre, and more importantly within the television medium in Brazil as the couple challenged the way lesbians were historically portrayed in Brazilian television," observe Brazilian media scholars Antonio La Pastina and Samantha Nogueira Joyce.[11]

In May 2011, the Brazilian telenovela actually got around to a steamy, 40-second kiss between two women, Marcela and Marina, in the SBT (Globo's competitor) telenovela *Amor e Revolução* (Love and Revolution), set during Brazil's military dictatorship. The kiss aired exactly one week after the Brazilian Supreme Court had ruled in favor of gay civil unions, granting same-sex couples the same marriage rights as heterosexual couples.

The Brazilian kiss practically coincides with another kiss—this time in Peru. In the 2011 telenovela *Lalola*, Celeste, a declared lesbian, kisses Lola. However, the focus of the telenovela is not on gay relationships, but rather on an inveterate womanizer.

I've emphasized the issue of kissing here since its portrayal makes the way viewers see a relationship between two men or two women as very ordinary, a normal part of daily life. It removes any ambiguity from portrayed relationships and sends the message that the gay relationship is like the heterosexual one in its affectivity and passion. It means that the partners want to get married. Or they don't. It means that they adopt children. Or they don't. It means that they can be good, bad or every shade in-between. They can be faithful—or adulterers. They can fall in and out of love, and have outrageous crushes on people who don't reciprocate. They are sexual beings (or, if they are not, it's because they choose not to be) just like all the heterosexual couples in telenovelas. In other words, it's what straight people have long seen as normal in their daily lives—and in telenovelas. It's what one might call the new "normal," a trend that is not by any means true of all telenovelas, but becoming increasingly frequent both in Latin America and in U.S.-based Spanish language television.

Going All the Way

So when and where, talking of "normalization," did the first full sexual encounter between two men air in a Latin American telenovela?

Well, Colombia may claim the first lesbian kiss and Argentina the first passionate kiss between two men, but Brazil hosts the first gay sex scene in bed with the 2016 telenovela *Liberdade, Liberdade* (Freedom, Freedom), an 18th-century period piece. Andre and Colonel Tolentino have been attracted to each other for months, but they finally undress and make love. Afterward, the couple lies on the bed naked, holding hands.[12]

The dialogue between the two men is a coming-out scene:

Tolentino: My only friend is you. You, Andre. A sensitive man. Can you understand the mysteries of life. The turns that the world gives. The surprises that life holds.

Andre: Surprises about ourselves.

Tolentino: Yes. You said one day. We all have a second nature. Sometimes it remains hidden.

Andre: But not forever . . .

The undressing scene that follows is slow and sensual, evolving from shyness with a tinge of shame to tenderness, romanticism and confidence. It is, in short, a beautiful love scene.

"I am very happy to be representing this story," Caio Blat, who plays Andre, told the press. "It adds to the feeling of the show, addressing various forms of prejudice and discrimination."

"This is a mature telenovela," he added. "People realize these are contemporary issues that are being addressed in a historical context."

A Catholic organization protested, charging the telenovela "wanted to take the devil into viewers' homes," and evangelicals have called the sex scene "a sexual assault on the Brazilian family."[13]

But the telenovela—although a historical one—allowed gay viewers to identify with the protagonists. Facebook, Twitter and gay websites were abuzz with commentary about the scene.

A person who identified himself as "Billy Budd" wrote on a gay website:

I cried like a baby when I watched this scene. It is the FIRST scene between gay men in Brazilian television. It was masterfully crafted, well acted, beautifully lit, and the actors are gorgeous. It is a LOVE scene, not a sex scene. It is romantic and in very good taste. The music is from the classic gay movie "Death In Venice" (1971). It is the adagietto from Mahler's fifth symphony.[14]

Throughout Latin America, other telenovelas have implied sex scenes (such as in the case of Jenifer and Eleanora), but *Liberdade, Liberdade* is as explicit as any heterosexual sex scene in a telenovela. In the melodramatic rhythms of telenovelas, kissing is extremely important. A kiss is the moment when the viewer knows that the kissers are now a couple—and are usually going to be so for a while. More than a conquest of one side or another, it is the statement of a bond.

Sex scenes can be ambivalent in the Latin American telenovelas, but as "Billy Budd" astutely observes, *Liberdade, Liberdade* shows a love scene, not a sex scene. The physicality between same-sex couples normalizes the relationship between the couple. It is no longer a relationship that the viewer can surmise but not actually see. Historically, the lack of sexuality in gay relationships shown in telenovelas reflects the silence of Latin American society in the face of gayness: everyone knows Uncle José is gay, but no one talks about it; everyone knows the hairdresser or fashion designer is gay, but no one talks about it, just enjoys the touch of comic relief. Seeing gay relationships expressed in the same ways and degrees that heterosexual relationships are depicted opens the viewer to a new perspective.

Doing Away With Invisibility

Women have long been able to see themselves in telenovelas, and gays are beginning to do the same. Telenovelas are gradually doing away with the invisibility of the gay community.

An Obitel report points out that

> [telenovelas] have become a space for discussion of both sexuality and homophobia. This scenario led us to stress the importance of the space for discussion allowed by telenovela plots and characters and identify it as a characteristic trait of Brazilian telenovelas.[15]

Homophobia in Brazilian telenovelas and beyond is mainly expressed through family relationships, in which parents reject their offspring because of their gayness. However, at least one Brazilian telenovela takes on the issue of violence against gays. *Duas Caras* (Two Faces), a 2007 telenovela extensively discussed in this book's chapter on race, depicts a mob scene of evangelical Christians who go to the favela to storm the house of two gay men and their very pregnant coworker and housemate, Dália. Bernadinho and Heraldo are planning to register the baby with two fathers. Furious about what it considers the immorality of the three housemates, the crowd moves through the neighborhood, hurling stones at the house and hitting Dália in the head. Bernadinho and Heraldo are roughed up; Dália escapes. The crowd enters the house and destroys the bed by stabbing and ripping it. The rioting stops only when a powerful politician fires off a single gunshot and the mob disperses.

The scene underlines an interesting tension between normalizing gay relationships in telenovelas (and through legislation) and showing the hate-mongering that prevents or endangers those relationships. Many Latin American countries have very progressive gay rights laws. In 2003, Brazil became the first Latin American country to recognize same-sex unions and was among the earliest to allow gay couples to adopt children. Yet, despite these laws, sexually liberal attitudes, and its reputation for gay carnival, it has one of the highest rates of antigay violence in Latin America. In mid-2016, the non-governmental group Grupo Gay da Bahia estimated that nearly 1,600 gay people have died in hate-motivated attacks in the last four and a half years. The group, which tracks the deaths through published newspaper articles (which may mean the figure is on the low side), says that at least one gay or transgender person is killed on a daily basis in Brazil.[16] Thus far, telenovelas have mostly portrayed the issues of identity and equal rights, rather than tackling hate crimes. *Duas Caras* seems to be a notable exception.

Although Brazil has taken the lead on dealing with LGBTQ themes, other countries are not far behind, and indeed may even be ahead in terms of their portrayal of transgender people. In Argentina, a transgender actress known as Florencia de la V played the role of a transgender daughter in the 2004 telenovela *Los Roldán*. Colombia bought the rights to a remake, and in 2006 the transgender Laisa Reyes, in *Los Reyes* (The Kings), was played by Endry Cardeño, a real-life transgender actress. Laisa returns from Europe, where she has had a sex change, and is warmly embraced by her family. Cardeño, in turn, is embraced by the enthusiastic Colombia public, and she is featured on the cover of the prestigious Colombian magazine *Soho*. There was also a Mexican remake known as *Los Sánchez*.

In Peru, another socially conservative country, one of the first transgender portrayals was that of Josi, a transgender character in *Los de arriba y los de abajo* (1994). In 2014, Comando Alfa portrays a transgender sister sympathetically. The 2014 Obitel report notes that these representations, although few and far between, have "begun to generate empathy and coexistence."

"Telenovelas have played an active role in representing sexual minorities," says Mauro Pereira Porto. "[T]here is an important pluralization in the way television fiction has represented sexual minorities, although stereotypes and stigmas persist and telenovelas continue to face major difficulties in representing the social perspective of gays and lesbians."[17]

Even the most socially conservative countries in Latin America have been portraying gay characters for years. In Chile, for example, a gay personality was shown in the 1981 *La madrastra* (The Stepmother). The stereotyped role was as an effeminate bartender, an object of humor. However, in the social context of the repressive dictatorship, just showing a gay man was significant. The second gay personality, according to Bernardo Amigo, María Cecilia Bravo and Francisco Osorio, did not appear until 12 years later in *Marrón glacé* (Machos).[18]

"During this period, in spite of the risk represented by Pinochet for the consolidation of human, civil and political rights, Chileans began to energetically insist on recognition and rights for ethnic, cultural and political communities," say the authors.

The gay character in *Marrón glacé*, Pierre la Font, is the head chef in an exclusive restaurant. While his portrayal has elements of the humorous stereotype, he is an integral part of the telenovela, appearing day after day and not just in situations that might evoke laughter. The telenovela appeared around the time the gay liberation movement there was presenting a proposed bill to reform homophobic laws.

In Chile, the real break with the stereotypes comes with the 2003 telenovela *Machos* in which one of six brothers, sons of a very machista father, is gay. He's not effeminate; some of his brothers accept him, and others do not; the father rejects his son's sexuality completely.

Amigo, Bravo and Osorio observe that the gay son is presented in a very favorable way: "sensible, determined, caring and understanding." At the same time, they say, he is victimized by rejection and misunderstanding "by those who are inflexible, anachronistic and violent. . . . In *Machos*, for the first time [in Chile], a gay person is vindicated."

By 2009, in the telenovela ¿*Dónde está Elisa?*, there's the first representation of gay relationships, when a successful married lawyer falls in love with his wife's gay friend. Since then, gay roles have become much more frequent in Chilean teleno-velas, although the society is still considered to be socially conservative.

The three authors conclude that while the telenovela is not the change agent in the social debate, it can "have a multiplying effect and solidify these changes. . . . In this sense, telenovelas are an interesting index of the realities of social complexity."

The pattern continues throughout Latin America. As the gay community begins to agitate for rights, their representations increase in telenovelas, and as sympathetic representations increase, gays and their allies find more opportunities to gain acceptance on a personal level and to obtain changes on the legislative front.

Brazil in the Vanguard

In much of Latin America, the inclusion of gay figures in a serious, respectful light has been gradual. Brazil, while having had its fair share of comic-relief gay roles, started to portray serious gay characters in relationships quite early. Antonio La Pastina and Samantha Joyce, in an insightful article on the history of gayness in Brazilian telenovelas, discuss a listing of popular gay characters in *Época* magazine, published in 1999 just as a telenovela protagonist, Uálber, is about to come out to his mother in the 1999 series *Suave Veneno* (Smooth Poison). The list is surprisingly long (in chronological order): Inácio (Dênis Carvalho), the sensitive millionaire in *Brilhante* (1982, Globo Network); Mário Liberato (Cécil Thiré), the villain adored by the audience in *Roda de Fogo* (1986, Globo Network); Zaqueu (João Alberto), the butler in *Pantanal* (1990, Manchete Network); Sandrinho (André Gonçalves) and Jéfferson (Lui Mendes), a young couple in *A Próxima Vítima* (1995, Globo Network); Sarita Vitti (Floriano Peixoto), pioneer drag queen in Brazilian televi-sion in *Explode Coração* (1996, Globo Network); and Rafael (Odilon Wagner), the bisexual father who leaves his wife for a young man in *Por Amor* (1997, Globo Network).[19]

In recent years, Brazil has burst into the forefront of gay-themed telenovelas and those with strong gay characters. The 2012 *Insensato Coração* (Restless Heart) portrayed six gay characters, ranging from the businessman to the waiter, distrib-uted among the many subplots, although as we mentioned before, it stopped short of overt sexuality expressed through a kiss. Statements in favor of gay rights were strengthened by the characters (gay or not), showing an ample view of gay move-ments' demands from the perspective of different social classes. Just like we saw in the case of Chile, the telenovela was broadcast while there was a bill being debated in the Brazilian Congress on sexual diversity (PLC 122/2006).

In 2014 alone, three telenovelas with strong gay figures were shown in Brazil: *Amor à Vida*, *Em Família* and *Império*. These telenovelas explored the complexity of family and love relationships through their main characters and illustrated the ambiguous behavior of Brazilian society toward traditional family values and the new family arrangements created by sexual and gender diversity.

The stereotypes still appear throughout Latin America (and indeed in the telenovela-inspired U.S. series such as *Ugly Betty*, which keeps the portrayal of a flamboyant gay designer from the original *Betty la fea*) (Figure 4.2), but interesting and serious gay characters are becoming much more frequent. Indeed, some of the tensions of representation can be seen in *Ugly Betty* itself, set in a very Latino Queens, where Betty's nephew Justin comes to terms with his own gayness. His father—despite his macho attitudes—ends up defending him on a New York subway after the teenager is exposed to gay-bashing remarks. The recognition in this telenovela-influenced series—as in Latin American telenovelas in general—seems to be that the effeminate stereotype can coexist along with tales of lawyers, football players and even hired assassins.

Some ask whether the presentation of gays as effeminate is still "a step forward" because it is inclusive to the presence of gays in daily life or whether it is counterproductive because it plays into stereotypes. Julee Tate, in her fascinating article, "From Girly Men to Manly Men: The Evolving Representation of Male Homosexuality in Twenty-First Century Telenovelas," brings up the interesting question, drawing on work by Silvia Paternostro, that in many Latin American countries, the active partner is not necessarily considered gay, thus complicating the interpretation of telenovelas throughout the continent.[20]

FIGURE 4.2   *Yo soy Betty, la fea*, 1999, Produced by María del Pilar Fernández.

She observes that these characters are flamboyant in the way they dress and speak, and almost seem like a parody of gay men, rather than a realistic depiction, noting,

> [T]his characterization raises questions and concerns. While it may be interpreted in a positive light that the telenovela industry is including gay characters in their scripts, the tendency to portray these individuals in a caricaturesque manner is essentializing and suggests that there is only one kind of gay man: an effeminate, or girly, man.

Tate points to the frequency of gay designers in the fashion industry as a common recurrence in telenovelas (Hugo Lombardi, the flamboyantly petulant fashion designer in *Betty la fea*, immediately comes to mind), and Tate makes reference to Gregory in *Sabor a ti*, a Venezuelan production, and Federico "Fico" in *Soledad*, a Peruvian telenovela. In both telenovelas discussed by Tate, the gay characters work in the fashion and advertising industries (note that they are professionals) and dress in loud colors and styles, speaking in cadences that are associated with effeminate manners. Gregory hangs out with the beautiful models in a platonic way and is accepted as "one of the girls."[21]

Fico sports makeup, and gorgeous women inhabit his social life in a non-sexual way. Neither character has a relationship or love interest with another man during the telenovela. This nonsexual portrayal of gays in Latin American telenovelas is one of the reasons that I chose to begin the chapter with a history of kisses; the evolution of gay telenovela characters is not only between effeminate and non-effeminate (to avoid using the word "masculine"), but between non-sexual and sexual.

One of the more modern representations on this spectrum is the 2003 Peruvian-Venezuelan telenovela *La mujer de Lorenzo* (Lorenzo's Woman), which features once again a fashion designer, but with the big difference that Giacomo, who has both a teenage son and an ex-wife, is not effeminate or flamboyant. Many episodes go by before the viewer—and some of the characters in the telenovela—figure out that Giacomo is gay or bisexual. Tate refers to this lapse in time as "'after-school special' effect—the didactic message being that not all gay men are effete."

Giacomo decides to date a woman called Nati in an attempt to hide his sexuality, and he finally ends up confessing to her that he is gay. Nati finds this hard to believe, asking him incredulously, "Isn't Toni your son?" He explains that he was young and already had doubts about his sexuality when his wife Alicia got pregnant. Nati replies, "Giacomo, I know homosexuals. Believe me, none is like you. They are . . ." Giacomo replies that the majority of gay men are not effeminate, but are "like him."

Tate points out that Giacomo is commenting as much on the sexuality of men in the general society as on the specific portrayal of these men in telenovelas where, as has been seen in previous examples, the majority of gay characters are portrayed as effeminate to the point of being comedic. Giacomo's portrayal as a masculine gay man and his direct challenge of the idea that gay equals effeminate is not common in Latin American telenovelas, but does appear in places as disparate as Mexico and Cuba.

But although the telenovela discusses Giacomo's sexuality in a frank and open way, it never shows him as a masculine gay man involved with a sexual partner of the same sex.

As early as 1999, Mexican television was showing an image of masculine gays, although in this case, the plot may be "justified" by the fact that one of the couple is a Mexican-born immigrant in San Francisco, suggesting that he may be bringing different cultural values of what it means to be gay.

La vida en el espejo (Life in the Mirror) looks at the lives of Mauricio, a wealthy Mexican in his 20s, and Jim, a Mexican-American. In the beginning of the telenovela, Mauricio is romantically involved with a young woman, but begins to question his sexuality. He says that he wants to stay chaste until he is married, and reacts with force when Jim, a gay friend, suggests he might be also. He eventually finds he is in love with Jim, and they become a couple. Both masculine types, they are accepted by their families and friends, but the sexuality between the two is only insinuated, leaving most everything to the viewer's imagination. Yet, it marks a first for Mexican telenovelas in putting the issue of gayness as an issue involving love, emotion and self-identity, rather than ridicule and shame.

The 2007 Mexican Televisa comedic telenovela *Yo amo a Juan Querendón* presents another gay masculine image, Gaytán Pastor, an executive in a food distribution company who dresses in reserved but fashionable business suits. He is openly gay. He pursues guys, most often without much luck. Gaytán is smitten with Juan, a hypermasculine man from rural Mexico, whom he decides to employ as his personal chauffeur. Juan understands his boss's intentions, but takes the job out of necessity. He finally confronts Gaytán and says he is tired of being harassed. Gaytán maintains his job and professional relationships even though he openly admits he is gay, but that does not keep the barbs from flying—especially because of his pursuit of Juan.

Toward the end of the telenovela, Gaytán trades his infatuation for Juan for that of Heriberto, who also is a hypermasculine rural Mexican with little education. Heriberto flees back to his hometown because he is so offended and upset by Gaytán's overtures, but he eventually comes back, confessing to a close woman friend, Yvonne, that he is confused about his feelings for Gaytán. Yvonne ends up asking Gaytán about his coming-out process; he gives her a list of books he read while he was in therapy to deal with his own feelings at the time, and Yvonne shares the list with Heriberto. After Yvonne lures both to a gay club (neither knowing the other is there at the same time, a comedic but supportive act of matchmaking), Heriberto starts dancing with a man he has just met. Gaytán spots the dancing pair and becomes enraged, but Heriberto quickly confesses to

Gaytán, "You moved me with things I didn't know I had inside. I believe I am in love with you. I have never felt this way about anyone." The two hold hands, and the following morning arrive at the office together. Coworkers stare, but they don't mind. The couple continue to lead a normal life (in queer studies, this is known as "heteronormative"), working out with Gaytán's brother and sister-in-law, dining and spending leisure time with other couples.

At the same time that many of these telenovelas reflect a normalizing of gay relationships, gay hairdressers and fashion designers persist. Nevertheless, one can say that a multiplicity of models is being offered to the telenovela viewer.

While I welcome the shift to normalization in the portrayal of gays in Latin American telenovelas (and U.S.-based telenovela-influenced hybrids), I don't necessarily think that the persistence of the portrayal of highly effeminate men is a bad thing, as long as it is not the only way to be gay. After all, if one goes to a gay rights parade in Boston or New York or Rio, one sees gay men portraying themselves as drag queens or highly effeminate figures—and that's alongside proud gay (and sometimes married) couples of both sexes strolling their baby carriages, hypermasculine big gay guys and transgender beauties. There doesn't necessarily have to be a continuum from effeminate to "just like us" portrayals, in my opinion.

Tate, whose essay is the most thorough I have found on the subject, warns us (but she does see it as a negative thing) that the shift does not mean that telenovelas will stop portraying gay characters as extremely effeminate and as a way of providing comic relief, adding, "Only time will tell if Juan Querendón is an aberration or, rather, a sign of change."

One might add that a shift in attitudes toward the depiction of gays in a Mexican telenovela does not just have impact in Mexico. Telenovelas do not only stay in their country of origin, but move between countries, inspiring dubbed versions and remakes. Brazilian telenovelas, for instance, are exported to more than 140 countries worldwide.

Says Samantha Nogueira Joyce, "[Telenovela] programs bring political events, news, and trends to the fore, as well as questions about ingrained traditions such as gender roles and sexuality. They therefore function as a type of public sphere...."[22]

Transitions in Cuba

Cuba is a good example of how the telenovela involving gayness reflects in the public sphere. For many years, Cuba was one of the most overtly homophobic countries in Latin America and the Caribbean, even sending gays to gulag-type camps in the 1960s and '70s for "rehabilitation." Many of the Cubans who fled the island in the Mariel boatlift exodus of 1980 were gay Cubans who felt under threat.

Unlike in many Latin American countries, it was a movie—rather than telenovelas—that opened up the discussion about a delicate subject. In 1993, Cuban director Tomás Gutiérrez Alea's *Fresa y chocolate* (Strawberry and Chocolate) had a gay protagonist and criticized the antigay prejudice and the unjust treatment suffered by gays. The film, the first of its type in Cuba, caused much controversy both within Cuba and internationally. Although it aired widely in theatres, it was not shown on Cuban television.

Another significant factor in the panorama of the treatment of gays in Cuba is that Mariela Castro, the daughter of Cuba's President Raúl Castro, runs a state-affiliated gay rights organization (she is straight).

In this context, in 1998, Cuban television (which is state-owned) made a foray into a telenovela with a lesbian theme. *La otra cara de la moneda* (The Other Side of the Coin) depicted all sorts of controversial subjects: alcoholism, prostitution, domestic violence, drugs and a love story between two women. However, only three episodes revolved around the lesbian couple, and one of the women is conveniently killed in a train wreck by the fourth episode. There were no kisses, no bedroom scenes, only an implied relationship that had to be ended almost as soon as it started.[23]

In 2004, on the other hand, *El balcón de los helechos* (The Fern Balcony) told the story of two women who lived together happily and were raising a small boy. Again, the relationship is not explicit, and physical affection (what we see in any case) is directed toward their young son, rather than each other. But no one gets killed in a train wreck.[24]

But the telenovela that aroused the most talk about gayness was the state-produced 2006 telenovela *La cara oculta de la luna* (The Dark Side of the Moon). The telenovela was aimed at social change, but not to improve gay rights (or stir up latent homophobia), but rather "to promote sexually responsible behavior among Cubans."[25]

The telenovela depicts the individual stories of three men and two women living with HIV infection, the precursor to AIDS. One of those people is Yassel, an extremely handsome (think dreamy telenovela hero) and hard-working construction worker who falls in love with Mario, an openly gay lawyer.

Yassel is happily married and has a seven-year-old daughter. He is passionately in love with his wife, and that doesn't change after Mario comes along. He desires them both. Yassel's father won't accept that his son is gay (there's no talk about bisexuality); however, the mother is more understanding and eventually convinces her husband not to reject their son because of his sexuality.

Although the sex scenes with the wife, Belkis, are very explicit and passionate, *La cara oculta de la luna* does not even show a kiss between Yassel and Mario. They gaze romantically into each other's eyes over a glass of wine.

Belkis suspects Yassel of having an affair with another woman, but when she discovers that his extramarital interest is a man, she screams at him, "You're not a man, not a woman, nothing. I don't want to see you again!"

She files for divorce and gets custody of the little girl. He contracts HIV, the human immunodeficiency virus that can lead to AIDS, and his relationship with Mario falls apart. It was said to be the first time Cuban television had portrayed gayness openly, and it is also relatively rare that Latin American telenovelas deal with bisexuality (although a few notable exceptions have been discussed in this chapter).

Cuban viewers were surprised that such a virile man as Yassel could fall in love with another man. "People were totally torn about this telenovela," observed Geydis Fundora, a Cuban sociologist, who does not study telenovelas formally, but watches them at least once a week with her parents in Cuba ("What sociologist could avoid that temptation?" she asks).

> Some loved *La cara oculta* and saw it in terms of bringing the subject of homosexuality to light. But it aroused a lot of homophobia and people, especially older people who had been influenced by the extreme anti-homosexuality of the Cuban revolution in the 1960s and 70s, would call Yassel a fag and all sorts of names.

An example of this attitude came up in messages sent to the National Center for Sex Education (CENESEX) website. One viewer, who identified himself as Angel Padrón Hernández from Camagüey province, talked about some of the attitudes there, "I heard one of my neighbors at the grocery when she was saying, 'We have to beware of faggots. Men are no longer having affairs with women, but with other men.'"

Indeed, that was one of the nerves the portrayal of Yassel struck. Julee Tate, in her analysis of gays in telenovelas, points out that the common attitude throughout the continent is to assume that to be feminine is to be gay, so therefore to be masculine is to be straight, regardless of whom one sleeps with. This analysis did not work for Yassel despite his good-looking and traditional masculinity; I believe that is because Mario is not a "conquest" but a deep love for which Yassel is willing to risk his home and family life.

The issue of bisexuality is also treated in a different manner than in other Latin American telenovelas (when it is treated at all), because the bisexual protagonist, unlike the protagonist in the Brazilian 1997 telenovela *Por Amor*, does not discover his gayness and decide to leave his wife; rather he is equally in love with and desires two people of different sexes.

La cara oculta was so polemic that Cuban state television decided to host a panel to discuss the series and invited viewers to call in.

"From now on, these themes will have to be discussed with more frankness," said Fredy Domínguez, the telenovela's scriptwriter. One man called in, declaring that he was offended with the presentation of homosexual relationships "as if they were natural." "It compels us to be better people, to be more tolerant," said panelist Manuel Calvino, a Cuban psychologist. "The show isn't a work of art; a lot of criticisms could be made," Mariela Castro, CENESEX director, added in an interview with the Associated Press. "But the debate is satisfying."[26]

Indeed, whether it is in regards to Cuba, Argentina, Brazil or Mexico, Mariela Castro's words are relevant to the evolving nature of gay portrayals in telenovelas. The 2015 Obitel report notes:

> The portrayal—or lack thereof—of homosexuals and homosexual love is thus highly significant, as the genre contributes to the general cultural acceptance of issues and in so doing can open up real-life possibilities to a segment of the population that traditionally faces discrimination.

The report, which focused on gender issues in telenovelas, pointed out that the depiction of different gender roles—including LGBTQ characters—establishes a dialogue with everyday life and the way the ordinary person perceives gender.[27]

Gay-themed telenovelas underline the fact that telenovelas put subjects on the table that people are not prone to discuss openly. They also reflect the importance of ordinary individuals—in this case, the LGBTQ community—seeing themselves on the screen. And they are a magnificent example of how telenovelas circulate from country to country, influencing other productions and even social policy. While LGBTQ activists in Argentina, for example, took their cues from U.S. gay rights activists in using the media to lobby for rights, chatrooms, websites and gay forums reflect how intensively U.S. viewers—sometimes Latino, sometimes not—are looking to Latin American telenovelas for frank expressions of sexuality. The periphery, as it were, is now having an impact on the center—Latin American telenovelas are influencing U.S. culture, as well as vice versa.

The productions are also consciously packaged for other countries. For instance, *Amor à Vida*, the 2013 Brazilian telenovela with the passionate kiss, was sold as *Rastros de Mentiras* (Traces of Lies) to TV Azteca in Mexico in 2014. In 2016, the Spanish-language telenovela won an award from GLAAD, the U.S.-based organization that monitors LGBTQ representations in the media.[28]

Thus, viewers in more socially conservative countries may see these telenovelas. They may reject the positive roles outright or they may see the situations as something that only happens in Brazil. But just as my Ecuadoran friend saw an educational message in learning about rape from a Venezuelan telenovela and my Puerto Rican friend totally thought the message inappropriate, the telenovelas operate in a public sphere in which viewers can make up their own minds.

When telenovelas got their start in the 1950s and 1960s, people would gather around to watch them. Sometimes it would be the entire family; sometimes it would be the children and the nanny; sometimes a community group looking at one lone privileged television. Programs were discussed in the home, at the bar and in the office. They still are, but now the conversation also flies through the Internet, on Twitter, through message boards and Facebook, as well as word of mouth and daily interactions.

The roles of gays in telenovelas have influenced, reflected and strengthened legislation about equal rights, whether it be non-discrimination laws or gay marriage. The new virtual conversations, like the telenovelas themselves, cross national borders. Telenovelas become mirrors for gender and sexuality, transcending borders, generations and social class. They may, as always, be vehicles for romantic dreams, but they are also places where the reflection of oneself becomes a place of power.

Notes

1 Las2orillas, "El encuentro erótica de la diva y Margarita Rosa en Los pecados de Inés de Hinojoso marcado la vida de la diva que hoy llega a los 60 años," May 12, 2016, www.las2orillas.co/el-pecado-de-amparo-grisales-que-escandalizo-a-colombia dalizo-a-colombia.
   Also see "Vuelve la historia de 'las Hinojosa', para quienes se la perdieron," *El Tiempo*, October 14, 2014. The 1988 telenovela was shown again in 2014 and still stirred controversy.
2 Omar G. Encarnación, *Out in the Periphery: Latin America's Gay Rights Revolution* (New York: Oxford University Press, 2016), 143–144.
3 Personal correspondence, November 26, 2016.
4 www.eltrecetv.com.ar/farsantes. Also see the Club De Fans De Guille Y Pedro Farsantes Facebook page: www.facebook.com/Club-De-Fans-De-Guille-Y-Pedro-Farsantes-510081359077256/.
5 Carlos Gustavo Halaburda, "We Demand a Happy Ending for Pedro and Guillermo: Love, Society and the Queer Politics of the Latin American Telenovela," *Sojourners: Undergraduate Journal of Sociology*, University of British Columbia, 2014, 6, http://soci.sites.olt.ubc.ca/files/2013/02/SOJOURNERS-VOL-6-7-FINAL.pdf#page=30.
6 #BBCtrending: "'Historic' gay kiss on Brazilian TV," February 3, 2014, www.bbc.com/news/blogs-trending-26020533.
7 Maria Immacolata Vassallo de Lopes and Guillermo Orozco Gómez, eds., *Gender Relations in Television Fiction*, Ibero-American Observatory for Television Fiction (Obitel) 2013 Yearbook (Porto Alegre, Brazil: Editorial Sulina, 2013), 77.
8 "Novela Amor a Vida—Novela protagoniza primeiro beijo gay da emissora," January 2, 2014. www.noticiasbr.com.br/novela-amor-a-vida-novela-protagoniza-primeiro-beijo-gay-da-emissora-133736.html.
9 Fréderic Martel, *Global Gay: como la revolución gay está cambiando el mundo* (Madrid: Taurus, 2013), 56.
10 #BBCtrending: "'Historic' gay kiss on Brazilian TV," www.bbc.com/news/blogs-trending-26020533.
11 Antonio La Pastina and Samantha Nogueira Joyce, "Changing GLBTQ Representations: The Sexual Other in Brazilian Telenovelas," *Lumina*, 8, no. 2, December 2014, *Revista do Programa de Pós-graduação em Comunicação*, Universidade Federal de Juiz de Fora / UFJF, www.researchgate.net/profile/Antonio_La_Pastina/publication/273525627_Changing_GLBTQ_representations_The_Sexual_Other_in_Brazilian_Telenovelas/links/55056a0f0cf2d60c0e6be69f.pdf.
12 Dan Avery, "Brazilian Telenovela Airs Country's First Gay Sex Scene," July 12, 2016, www.newnownext.com/brazilian-telenovela-first-gay-sex-scene/07/2016/.
13 Josh Lee, "Brazilian TV Show Makes History with Country's First Televised Gay Sex Scene – Watch," *Attitude*, July 18, 2016, http://attitude.co.uk/brazilian-tv-show-makes-history-with-countrys-first-televised-gay-sex-scene-watch/.
14 Billy Budd, comment on "Gay Couple Gets Intimate on Brazilian Telenovela for the First Time Ever," www.queerty.com/gay-couple-gets-intimate-brazilian-telenovela-first-time-ever-20160715.

15 Maria Immacolata Vassallo de Lopes and Guillermo Orozco Gómez, eds., *Transmedia Production Strategies in Television Fiction*, Ibero-American Observatory of Television Fiction (Obitel) 2014 Yearbook (Porto Alegre, Brazil: Editorial Sulina, 2014), 149–50.
16 "Grupo Gay da Bahia," www.ggb.org.br/ggb-ingles.html.
17 Mauro Pereira Porto, *Media Power and Democratization in Brazil: TV Globo and the Dilemmas of Political Accountability* (London and New York: Routledge, 2012), 139.
18 Bernardo Amigo, María Cecilia Bravo and Francisco Osorio, "Telenovela, recepción y debate social/Soap operas, reception and social debate," *Cuad.inf*, no. 35 Santiago 2014, www.scielo.cl/scielo.php?pid=S0719-367X2014000200009&script=sci_arttext.
19 Antonio La Pastina and Samantha Nogueira Joyce, "Changing GLBTQ Representations: The Sexual Other in Brazilian Telenovelas," *Lumina*, 8, no. 2, December 2014, *Revista do Programa de Pós-graduação em Comunicação*, Universidade Federal de Juiz de Fora / UFJF, www.researchgate.net/profile/Antonio_La_Pastina/publication/273525627_Changing_GLBTQ_representations_The_Sexual_Other_in_Brazilian_Telenovelas/links/55056a0f0cf2d60c0e6be69f.pdf.
20 Julee Tate, "From Girly Men to Manly Men: The Evolving Representation of Male Homosexuality in Twenty-First Century Telenovelas," *Studies in Latin American Popular Culture*, 29, no. 1, 2011, 102–114. https://muse.jhu.edu/.
21 Ibid., 107.
22 Samantha Nogueira Joyce, "A Kiss Is *(Not)* Just a Kiss: Heterodeterminism, Homosexuality, and TV Globo Telenovelas," *International Journal of Communication* 7, 2013, 48–66.
23 Gary Marx, "Helping Cubans Realize 'What It Means to Be Gay,'" *Chicago Tribune*, June 4, 2006, http://archive.globalgayz.com/caribbean/cuba/gay-cuba-news-and-reports-2003-07/.
24 Mariel Cuesta, "Other Islanders on Lesbos: A Retrospective Look at the History of Lesbians in Cuba," in Thomas Glave, ed., *Our Caribbean: A Gathering of Lesbian and Gay Writing from the Antilles* (Durham, NC: Duke University Press, 2008), 138.
25 Cubavision official website, *La cara oculta de la luna*, May 16, 2007, www.cubavision.info/live.html.
26 Andrea Rodríguez, " Cuban soap's gay story starts dialogue," http://archive.globalgayz.com/caribbean/cuba/gay-cuba-news-and-reports-2003-07/, Associated Press, June 18, 2006.
27 Maria Immacolata Vassallo de Lopes and Guillermo Orozco Gómez, eds., *Gender Relations in Television Fiction*, Ibero-American Observatory for Television Fiction (Obitel) 2015 Yearbook (Porto Alegre, Brazil: Editorial Sulina, 2015), 78.
28 "Lista de ganadores 27ta entrega de Premios GLAAD en Los Ángeles - The Beverly Hilton, 2 de Abril, 2016," www.glaad.org/releases/lista-de-ganadores-27ta-entrega-de-premios-glaad-en-los-%C3%A1ngeles-beverly-hilton-2-de-abril.

Bibliography

Amigo, Bernardo, María Cecilia Bravo, and Francisco Osorio. "Telenovela, Recepción y Debate Social/Soap Operas, Reception and Social Debate." *Santiago de Chile, Cuadernos.inf. com*. no. 35, 2014. www.scielo.cl/scielo.php?pid=S0719-367X2014000200009&script=sci_arttext.
Avery, Dan. "Brazilian Telenovela Airs Country's First Gay Sex Scene." July 12, 2016. www.newnownext.com/brazilian-telenovela-first-gay-sex-scene/07/2016/.
#BBCtrending: "'Historic' Gay Kiss on Brazilian TV." February 3, 2014. www.bbc.com/news/blogs-trending-26020533.
Encarnación, Omar G. *Out in the Periphery: Latin America's Gay Rights Revolution*. New York: Oxford University Press, 2016.

Halaburda, Carlos Gustavo. "We Demand a Happy Ending for Pedro and Guillermo: Love, Society and the Queer Politics of the Latin American Telenovela." *Sojourners: Undergraduate Journal of Sociology.* Vancouver: University of British Columbia, 2014, 6. http://soci.sites.olt.ubc.ca/files/2013/02/SOJOURNERS-VOL-6-7-FINAL.pdf# page=30.

Joyce, Samantha Nogueira. "A Kiss Is *(Not)* Just a Kiss: Heterodeterminism, Homosexuality, and TV Globo Telenovelas." *International Journal of Communication*, 7, 2013, 48–66.

La Pastina, Antonio, and Samantha Nogueira Joyce. "Changing GLBTQ Representations: The Sexual Other in Brazilian Telenovelas." *Lumina*, 8, no. 2, December 2014. www.researchgate.net/profile/Antonio_La_Pastina/publication/273525627_Chang ing_GLBTQ_representations_The_Sexual_Other_in_Brazilian_Telenovelas/ links/55056a0f0cf2d60c0e6be69f.pdf.

Las2orillas. "El encuentro erótica de la diva y Margarita Rosa en *Los pecados de Inés de Hinojoso* marcado la vida de la diva que hoy llega a los 60 años." May 12, 2016. www.las2oril las.co/el-pecado-de-amparo-grisales-que-escandalizo-a-colombia dalizo-a-colombia.

Martel, Fréderic. *Global Gay: como la revolución gay está cambiando el mundo.* Madrid: Taurus, 2013.

Marx, Gary. "Helping Cubans Realize 'What It Means to Be Gay.'" *Chicago Tribune,* June 4, 2006. http://archive.globalgayz.com/caribbean/cuba/gay-cuba-news-and-reports-2003-07/.

Pereira Porto, Mauro. *Media Power and Democratization in Brazil: TV Globo and the Dilemmas of Political Accountability.* London and New York: Routledge, 2012.

Tate, Julee. "From Girly Men to Manly Men: The Evolving Representation of Male Homosexuality in Twenty-First Century Telenovelas." *Studies in Latin American Popular Culture*, 29, no. 1, 2011. https://muse.jhu.edu/.

Vassallo de Lopes, Maria Immacolata, and Guillermo Orozco Gómez, eds. *Social Memory and Television in Ibero-American Countries*, Ibero-American Observatory of Television Fiction (Obitel) 2013 Yearbook. Porto Alegre, Brazil: Editorial Sulina, 2013.

Vassallo de Lopes, Maria Immacolata, and Guillermo Orozco Gómez, eds. *Transmedia Production Strategies in Television Fiction*, Ibero-American Observatory of Television Fiction (Obitel) 2014 Yearbook. Porto Alegre, Brazil: Editorial Sulina, 2014.

Vassallo de Lopes, Maria Immacolata, and Guillermo Orozco Gómez, eds. *Gender Relations in Television Fiction*, Ibero-American Observatory of Television Fiction (Obitel) 2015 Yearbook. Porto Alegre, Brazil: Editorial Sulina, 2015.

5

BLACK, WHITE AND BROWN
Telenovelas and Race

The slave was fleeing. The slave was fleeing from the horde of men with guns and their barking dogs. The slave was white. And she was beautiful.

Isaura, the protagonist of *Escrava Isaura*, a 1976 Brazilian telenovela with a 2004 remake by the same name, was not only beautiful, but cultured, kind, gentle, an adept piano player and well read. But a slave she was. The love child of a white foreman, Miguel, and a black slave, Juliana, Isaura was raised by the plantation mistress after Juliana was whipped to death shortly after childbirth.

"They say slaves don't have souls. I don't believe that," declares Gertrudes, calling to see the infant Isaura after the death of her mother. "Forgive me, Juliana." She takes the baby in her arms and decides to raise her as a daughter—but keeping the status of slave.

As in many telenovelas throughout Latin America and over time, the protagonist is not black, at least by Latin American standards. In the United States, the concept of race—particularly in regards to blackness—has historically been determined by the one-drop rule. If you have one drop of black blood, you are black. Although U.S. society has become more flexible in terms of categories like "biracial," people—even President Barack Obama, who had a black father and white mother—are defined in terms of their black blood. In Latin America, however, race is determined by skin color, and often the perception is influenced by social class. That's also true of indigenous people. Black and indigenous people, in fact, clearly defined as such, are seldom seen in telenovelas. If they are, they are often the docile servants, the bodyguards, the prostitutes, the beloved nannies or the young maids from the countryside. They border on invisible or, sometimes, comical figures. Yet black (and sometimes indigenous) characters have sometimes played important roles in telenovelas since the 1952 Cuban telenovela *Derecho de nacer*. Historical novels, a handful of biopics and a handful of more traditional formats with strong black characters resist the trend of invisibility. A good example is the 1976 *Isaura*.

Isaura, no matter how white she looked, was trapped by her social status: she was born a slave, the daughter of a slave, and although her father tried to purchase her freedom over the years, she remained a slave. When her godmother Gertrudes, the plantation mistress, died, she was left without protection.

Although the protagonist is perceived to be white, the historical telenovela, set 20 years before Brazil's emancipation, roots the story very much in the history of blackness and slavery. The black characters are noble and they are individuals—not caricatures.

"The Negro is not a slave," declares João, the eldest of the slaves. "He has been enslaved." He is aware that he is the son of African royalty, and lends a stabilizing dignity to the slaves on the plantation owned by Commander Almeida—no matter how they are treated.

Each telenovela episode starts with an image of broken chains, but there are constant reminders that those chains have yet to be broken.

When the plantation owner buys Juliana, Isaura's mother, his comments are highly sexual: "Look at those breasts, those legs; she will be a good breeder."

Juliana is whipped to death—despite being a good property—because she refuses her master's advances and instead becomes pregnant by the man she truly loves and who has befriended her, Miguel. She takes the sexual initiative with her benefactor—which is something most women in this telenovela do not get a chance to do.

Indeed, sometimes the enslavement of blacks seems to emphasize the near-slave status of women. "You will do what I want," the plantation owner's evil son, Leôncio, tells his new bride. "You are mine now."

All sorts of freedoms are at stake in the telenovela—slavery, women's emancipation, class status. The story of Isaura was based on an 1875 novel of the same name by 19th-century Brazilian abolitionist writer Bernardo Guimarães. The telenovela was criticized by the Afro-Brazilian movement for casting a white actress as the protagonist, but the series does feature a strong ensemble of black characters. Indeed, I would contend that precisely because of the fact that Isaura is a white-skinned slave, the telenovela underlines the extreme cruelty of slavery.

Even before her escape and subsequent pursuit, Isaura is highly aware she is a slave. Gertrudes's lecherous son, who becomes her owner after his parents die, is constantly trying to impose his sexual will on her. She frequently reminds would-be suitors of another social class, "I am not a *señorita*; I am only a slave."

She—and everyone else around her—nevertheless is aware that her pale skin carries with it certain privilege. André, João's son (and considerably darker skinned), proposes that they try to escape together. "We can say that I am your slave and you are my mistress," he says.

Isaura would prefer to wait for her white father, Miguel, to purchase her freedom, but she accepts the proposal as an alternative if that doesn't happen. André is in love with Isaura, and she cares for him, but not romantically.

Unfortunately, another slave, Rosa, overhears the conversation and reports the couple as planning to flee. Rosa and André had been lovers when they were younger; Rosa is now the slave mistress of Leôncio, which gives her a certain type of power over Isaura. She does not hide her bitterness.

"When you were playing the piano, I was cutting sugar cane," she lashes out at Isaura. "When you were getting your music classes, I was hauling firewood."

The ensemble of black characters—and I would include Isaura here—provide perspectives on the slave experience, on the black experience. João and his sister-in-law, Joaquina, are the older voices of wisdom, the link to the African past. They were captured from a runaway slave community, although the telenovela does not give us the backstory of how they got there. They have had the experience of living together in community, and that allows them to maintain their strength despite their slave status. Joaquina knows all the herb potions and secrets of the African past. Despite a high and somewhat comic voice tinged with the lilts of Africa, Joaquina has to be taken seriously; she has the courage to tell the truth and to risk her own life giving a sleeping potion to the guards so André can escape. Joaquina and João may engage more in passive resistance and acceptance of their position than Rosa, André and even Isaura, but they do so with immense dignity. André, João's son and Joaquina's nephew, has inherited their dignity.

After Rosa reports that André and Isaura are planning to flee, André is sent to a prison-like solitary cell on the plantation without food or water, then released to be strapped to a stake, the same kind of stake where Isaura's mother was whipped to death.

João laments, as he watches his son's punishment, "Who would ever think the grandson of royalty would endure treatment like this?"

But it is Rosa—in her anger and jealousy—who carries the seeds of black fury. At first, we do not like her. She is needlessly jealous of Isaura. She is needlessly jealous of André. And she is a tattletale. She sleeps her way to (relative) power with Leôncio.

But we learn when she comes to visit André at the stake that they have actually been lovers, a fact that has been kept from the viewer until that point. "That is before I learned you were sleeping with everyone," he retorts, when she invokes their former relationship. At the beginning of the telenovela, she does not know who her father is. It is only later—when Leôncio has married an upper-class and slightly older woman named Malvina—that she learns that her father is Sebastião Cunha, Malvina's father.

Cunha's wife had become jealous of Josefa, her husband's slave lover. When Josefa becomes pregnant with Rosa, she is sold to Commander Almeida and Gertrudes.

A mistreated Josefa dies after childbirth, and Cunha is led to believe the child has died too. He learns otherwise only 20 years later, when Rosa confronts him after finding out who her father is.

There is more cause for bitterness. In essence, she sees that she has nobler blood than Isaura. Her biological father is of higher social class than Miguel, Isaura's father, but Cunha rejects her. The children of slaves are slaves; they are bastards; they have no standing, and this irony is made even worse when her father eventually purchases her to be his slave.

Sebastião Cunha, a distinguished and patriarchal figure with olive skin, becomes the vehicle in the story for questioning the myth of the time about racial purity. Cunha's son Enrique has fallen in love with Isaura in his many visits to the Almeida plantation to visit his sister Malvina. He wants to marry her and asks his father to lend him money so he can free her. His father declares, "I won't lend you the money. You can do anything you want with her, but you are not going to marry her. Do you think I want grandchildren with African blood?"

"You're not so white yourself," Enrique retorts. "Did you get that color from hours in the sun? Every Brazilian has a bit of black and Tupi [indigenous] in him."

"I'm Portuguese; I'm pure," retorts Cunha.

Of course, Enrique's reaction is a projection of the concept of racial democracy—that every Brazilian is a mix. But at the same time, through the difference in status between Rosa and Malvina, both the daughters of the same father, the telenovela underlines that the cultural legacies are different, that slavery shaped black heritage.

Isaura tells the stories of many types of black experience. The story takes many twists and turns as Isaura is hunted in her flight. She passes for white, taking the name of Doña Elvira, and falls in love with Don Alvaro, one of the richest (and most progressive) men in Brazil. But at a ball with Alvaro, a man recognizes Isaura from Leôncio's newspaper ads about his runaway slave. She is returned to the plantation, but Alvaro eventually manages to rescue her.

The telenovela became a runaway sensation around the world. It was sold to more than 80 countries. In 1986, it was the first telenovela screened in Poland, and the most popular in the history of the country, sometimes reaching as high as 92 percent of the television-watching audience. *Escrava Isaura* was the first series in China with a non-Chinese protagonist.[1]

When Russians were allowed to own small plots of land in the 1980s, they dubbed them "fazendas," the Portuguese word for "farm," often used in the telenovela. Later, another word borrowed from a Brazilian telenovela would work its way into the Cuban vocabulary; an independently owned, non-government small restaurant in Cuba is known as a *paladar*, the name of a chain of family-owned restaurants in the telenovela *Vale Tudo*. The 1988 telenovela was aired in Cuba in the 1990s, around the same time the Cuban government started issuing licenses to the small businesses.[2]

Extremely popular in Eastern Europe, even when it was Communist, *Escrava Isaura* can be seen as a quest for freedom. In Hungary, viewers purportedly took up a collection to purchase Isaura's liberty. The message of a slave in faraway Brazil in a long-ago historical context did not have to face censorship.

Telenovelas bring to the fore conversations people don't tend to have—whether it's freedom in Communist Eastern Europe or race relations in Latin

America. Although *Escrava Isaura* is clearly set in Brazil, it presents situations experienced in any Latin American country with a history of slavery and subsequent racial mixing.

The runaway slave community in Colombia could have been San Basilio de Palenque, for example, a community close to Cartagena that has produced four world-champion boxers. The plantation could have been in Venezuela or the Dominican Republic or Ecuador.

It is a story with which viewers in Latin America—and beyond—can identify, and yet it asks some uncomfortable questions. What does it mean to be black? Is slavery only an economic relationship or one intrinsically based on race? Does race really change with a change in class status? Are we all racially mixed? And if we are, is that because of love (Miguel and Juliana) or because of rape? Should we accept our status, hoping to be emancipated (Isaura until she could no longer wait) or boil in anger like Rosa?

The questions become even more important in the context of Latin American perceptions about race. In Brazil, there's the concept of so-called racial democracy, the notion that Brazil has somehow escaped racial discrimination because its citizens do not see each other through the lens of race. Brazilian sociologist Gilberto Freyre in his 1933 book, *The Master and the Slaves*, contended that the close relationship between slaves and their owners before emancipation meant that strict racial categories were meaningless. He also argued that continued mixing of the races would lead to a "meta-race" or a race beyond races.[3]

The concept is not far from the Mexican concept of *la raza cósmica* (the cosmic race) originally coined by philosopher José Vasconcelos to describe the mixing of the races into one Mexican and postracial culture.

Escrava Isaura invites viewers to think about these questions, even as they are following the sagas of love and vengeance, hope and hopelessness. It is not alone of telenovelas using a historical backdrop to explore racial issues.

La Esclava Blanca

At first glance, it might seem that *La Esclava Blanca* (The White Slave), a 2016 Caracol production distributed widely throughout Latin America and aired on the U.S.-based Telemundo, was another remake of *Esclava Isaura*, the Spanish-language version of *Escrava Isaura*.

But the story of love and vengeance, set in colonial Colombia, is entirely different. The telenovela does similarly show sexual violence against slave women and general mistreatment of slaves. Like *Esclava Isaura*, the story portrays the deep relationship between the "white" protagonist and the black, dignified slave community that nourished her. But Victoria, the slave of the title, is actually white, not the product of relationship between a white man and a black woman.

La Esclava Blanca recounts how Victoria, the infant daughter of a prosperous white plantation family, is orphaned when greedy landowners burn down the plantation and murder her family in the arson attack. She is rescued by black slaves, spearheaded by her suckling nurse. They later escape to a free slave community and raise her as one of their family. The Spanish military discover the community and destroy it. Victoria Quintero is sent to a convent in Spain and returns as a wealthy Spanish duchess with an assumed identity to avenge her black family, freeing them from the shackles of slavery, and to reunite with her true love. The official Caracol page notes, "For Victoria, everyone is the same color, which is why she won't rest until she claims justice and becomes a true heroine."[4]

Again, we are dealing with the meaning of blackness. Should Victoria be considered culturally black because she was raised by a black family? What does it mean that blacks were her emancipators by rescuing her from orphanhood?

The telenovela was perhaps the first to deal with the issue of slavery in Colombia, although *Esclava Isaura* was aired widely on several different occasions and had sparked earlier discussion about Colombia's slaveholding history.

Yesenia Barragán, a historian of Afro-Latin America, asserts in a blog post, "the show engages in a violent historical revisionism by centering the fantastical travails of a white woman who ostensibly holds the key of freedom for the region's enslaved."

Her argument makes historical sense, although I would argue that it does not necessarily make melodramatic sense: Victoria Quintero is a powerful icon, evoking the emotions with her plight.[5]

But Barragán brings up several points that help us to understand the role of race in telenovelas, when it is treated at all. *La Esclava Blanca*, she writes,

> seeks to rewrite the place of white women in the history of slavery in Colombia. No doubt, at times *La Esclava Blanca* graphically depicts the emotional and physical violence wielded by white women slaveholders, both young and old. But ultimately, the white, Virgin Mary-like would-be-slaveholder-turned-slave-redeemer Victoria Quintero absolves the racial consciences of (white and *mestizo*, or mixed race) Colombian and Latin American viewers in a country where anti-black racism is alive and well.

Barragán also notes that the telenovela feeds into the concept—or "myth"—of a postracial society, in which black, white and indigenous are mixed, a racial democracy or a cosmic society.

Many Colombians objected to the "exaggerated" violence depicted in the telenovela, she observes. In February 2016, Caracol in response organized and broadcast a half-hour television program to treat the historical validity of the telenovela. Colombian slavery scholar Rafael Antonio Díaz and Afro-Colombian activist Juan de Díos Mosquera reaffirmed to the Colombian viewing public the violent nature of slavery in Colombia and elsewhere.

As in the case of Afro-Brazilians with *Escrava Isaura*, Afro-Colombian activists objected to the fact the protagonist was a not a black woman, and objected that few Afro-Colombians can find acting roles beyond stereotypical parts. The difference, of course, is that the protagonist in *Isaura* is, in U.S. terms, black, while the protagonist in the *Esclava Blanca* has only been raised by blacks.

Afro-Colombian anthropologist Rudy Amanda Hurtado Garcés organized a digital boycott of the program for the series premiere.[6]

The intent may have been to conduct a symbolic boycott, but instead the Facebook page turned into a lively (and generally quite civilized) venue of discussion of both the program and the issue of race.

Says a blogger who signs as Tiaret Kimya, "A telenovela like the *Esclava Blanca* continues to spread stereotypes that will keep on generating violence ... [it] reproduces propaganda harmful to our black community with this type of representation that destroys under the guise of fiction."

A person who identifies herself as Adriana Briceño comments,

> It's only a television program that's made to entertain, what a shame that you [boycott organizers] are doing your own form of discrimination. The telenovela reflects the pain and abuse they [the slaves] were subjected to. It hurts that we ourselves generate violence ... should Holocaust survivors oppose films and series made about their suffering? They are conscious that the entire world should know their history.

While the boycott Facebook page evoked a discussion from a basically Colombian audience, Barragán's article drew more than 50 comments from mostly U.S.-based viewers (judging from names, both Latinos and non-Latinos), who had seen the series on Netflix.

"As an ordinary viewer, I didn't analyze the episodes the way the writer of this article probably did, so I can't judge the accuracy of the show or the ramifications of this novela to the Colombian (and international) population," writes a person who signs as Posada Pimental.

> I was drawn in to the story-line because of the characters. I cheered for the protagonists and squirmed whenever the antagonists got away with their evil deeds ... To think of this show as anything more than entertainment media would be looking for things to complain about ... What if the daughter of slave-owners was saved by slaves from being murdered and was then raised in a community of runaway slaves? You wouldn't be able to tell the story any other way because in that region, during that time period in the show, only rich, white men could buy and sell slaves. It shouldn't be a surprise that Victoria is white.

And one commenter, who identifies herself as Phyllis, inadvertently draws the whole question of racial categories into question. Although she does not identify as North American, her comments seem to suggest that she is watching the telenovela from the parameters of a U.S. "black, white and Hispanic" categorization.

"We just finished watching this on Netflix and found it very interesting," says Phyllis. "We couldn't understand why the masters were considered as white people who clearly looked Latin and spoke Spanish."[7]

On a different blog called "boriquachicks," founder Omilani Alarcón, a Puerto Rican Cornell graduate who went on a Fulbright-Hayes grant to study Yoruba in Nigeria, describes her discovery of *La Esclava Blanca*. She was talking to a group of friends while "Spanish TV" was playing in the background, and they began to discuss how Afro-Latinos are nowhere to be found on Spanish-speaking television.[8]

"At that point Black people had only been the *criadas* (nannies) or docile enslaved hopeless beings—always in the background or minimized as an object . . .," she wrote. She noted that the biopic *Celia* was the first she had seen in which black actors and actresses play important roles, and that many of them would appear again in the *Esclava Blanca*. She acknowledged that the series had been criticized for violence and sexual content, but "we were raped historically and regarded as property . . ."

She added that she had never (and she wrote that in all capital letters) seen a portrayal on English-language television of white people praying to an African ancestor for strength, concluding that she rejected criticisms of *La Esclava Blanca* "as just another *Great White Hope* series."

The variety of spontaneous intellectual commentary, blogs and Facebook posts, as well as the official Caracol outreach that included a web page, a Facebook page and the television segment on the slave experience, illustrate how telenovelas put controversial issues in the public eye.

Colombians—and Latin Americans and U.S. viewers—began to debate the slavery experience, the black experience and the nature of race. Neither *La Escrava Isaura* nor *La Esclava Blanca* resolves any of these questions, but the important thing is that they have raised these questions.

Another historical telenovela worth mentioning briefly here is the 1996 Brazilian *Xica da Silva* (Figure 5.1), a telenovela about a beautiful slave who married a white man in colonial Brazil. Nude female body exposure appealed to a male audience, while the history of a black Brazilian also appealed to black viewers. Xica was popularly known as "the slave who became a queen," a historical figure who actually lived in the 18th century (unlike the fictional Isaura or Victoria).

Starring Taís Araújo, the first black actress to play the leading role in a Brazilian telenovela, the telenovela was very polemical not only because of its frank treatment of slavery, but because of its highly erotic scenes.

O. Hugo Benavides points out that despite the Afro-Brazilian actress and the biographical documentation of Xica's life, the telenovela still does not achieve a close representation of the slave experience:

> The problematic portrayal of black characters in the telenovela *Xica* as not only racially but also culturally distinct in terms of religious practices (e.g. belief in African Orixas); linguistic dialects (use of slang and "low-class"

FIGURE 5.1 Victor Wagner and Taís Araújo in *Xica da Silva*, 1996, Walter Avancini.

speech); cultural celebrations (e.g. distinct wedding ceremonies), sexual mores (e.g. presence of not only rape and abuse but also lust for the white other) has made the genre a target of criticism for putting forth a biased and racist representation of the slave and former slave population.[9]

The discussion of the representation of slavery in telenovelas continues to put the issue of how race is portrayed in the public sphere. It keeps the chatrooms busy and conversations going—which, I contend, is the most important social role of the telenovela. For black and white viewers alike—and every shade in between—the telenovelas do more to evoke and explain a painful past to the general public than any textbook ever could.

Our Lives: The Black Biopic

In the slavery telenovelas, one sees black faces, and although those represented are either slaves, freed slaves or runaway slaves, they are nevertheless on the screen night after night. In the context of these series, they are no longer invisible, no longer relegated to the minor roles.

I've known subjectively—as most telenovela viewers do—that the average telenovela character is whiter, thinner, blonder and more green-eyed than most of the population in Latin America.

I'd never seen any quantitative research on the subject until I discovered a detailed 2002 study of Spanish-language television in the Los Angeles area by Illinois State University professor Rocio Rivadeneyra. I would suspect the numbers have slightly improved, but not by much.

Rivadeneyra looked at whether darker-skinned characters were portrayed with low status and as being sexual objects. Looking at three Spanish-language networks (Univision, Telemundo and Telefutura), she coded 13 Latin American telenovelas from Venezuela, Colombia, Brazil and Mexico. In the 19 episodes of each novel coded with the help of three students, Rivadeneyra encountered 466 speaking characters; 32 were coded "as being of olive tone" and only 6 as "dark skinned." That is pretty much what I would have expected.

Another finding was also anticipated: darker skinned characters were played as "more sexualized." However, she did have a surprising finding:

> Unexpectedly, we found that characters with dark skin were more likely to be represented in the extremes of social class with very few in the middle class. Characters with dark skin were more likely to be portrayed as upper class compared to characters with lighter skin.[10]

Her study confirmed for me my subjective observation about black characters in telenovelas; the unusual finding about upper-class blacks piqued my curiosity. Certainly Xica would qualify as wealthy (although the Brazilian telenovela was not part of the sample), and I started to think about how the recent wave of biopics (called *bionovelas*), particularly in Colombia, are projecting those positive, successful images.

The 2015 Colombian telenovela *Celia*, based on the life of the Cuban salsa singer Celia Cruz, is very much in the rags-to-riches telenovela scheme, but it is her talent, not a princely suitor or a long-lost uncle, that puts her into the ranks of the rich and famous.

The telenovela, produced by Fox TeleColombia for RCN and Telemundo, deals with the barriers Cruz had to face not only as an Afro-Cuban, but as an Afro-Cuban woman. The official RCN website for the telenovela stresses the transformation, "Her talent, her voice and her charm were transforming her and she went from being a poor, skinny, little black girl to the most loved and successful Latin American woman in all of the music world."

The telenovela traces her passion for singing in 1950s Cuba to her becoming the lead singer of the musical group "La Sonora Matancera." After the revolutionary government came to power, she went into exile with her husband, Pedro Knight, and became the most renowned figure of salsa music—which at that time was an all-male genre.[11]

Like the slavery-themed telenovelas, this biopic faced ample criticism, both about its casting and historical accuracy. Websites—particularly Miami Cuban websites—complained that the majority of actors and actresses were Colombian, not Cuban (the role of Celia was played by Cuban singer Aymee Nuviola, but many supporting roles were indeed Colombian). Miami's *El Nuevo Herald* also covered the controversies extensively, including that of how accurate a historical telenovela has to be.

Omer Pardillo Cid, Celia Cruz's estate executor, after a long litany of objections to the factual accuracy of the telenovela, finally admits, "The telenovela has revitalized the life and legacy of Celia for new generations."[12]

The issue of accuracy touches deeply on the issue of identity, as does the issue of casting: who has the right to tell the story and how. One of the scriptwriters, Andrés Salgado, justified the historical errors (for example, placing the Castro rebellion earlier then it actually occurred) by saying that as a telenovela, it is "not a historical document, but a dramatic series."

Ironically, it's not the first time Celia Cruz's name has been associated with a telenovela. She actually played in two of them. Ana M. Lopez, in her essay "Our Welcomed Guests," recounts how Cruz played the role of "la negra Lucumé," an elderly Afro-Cuban *santera*, in the 1993 *Valentina*, a Mexican Televisa comeback vehicle for actress Verónica Castro.

The plot revolves around a botched murder on a cruise ship, which lands the intended victim, who can't remember anything, on a mythical Caribbean island (actually Quintana Roo in Mexico).

> Cruz's character, "imported" from the Caribbean and dropped into an inappropriate Mexican context, was obviously meant to be the serial's trump card for the US Hispanic market. Cruz's popularity and the audience's curiosity in seeing her acting rather than singing were activated before the telenovela's premiere. . . . Univision featured Cruz in its talk shows, devoted a special 1-hour homage to her "Cubanness" hosted by the Cuban-born Cristina Saratequi and featured her as much as Verónica Castro in commercials and the telenovela's pre-credit sequence.[13]

After reading about that episode in Cruz's life (she also played the part of a nanny, "la negra Macaria," in another Mexican telenovela in 1997, *El alma no tiene color* [The Soul Has No Color], and acted in the 1992 film *Mambo Kings*), I imagined the kind of licenses taken in her biopic wouldn't have bothered her one single bit. I couldn't find an explanation of why she had participated in the telenovelas or the film, but I can only imagine that the role of a strong black Afro-Cuban priestess appealed to both her sense of Cuban nationality and her identity as a black woman—an identity projected strongly to the viewers in *Celia*.

Andrés Salgado, the co-scriptwriter for *Celia*, had previously created (with Natalia Ospina) another black-centered Colombian biopic telenovela, *El Joe, la leyenda* (Joe, the Legend), based on the life of Joe Arroyo, a Colombian salsa singer and composer. It's a love story, as well as being a story about music, and shows how Joe desperately seeks out the aristocratic Jacqueline Ramón, with whom he had had a passionate affair during the Barranquilla Carnival during the '70s. Joe, a singer in the Protesta band at the time, does not know that Jacqueline's father is a powerful music entrepreneur. A rival for Jacqueline's hand convinces her father that his daughter should have nothing to do with someone who is "black and poor." He eventually marries Jacqueline (his second marriage) and rises to fame by blending a variety of rhythms from the African diaspora in an original style. Shakira performed one of his songs, "En Barranquilla Me Quedo" (I'll Stay in Barranquilla), in Las Vegas at the Latin Grammys in 2011.[14]

The series is Afro-centric, and not just because Joe (who died in 2011) was black. His music was a new sound that came out of the African diaspora; Joe became an inspiration to many other young black musicians. Moreover, visually, the telenovela takes us to black places such as San Basilio de Palenque, formerly a runaway slave community on the Colombian coast; the black neighborhoods of Cartagena and Barranquilla; and to celebrations with deep roots in the diaspora such as the Barranquilla Carnival.

The telenovela, like *Celia*, received criticisms for historical inaccuracies—in particular, for the portrayal of the romance between Joe and Jacqueline (who is white), and the role she played in shaping his career.

Another Colombian bionovela of a famous black figure—the world boxing champion Antonio Cervantes Reyes, known as Kid Pambelé—was based on the book by Alberto Salcedo Ramos, *El Ojo y la Oscuridad* (The Eye and the Darkness). Director Andrés Cortés said that in *Kid Pambelé* he wanted to paint all of Pambelé's ups and downs, his rise to fame from his humble beginnings in San Basilio de Palenque to his boxing championship to his fight against addiction.[15]

These bionovelas, like the slavery novelas, are important in several ways. They are allowing black people to see themselves on the little screen and in a positive light. They allow non-black people to recognize blacks as part of their community and history. Even the debates about historical inaccuracies are significant, because they show that readers are paying attention to history.

Ways of Blackness

University of Michigan professor Yeidy M. Rivero, originally from Puerto Rico, notes that Puerto Ricans often had to watch Brazilian films to see people of their own skin color. Yet, somewhat ironically, the first film with a black protagonist was filmed just an island over in Cuba in 1952. *Derecho de nacer,* based on a Cuban radionovela of that name (and discussed in Chapter 1), had a black heroine, Mama Dolores, who rescues her employer's daughter's illegitimate son, who has been ordered at birth to be killed by his grandfather. The black nanny raises the child on her own, and he believes that he is Mama Dolores's biological son and that his father was most likely white.

"[I]n terms of racial signification, these scripts [*Derecho de nacer* and other early radio- and telenovelas] positioned black women as content with their class and racial position in the telenovela's fictional social space," observes Rivero. "Although the negra characters seem to be integral to the narrative and were constructed as sacrificing heroines, they never challenged their racialized, gendered or class status."

Unlike in the slavery telenovelas, the black characters in the early telenovelas never faced "systematic racial oppression," Rivero adds, although they sometimes suffered mistreatment at the hands of individuals.[16]

Sometimes the black characters weren't even black. *El hijo de Angela María,* a Puerto Rican telenovela aired by Telemundo in 1973, included two maid characters, Panchita and Chianita, who were white actresses in blackface. Chianita, as described by Rivero, was a "black and humble jibara (Puerto Rican peasant)," a clownish figure.[17]

Puerto Rican black rights activist Sylvia del Villard protested the use of blackface, but was simply told "there are not enough black actors to play the parts." The issue of blackface also became controversial in Brazil's TV Globo telenovela version of *A Cabana do Pai Tomás* (Uncle Tom's Cabin), in which the famous and popular white actor Sergio Cardoso had his skin painted black and stuffed cotton inserts into his nose and lips to conform to racial stereotypes. Again, the network's justification seemed to be that no black actor could match Cardoso's star power.[18]

Colombia employed Afro-Colombian actors in its 1989 *Azucar* (Sugar), which takes place on sugar plantations. Indeed, black rural life is central to the plot. The black servant Sixta Lucumi has a child, Maximiliano Solaz, by sugar plantation owner Manuel María Solaz. He recognizes the child, but his wife Matilde feels betrayed and snatches the child. With her knowledge of magical arts, Sixta—torn by grief—casts an evil spell on the Solaz family that lasts for three generations. When a Solaz woman gives birth, she conjured, she will die the same day as her child is born. Each episode of the telenovela begins, "In order for sugar to be white, it needs black blood, black seeds and black fertile soil." The telenovela was remade in 2016, another opportunity for Afro-Colombian actors.

Much earlier, in 1969, RTI television in Colombia had aired a telenovela about gold miners in the isolated Pacific region of El Chocó. The telenovela, *El Candó*, featured one of Colombian's most famous black singers, Leonora González Mina, better known as "La Negra Grande de Colombia" in an acting role (as in the case of Cuban singer Celia Cruz, the telenovela capitalized on the singer's tremendous popularity to attract a wide audience). Although the telenovela appears to have several black actors, the protagonists were Julio César Luna, an Argentine immigrant to Colombia, and Ali Humar, who later became an icon of Colombian television.[19]

The participation of black actors and actresses is still an issue in telenovelas (although blackface was infrequent in the past and appears to be non-existent in the present). For example, the 2007 Brazilian TV Globo telenovela, *Duas Caras* (Two Faces), the first Brazilian prime-time telenovela to feature an Afro-Brazilian as the main hero, had a cast of 100 actors and actresses, but only 15 were played by black actors. Yet that's an improvement. According to Samantha Nogueira Joyce, the 98 telenovelas developed by TV Globo between 1980 and 1990 (with the exception of those that dealt with slavery) featured only 28 cases of individual Afro-Brazilians. Yet Brazil is 44 percent black.[20]

Perhaps having 15 Afro-Brazilians in one single telenovela is not such a discouraging statistic after all. Despite the numeric minority, *Duas Caras* puts blacks front and center.

Joyce observes, in a book in which she shows how this Brazilian telenovela debunks the myth of racial democracy, that

> Although Brazil has always had a racially and culturally diverse society, this diversity has not been reflected on television, especially not in telenovelas. While the genre has been the most popular program type in Latin America for the last thirty years, traditionally, when it comes to Brazil, African descendents have been virtually invisible or relegated to secondary roles. But this is changing. Writers and politicians have been making a conscious effort to introduce a more diverse cast as well as incorporate storylines that address matters of race and racism.[21]

The hero of *Duas Caras* is Evilásio Cao, a dynamic Afro-Brazilian founder of a Rio de Janeiro shantytown. Julia is a rich white filmmaker who has decided to make a documentary about the neighborhood. When her car has a flat tire and Evilásio approaches to help, she thinks he is a robber. When she realizes his identity, she goes to apologize.

Scriptwriter Aguinaldo Silva knew exactly what he was doing: exposing racism and the myth of racial democracy. He kept a blog in which he discussed the telenovela and the public's reaction.

He describes how Evilásio and Julia end up fighting as a result of a discussion around the table about racism, and discover they really want to kiss:

> Therefore it starts, amongst slaps and kisses, the post-modern Romeo and Juliet of *Duas Caras*: a romance that mixes racism and class struggle, the type loved by sociologists and by Labor Party followers. Will Barretão, the young woman's father, call Evilásio a "stuck-up nigger" or won't he? Stay tuned! . . . I promise: *Duas Caras* will be explosive! [Eu prometo: *Duas Caras* vai bombar!][22]

In the slavery telenovelas, racism is seen as a result of economic status; a slave is a slave (although *Isaura* in particular acknowledges the lighter one's skin, the lighter one's burden).

There's a powerful scene at the dinner table with a liberal senator Narciso Tellerman, Julia's lawyer father Paulo Barreto, Julia and Evilásio. When the senator declares enthusiastically, "If Brazil has a soul, it is a black one," Barreto asserts that he wouldn't think that way if he had a daughter, and she got involved with "one of them." There is a moment of silence. Then the senator replies, acknowledging indirectly that the comment was being made about Evilásio, that he would be proud to have a son-in-law like the shantytown organizer with such "character and dignity." Evilásio ends up leaving, and the senator and Julia follow him out. Julia apologizes for her father, but Evilásio asserts she is racist too, alluding to the fact that she initially thought he was a robber.

In a *Jornal O Día* editorial, S. Grimberg notes,

> Never before in the history of this country have racial prejudices been discussed as in *Duas Caras*. This is all people talk about regarding Aguinaldo Silva's story. After discussing the theme through the interracial couple portrayed by Evilásio (Lázaro Ramos) and Julia (Débora Dalabella), the author has spread the subject through all the other subplots. . . . It was about time this story is discussed in a telenovela. We are in a very good process of evolution. Just a while ago, the media were racist, the telenovelas were racist. Aguinaldo is helping to open up doors.[23]

Again, we have a mirroring effect. The telenovela is enabling the society to talk about themes it usually avoids, whether they be racism, miscegenation or black rights.

Joyce points out that the telenovela has an enormous power to influence attitudes and social changes. She adds that the high production values and timely actuality of *Duas Caras* "give the telenovela a certain realism [and] critics and fans alike sometimes refer to the telenovela as a 'mirror of reality.'"

She observes,

> The telenovela genre, as a medium that opens the door for discussion and unites all segments of society—men, women, rich and poor—facilitated and exacerbated the discussions involving race and racism, especially through the blatant racist dialogues and story line it presented its audience nightly for a period of time of nine months.[24]

Despite their rather uneven history of racial portrayals, Brazilian telenovelas have been widespread in Latin America in projecting black figures, as Yeidy M. Rivero observed from her television viewing in Puerto Rico.

Blacks have had significant parts in earlier telenovelas, particularly in Brazil— although not as protagonists. Milton Gonçalves played a faithful companion to the three brothers Courage in *Irmãos Coragem* (The Courage Brothers) in 1970; the white heroes were accompanied by their loyal black sidekick. Gonçalves, a trained theatre actor, also played a European-educated black psychiatrist in the 1995 *Pecado Capital* (Capital Sin). According to Joyce, Gonçalves had asked the writer, Janet Clair, to create a role for him in which he would have to wear a suit and tie. Clair created the psychiatrist role and wanted to feature an interracial romance, but the idea was nixed both by government censorship and pressures from the public. That same year, the Noronhas were a black middle-class family in *A Próxima Vitima* (The Next Victim)—a kind of innocuous role model. The 1994 *Da Cor do Pecado* (The Color of Sin), a love triangle involving an Afro-Brazilian, like *Duas Caras*, addressed strong racial prejudice.

More recent telenovelas with strong black characters include *Lado a Lado* (Side by Side), a post-slavery telenovela that depicts a moving and lasting friendship between a wealthy white woman and a humble black woman in 20th-century Rio de Janeiro. And then there's *Vitória*, a very popular 2015 telenovela that features a successful black engineer and lavish upper-middle-class lifestyles (of course, I couldn't help but be reminded of Rivadeneyra's findings about blacks in telenovelas being overrepresented at the extreme ends of the economic spectrum).[25]

I have to admit here that my favorite recent black role in a telenovela isn't Brazilian. It's the role of Mariana, the 20-something Afro-Colombian in Betty's office support group *El cuartel de las feas*—the Ugly Women's Club. Yes, Mariana is far from ugly, and she's probably in the club because she's black and therefore an outsider. Yes, she reads tarot cards—which might invoke the kind of sorcery associated with black characters. But she's not hypersexualized, as many black women have been portrayed. She's not very poor or, for that matter, very rich. She likes to gossip; she wants to be a model; she watches her weight, and she's only interested in dating successful men. And yet with her Afro-Colombian hairdo, there's no ambiguity about her racial identity. Mariana is Mariana, a complex and endearing character who shares many things in common with her white friends.

We never see any racist actions against her, but at the end of the day, she's in the Ugly Women's Club only because she is black.

The Brown Indian: Absent but Emerging

Bruno Cárcamo looks earnestly at the camera in the YouTube video:

> We are concerned with the enpowerment of the Mayan language within mass media and we want to convey that Mayan culture is as good as any other and has expressions with which it's possible to make telenovelas, science fiction and any other genre.

Cárcamo is the director and producer of the first Mayan-language telenovela, which he says is the first telenovela in any indigenous language. Taking place in Quintana Roo, Mexico (ironically, perhaps, where Celia Cruz's fictional shipwreck island was filmed in *Valentina*), and in New York, the telenovela employed all indigenous actors.[26]

The viewer is treated to both the lush scenes of tropical Mexico with a musical soundtrack punctuated by bird cries and to the urban cityscapes of New York, where the director lives.

It's on a New York street that a Mayan actor observes to a passerby, "This is the story of Mayan rebirth."[27]

The 21-episode telenovela was broadcast on Mexican state television TV7 Plus—belonging to the Radio and TV System of the state of Quintana Roo—from July 1, 2013, on. The telenovela is slow compared to the pace of most telenovelas, and the scenes are rather chaste, with timid kisses. Its central purpose was to recover the language. As Cárcamo observes, after 6 p.m., when the commercial Spanish-language telenovelas come on, Mayans stop using their own language.

"The idea was to show a real situation that actually happens, of how we Mayans go and come back and sometimes we forget who we are," observed Hilario Chi, who translated the Spanish-language script into Mayan.[28]

In Mexico some 6.6 million people speak Mayan (it's also spoken in parts of Guatemala).

Bolivia and Peru, as well as other Latin American countries with large indigenous populations, have expressed interest in airing the telenovela.

The existence of this Mayan-centered film got me thinking about the indigenous portrayals in telenovelas. I could find only one telenovela in which indigenous actors played native peoples, in secondary roles. That's in the 1996 Brazilian telenovela *O Rei do Gado* (The Cattle King), which is a love story revolving around a land dispute.

One of the complicating factors in looking at telenovelas in this perspective is the mere question—as with blacks—of who is indigenous. Complicating the matter is the great diversity of indigenous cultures (or lack thereof) in Latin American countries. Guatemala, for example, has an indigenous majority, with many using their native languages and traditional dress. Bolivia has an indigenous president, Evo Morales, and a strong indigenous middle class. In some countries, the indigenous communities live in remote places, with a lifestyle little affected by the developing world. But in many countries, indigenous people are Indians in the countryside and peasant-urban dwellers when they migrate into cities.

Mexico is the country with the largest indigenous population that is also a telenovela-producing country. And despite the production of *Baktun*, indigenous people are not seeing much of themselves on the small screen. Yet, as with the case of blacks in telenovelas, one can find examples—and early ones at that.

The telenovelas were influenced by earlier films from Mexico's Golden Age of Cinema from 1939 and 1945, which, in the words of Angela Noble, was part of a reclamation that "took place across a range of cultural spheres, including the visual arts and film and, to put it crudely, involved a celebratory and yet deeply ambivalent representation of the 'Indian' as a national figure."[29]

A prime example of these films is the 1943 *María Candelaria*, directed by Emilio Fernández. María Candelaria, played by non-indigenous actress Dolores del Río, is presented in the movie as "una india de pura raza mexicana" (a pure-race indigenous Mexican woman) and as the epitome of true beauty.

The Golden Age films, and in particular *María Candelaria*, paved the way for a series of telenovelas. For example, there's the classic 1966 telenovela *María Isabel*, which was remade in 1997. Actually originating in comic book form, *María Isabel* (1966) tells the story of an indigenous girl from the countryside (we know she's indigenous because of her clothing, braids and speech patterns) who becomes close friends with her father's boss's daughter, Graciela. Graciela is sent off to school, gets pregnant and dies in labor. María Isabel raises the child, Rosa Isela, as her own. She works as a maid, and is made fun of for being the dark mother of a white, blonde baby. Ricardo, a rich lawyer who is a widower, hires her. He immediately asks her to use a uniform, which provides a transition from her indigenous clothing. But he also encourages her to learn to read and write and speak better Spanish. He compliments her on her "progress." They fall in love, and, of course, complications ensue.

The telenovela, created by expatriate Chilean director Valentín Pimstein, was groundbreaking because it was the first in which the protagonist was an indigenous character. The actress certainly wasn't; she was played in the 1966 series by Silvia Derbez, the daughter of a French businessman and a Mexican mother, and in the 1997 telenovela by Adela Noriega, who is even more light-skinned. However, the 1997 remake did ground the series in the Huichol community of Nayarit; the actors wear intricate traditional embroidered garments and beaded jewelry, work at ordinary tasks, cook over wood in thatched huts. María Isabel as a child sings a little song in her Huichol tongue down by the river.

The racism on the part of Mexican society is portrayed as blatant. Graciela's father does not want her to be friends with that "savage." He tells María Isabel's father, "Your daughter is not equal to Graciela." When the two girls get caught playing together in Graciela's bedroom by Manuela, the father's secretary, they berate her—pointing to her indigenous features—"as if you weren't Indian yourself." But Manuela is well dressed in a stern suit and high heels, her high cheekbones set off by an austere bun; she scorns the label. María Isabel embraces her Huichol identity at the same time that she treasures a white, blonde doll Graciela gives her, a foreshadowing of her future as the mother of a white child.

Melixa Abaid-Izquierdo observes:

> María Isabel fell in love with her boss; race never mentioned as obstacle, but class. She transforms from a little Indian girl to a modern woman with Ricardo's help. . . . The story can be interpreted as instructional for the generation of young Indian women who migrated to urban settings. The show demonstrated that, as Indians, they would be discriminated against and mistreated. Despite this, they should stay proud, work hard, and be honest. In the process, the immigrant would leave behind the cultural signifiers of his/her ethnic origins, most notably clothing and speech . . . by migrating and doing all the right things "to progress." María Isabel represented Mexicans (especially indigenous Mexicans) having the ability to adapt to modern, urban life.[30]

Yet, while class is always at the forefront, race is ambivalent, perhaps part of a glorious past that is not so glorious (after all, we see María Isabel being mistreated by her family as a child). Race becomes a status that in some way can be "overcome," with help from people like Ricardo. María Isabel shifts from being a maid to a society lady, from indigenous to an unidentifiable member of the cosmic race.

Sofía Ríos, in a thought-provoking article, "Made-up Maids in Mexican Telenovelas," tells us that maids with their direct connection to an indigenous background provide an important point of reference to the public.

> Telenovelas could, thus, help tune us into the wider question that must be debated in Mexico: why is the issue of race so overlooked? . . . While *telenovelas* offer a space for the portrayal of Mexico's cultural and social diversity, this opportunity has not been seized. The experiences and features of Mexico's lower-class have merely been glamourized.[31]

Another Mexican telenovela, *Yara*, from 1979, stars the (non-indigenous) actress Angélica María, as a Lacandona indigenous woman from the jungles of Chiapas in the deep south of Mexico who comes to Mexico City looking for her father and, in the process, a better life. Again, the racism she faces is blatant, and she faces insults and brusque treatment. After many trials and tribulations, true loves and false loves and much in-between, she meets Mauricio, who helps her transform her appearance and become a famous singer.

An opening scene shows Yara and a companion dashing into Mexico City traffic in their long white robes. For a while, people who paid no attention to traffic were dubbed "Yara." Unlike in the case of María Isabel, *Yara* generated criticism for featuring a non-indigenous actress and for the rather one-dimensional portrayal of the character.[32]

In many of the rags-to-riches telenovelas, it's more difficult to interpret whether the protagonists are peasants or indigenous; so much depends on dress and language. The indigenous characters are most often maids, nannies or *brujos*, traditional witches. A popular telenovela in Mexico was the 1983 *El Maleficio*, which dealt with traditional witchcraft. The telenovela takes place in Oaxaca, a heavily indigenous state in the south of Mexico, but the series seems to use indigenous traditions only as a starting point.

More recently, there's *Amigas y rivales* (Friends and Rivals), a 2001 telenovela aimed at the teen audience. The storyline features four women from different social backgrounds, one of whom, Nayeli, works as a maid in the house of one of the wealthy girls, Jimena. Nayeli dreams of becoming a Hollywood star, and makes her way to the United States as an undocumented immigrant, where she falls on hard times. The actress who plays Nayeli does not have indigenous features, but she is the only one of the four with a *mestiza*, Indian mixed-race, appearance. Again, class instead of race seems to dominate the storyline.

In non-Mexican films, the invisibility of indigenous peoples seems to be about the same. For example, in a 2010 telenovela from Ecuador, Rosita the taxi driver was identified as an indigenous person by the storyline, although she was fair-skinned and had European features. The daughter of an indigenous woman from the mountains and a *mestizo* from the Ecuadoran coast, she was adopted by a family in the port city of Guayquil. She became the only woman working for a company called El Combo Amarillo, roughly the Yellow Cab Company.

And the indigenous theme manages to make its way into the Brazilian Brothers Courage telenovela, mentioned earlier in this chapter. One of the brothers, Jerônimo Coragem, is in love with Potira, his foster sister, an indigenous Brazilian raised by the Coragem family. For a while Jerônimo and Potira resist their passion for each other by marrying other people. However, they eventually break up their marriages and move in together. They are metaphorically punished with death: the police shoot Jerônimo and Potira in a dramatic finale. Potira, needless to say, is not played by an indigenous woman.

Yet, as director Cárcamo mentioned, indigenous people are heavy consumers of telenovelas. Maybe they are not seeing people like themselves on the small screen in terms of skin color, but the tales of rags to riches and of class mobility may be enough to provide a hopeful reflection and source of identification for their lives.

Indeed, we may be seeing more brown faces on the small screen as subjects evolve.

As O. Hugo Benavides notes, "It is not a coincidence that, with the popularity of melodrama and narco-drama, actors who are less upper and middle class and more rural and Indian have made their way onto movie and television screens."[33]

In the United States, two Honduran sisters, Victoria and Sophia Arzú, started Proyecto Más Color to convince Univision and Telemundo to get more black and indigenous actors into telenovelas and other programs in Spanish-language media. Through social media, they have been campaigning since 2014 to have more role models for young Latinos of color.[34]

Whether brown or black, these faces have not been absent from Latin American telenovelas. Themes involving race have spurred discussion throughout the Americas. The question is whether telenovelas will eventually represent Latin Americans and U.S. Hispanics in all the shades of their diversity on a consistent basis, night after night, episode after episode.

Notes

1 Daniel Biltereyst and Philippe Meers, "The International Telenovela Debate and the Contra-Flow Argument: A Reappraisal," in Ilan Stavans, ed., *Telenovelas* (The Ilan Stavans Library of Latino Civilization, Santa Barbara, CA: Greenwood, 2010), 38. Also see the April 17, 2016, post by Greg Childs, "A Telenovela, Slavery, and the Diaspora" for further discussion on the international impact of the telenovela, on the African American Intellectual History Society blog, www.aaihs.org/a-telenovela-slavery-and-the-diaspora/.

2 "Isaura: Slave Girl (1976–)," www.imdb.com/title/tt0142036/trivia.

3 Gilberto Freyre, *The Master and the Slaves* (New York: Alfred A. Knopf Incorporated, 1964) was first published in Portuguese in 1933 as *Casa-Grande & Senzala*.

4 "La Esclava Blanca: Capítulo Final," www.caracoltv.com/programas/telenovelas/la-esclava-blanca.

5 Yesenia Barragán, "*La Esclava Blanca*: The New Telenovela Rewriting Colombia's History of Slavery," African American Intellectual History Society blog, July 6, 2016, www.aaihs.org/la-esclava-blanca-the-new-telenovela-rewriting-colombias-history-of-slavery/.

6 www.facebook.com/events/796372277175060/ (page no longer available). All posts are from July and August 2016.

7 I've included Phyllis's comment because it shows how fluid the concepts of race are. For her as a North American, the "white" people in the telenovela aren't white because they "look Latin" and "spoke Spanish," i.e., they are Latino.

8 Omilani Alarcón, "*La Esclava Blanca*: White Fiction or Black Empowerment?" www.boriquachicks.com/2016/07/20/la-esclava-blanca-white-fiction-or-black-empowerment/.

9 O. Hugo Benavides, *Drugs, Thugs, and Divas: Telenovelas and Narco-Dramas in Latin America* (Austin: University of Texas Press, 2008), 9.

10 Rocio Rivadeneyra, "Gender and Race Portrayals on Spanish-Language Television," *Sex Roles*, 2011, Springer Science+Business Media, www.deepdyve.com/lp/springer-journals/gender-and-race-portrayals-on-spanish-language-television-M3wls5JYZG.

11 "Telemundo realizará 'Celia,' una serie sobre la vida de Celia Cruz," www.telemundo.com/entretenimiento/2015/07/15/telemundo-realizara-celia-una-serie-sobre-la-vida-de-celia-cruz.

12 Omer Pardillo Cid, "Albacea de Celia Cruz decepcionado con serie de Telemundo, February 9, 2016, www.elnuevoherald.com/entretenimiento/television/article593885 81.html. Translation is mine. Also see: www.cubaenmiami.com/serie-dedicada-a-celia-cruz-muy-criticada-en-miami/.

13 Ana M. Lopez, "Our Welcomed Guests," in Robert C. Allen, ed., *To Be Continued—: Soap Operas Around the World* (London and New York: Routledge, 1995), 268–269.

14 Leila Cobo, "Shakira Honored as Latin Grammy Person of the Year," *Billboard*, November 10, 2011, www.billboard.com/articles/news/465205/shakira-honored-as-latin-grammy-person-of-the-year.

15 Alfonso Díaz, "PAMBELE, nueva serie de RCN-NTN 24," www.youtube.com/watch?v=UvwqHiynktU.

16 Yeidy Rivero, *Tuning Out Blackness: Race and Nation in the History of Puerto Rican Television* (Durham, NC: Duke University Press, 2005), 23.

17 Ibid., 95.

18 Mauro Pereira Porto, *Media Power and Democratization in Brazil: TV Globo and the Dilemmas of Political Accountability* (New York and London: Routledge, 2012), 166.

19 The telenovela is not posted in whole or part on YouTube, and has been impossible to get through standard library and film seller channels.

20 Samantha Nogueira Joyce, *Brazilian Telenovelas and the Myth of Racial Democracy* (Lanham, MD: Lexington Books, 2012), 14.

21 Ibid., 1.

22 Samantha Nogueira Joyce, "Race matters: race, telenovela representation, and discourse in contemporary Brazil," (PhD [Doctor of Philosophy] thesis, University of Iowa, 2010), http://ir.uiowa.edu/etd/525.

23 S. Grimberg, "Discussão sobre racismo ganha mais espacio em *Duas Caras*," *Jornal O Día*, November 1, 2008, cited in Samantha Nogueira Joyce, *Brazilian Telenovelas and the Myth of Racial Democracy* (Lanham, MD: Lexington Books, 2012), 57. Translation is Nogueira Joyce's.

24 Samantha Nogueira Joyce, *Brazilian Telenovelas and the Myth of Racial Democracy* (Lanham, MD: Lexington Books, 2012), 30.

25 Matt Sandy and Morgann Jezequel, "Brazilian Soap Operas Slowly Cast Black Middle Class," April 11, 2015, http://america.aljazeera.com/multimedia/2015/4/brazilian-soap-operas-slowly-cast-black-middle-class.html.

26 Rachel Petersen, "Soap Opera for Cultural Preservation: Mexico's First Indigenous Soap Opera," August 16, 2013, https://rising.globalvoices.org/blog/2013/08/16/soap-operas-for-cultural-preservation-mexicos-first-indigenous-telenovela/.

27 "Trailer Baktun," www.youtube.com/watch?v=3yKGwkg2Q6w.

28 Entertainment Mexico Maya Soap Opera, www.aparchive.com/metadata/Entertainment-Mexico-Mayan-Soap-Opera/dd9d63776d3817dad4172744fe545cd7?query=killer+whale&current=1&orderBy=Relevance&hits=326&referrer=search&search=%2Fsearch%3Fquery%3Dkiller%2520whale%26allFilters%3D%2520Media%3AKeyword%2CClassical%2520music%3ASubject&allFilters=+Media%3AKeyword%2CClassical+music%3ASubject&productType=IncludedProducts&page=1&b=545cd7.

29 Andrea Noble, *Mexican National Cinema* (London and New York: Routledge, 2005), 87.

30 Melixa Abaid-Izquierdo, "The Cultural and Political Economy of the Mexican Telenovela," in Diana L. Ríos and Mari Castañeda, eds., *Soap Operas and Telenovelas in a Digital Age: Global Industries and New Audiences* (New York: Peter Lang, 2011), 93–110.

31 Sofía Ríos, "Representation and Disjunction: Made-up Maids in Mexican *Telenovelas*," *Journal of Iberian and Latin American Research*, November 16, 2015, 223–233, consulted online at www.tandfonline.com/doi/abs/10.1080/13260219.2015.1092647?needAccess=true.

32 To see what these non-indigenous actresses look like, take a look at Alejandro Zuñiga's program, "10 Actrices que han sido Indigenas en telenovelas!!" (Ten Actresses That Have Played Indigenous Characters in Telenovelas), www.youtube.com/watch?v=2sFgEavWWdY. Zuñiga boasts about these indigenous portrayals, but the women (with the exception of one or two) are obviously white. Indeed, they are much whiter than the typical *mestizo* (mixed-race) Mexican seen on your average street.

33 O. Hugo Benavides, *Drugs, Thugs, and Divas: Telenovelas and Narco-Dramas in Latin America* (Austin: University of Texas Press, 2008), 188.
34 "Proyecto Más Color," www.facebook.com/proyectomascolor/.

Bibliography

Abaid-Izquierdo, Melixa. "The Cultural and Political Economy of the Mexican Telenovela." In Rios, Diana L. and Mari Castañeda (eds), *Soap Operas and Telenovelas in a Digital Age: Global Industries and New Audiences*. New York: Peter Lang, 2011, 93–110.

Alarcon, Omilani. "La Esclava Blanca: White Fiction or Black Empowerment." www.boriquachicks.com/2016/07/20/la-esclava-blanca-white-fiction-or-black-empowerment/.

Barragán, Yesenia. "*La Esclava Blanca*: The New Telenovela Rewriting Colombia's History of Slavery." African American Intellectual History Society blog, July 6, 2016. www.aaihs.org/la-esclava-blanca-the-new-telenovela-rewriting-colombias-history-of-slavery/.

Benavides, O. Hugo. *Drugs, Thugs, and Divas: Telenovelas and Narco-Dramas in Latin America*. Austin: University of Texas Press, 2008.

Biltereyst, Daniel, and Philippe Meers. "The International Telenovela Debate and the Contra-Flow Argument: A Reappraisal." in Ilan Stavans (ed), *Telenovelas*. The Ilan Stavans Library of Latino Civilization. Santa Barbara, CA: Greenwood, 2010.

Cobo, Leila. "Shakira Honored as Latin Grammy Person of the Year." *Billboard*, November 10, 2011. www.billboard.com/articles/news/465205/shakira-honored-as-latin-grammy-person-of-the-year.

Freyre, Gilberto. *The Master and the Slaves*. New York: Alfred A. Knopf Incorporated, 1964.

Joyce, Samantha Nogueira. *Brazilian Telenovelas and the Myth of Racial Democracy*. Lanham, MD: Lexington Books, 2012.

Lopez, Ana M. "Our Welcomed Guests." in Robert C. Allen (ed), *To Be Continued—Soap Operas Around the World*. London and New York: Routledge, 1995.

Noble, Andrea. *Mexican National Cinema*. London and New York: Routledge, 2005.

Rivadeneyra, Rocio. "Gender and Race Portrayals on Spanish-Language Television." *Sex Roles*, 2011. Springer Science+Business Media. www.deepdyve.com/lp/springer-journals/gender-and-race-portrayals-on-spanish-language-television-M3wls5JYZG.

Padillo Cid, Omer. "Albacea de Celia Cruz decepcionado con serie de Telemundo." February 9, 2016. www.elnuevoherald.com/entretenimiento/television/article59388581.html.

Pereira Porto, Mauro. *Media Power and Democratization in Brazil: TV Globo and the Dilemmas of Political Accountability*. New York and London: Routledge, 2012.

Petersen, Rachel. "Soap Opera for Cultural Preservation: Mexico's First Indigenous Soap Opera." August 16, 2013. https://rising.globalvoices.org/blog/2013/08/16/soap-operas-for-cultural-preservation-mexicos-first-indigenous-telenovela/.

Ríos, Sofía. "Representation and Disjunction: Made-Up Maids in Mexican *Telenovelas*." *Journal of Iberian and Latin American Research*, November 16, 2015, 223–233, www.tandfonline.com/doi/abs/10.1080/13260219.2015.1092647?needAccess=true.

Rivero, Yeidy. *Tuning Out Blackness: Race and Nation in the History of Puerto Rican Television*. Durham, NC: Duke University Press, 2005.

Sandy, Matt, and Morgann Jezequel. "Brazilian Soap Operas Slowly Cast Black Middle Class." April 11, 2015. http://america.aljazeera.com/multimedia/2015/4/brazilian-soap-operas-slowly-cast-black-middle-class.html.

6

NARCONOVELAS

Beyond the News

Santiago Solano Rincón lifted himself to an upright position from the overstuffed couch in his Bogotá living room. It was well after 10 p.m. on a weekday night, but Christmas vacation had begun, and there were no bedtimes, just a lot of television. A documentary was beginning to be aired about the massacre at the Palace of Justice in 1985, and I started to explain what had happened there. "You don't need to tell me what happened," Santiago, then 11 years old, protested. "I saw it all on *Pablo Escobar, el patrón del mal* [Pablo Escobar, the Druglord]" (Figure 6.1).

Santiago had been born two decades after the tragedy in which the country's Supreme Court was decimated in a conflagration and crossfire after members of the M-19 guerrillas took over the Palace. Despite the fact that the kidnapped head of the Supreme Court telephoned from inside the building to plead with the army to hold off, the military retaliated with tanks and gunfire. More than a hundred people died in the attack, including half of Colombia's Supreme Court.

It was said that the guerrillas—at the behest of Pablo Escobar—had wanted to destroy documents connecting him with the drug trade. For Colombians, the Palace of Justice massacre marked a spiral into violence, a breach of the social contract, that is only beginning to show hopes of ending with the 2016 signing of a peace accord with the guerrillas in Havana.

For Colombians over 40, *Pablo Escobar, el patrón del mal* is a reminder of the bombs, the insecurity, the kidnappings, the horror of everyday life. It reinforces the collective memory of a time that many have repressed; it gives them—and us—the context and the drama. And for young Colombians like Santiago, the narconovela provides a historical context that he might not get in school or in a documentary he might just consider boring.

During Colombia's long armed conflict, people were not prone to talk about what had happened to them or their family members. It seemed to be inviting

FIGURE 6.1 *Pablo Escobar, el patrón del mal*, 2012, Directed by Carlos Moreno and Laura Mora, Image: Andrés Parra y Angie Cepeda.

trouble, many thought. *Pablo Escobar, el patrón del mal* provided a collective watching experience. Santiago watched the program with his grandfather and sometimes his grandmother and sometimes with his mother, a pediatrician who often works nights. In living rooms like Santiago's throughout Colombia, the program made the issue of drugs and the effect on the country into a national conversation.

Indeed, the 113-episode telenovela makes its relationship to memory quite explicit. At the beginning of each show, on a black background, the words "Who does not know history is doomed to repeat it" appear, just as much a trope as the parade of images depicting Escobar and his victims. A song plays as the images flash by, the same night after night, telling the viewer, "I will tell this story a thousand times. Never again. Do not delete it from your mind, to honor our dead who were cut down in such a foul way."

For many years, the national conversation about this story was silenced, or at least whispered in hushed tones among friends and family. Dago García, vice president of production of Caracol TV in Colombia, told Fox News Latino in 2013 that television producers refrained from exploring the subject matter for many years because they were afraid of reprisals from the druglords.

"The theme had been suppressed for different reasons, mainly because it was a topic that couldn't be discussed without having your life at risk," García said.[1]

The narconovela stirred visceral reactions, with some contending that these types of portrayals should not be shown, but whether one was for or against the programming, Colombians did not keep silent. The Ibero-American Observatory of Television Fiction (Obitel), in its 2013 annual report, notes that, "Fans reflected contradictory feelings about the actions of the trafficker, fueling the debate about the meaning of the fact and of the main character for the country," adding, "[The] disastrous cultural imprint of drug trafficking and particularly of Pablo Escobar, with the sequel of pain, tearing and tragedy that connotes for Colombians, acted as a protruding factor to grab the interest of the audience." But the report also observes that Colombians engage in many emotional debates about a possible vindication of the main character and his negative influence on the younger generation. The nature of the collective memory was challenged; people were talking about the period and what it meant.[2]

The conversation extended far beyond Colombia; the series was shown in at least 15 countries, including most of Latin America, much of Eastern Europe, Canada, Spain, France and other countries, and has been dubbed in more than five languages. Shortly after it premiered on Colombia's Caracol Television, it aired on the U.S.-based Telemundo, drawing nearly 2.2 million viewers the first night. It even spawned its own U.S.-based version, Netflix's popular *Narcos* series, now in its third season, also based on the life of Pablo Escobar. The Brazilian/Colombian/U.S. co-production is scheduled to run for at least two more seasons.[3]

The theme of drug trafficking had slowly been making its way onto the big screen for several years before the advent of the recent popular Colombian narconovelas (indeed, a 1986 Colombian narconovela took up the issue of the marijuana boom, discussed below). *El cartel de los sapos* (The Cartel of the Snitches), based on a book of the same name by former drug dealer Andrés López López, aired in 2008; *El Capo*, also based on the life of Pablo Escobar, appeared in 2009. Full-length feature films such as *Rodrigo D: No futuro* (1989), which depicted street children in Medellín caught up in the gritty drug trade; *La vendedora de rosas* (1998), loosely based on Hans Christian Andersen's "The Little Match Girl" and set in the tough slums; *Sicario* (1998), which portrays a youth caught up as a hitman in senseless violence; and *La virgen de los sicarios* (Our Virgin of the Assassins) all treated the subject in a quasi-literary manner, generally in the relatively safe and limited environment of the movie theatre.

In Mexico, narco-dramas such as *Orquidea sangriente* (Bloody Orchid), *El hijo de Lamberto Quintero* (The Son of Lamberto Quintero) and *La cueva de los alacranes* (The Scorpion's Cave) appealed to a more general public in a melodramatic way, often accompanied by *narcocorridos*, a Mexican folk genre from the borderlands that takes the drug traffic as its principal theme.

But the current wave of narconovelas enters viewers' living rooms night after night. Like the Mexican narco-dramas, they incorporate melodrama, but like the Colombian feature films of the 1990s and early 2000s, they are also highly realistic and invite the viewer to deal with the past.

Pablo Escobar, el patrón del mal, in particular, takes its strength from the telenovela structure and its careful attention to historical fact. This is not a coincidence. Camilo Cano, one of the producers of the narconovela, is the son of the crusading *El Espectador* newspaper publisher who was murdered by Escobar to silence the newspaper's courageous stance. Juana Uribe, vice president of Caracol TV and the series' co-producer, is the daughter of Maruja Pachón, who was kidnapped on Escobar's orders. Her uncle, the idealistic presidential candidate Luis Carlos Galán, was gunned down at a rally on Escobar's orders in August 1989.[4]

Pablo Escobar, el patrón del mal paints a portrait of the relentless violence on the streets of Colombia and in the halls of power, but it also describes to the viewer the full international context; the drug trafficking is not just a Colombian problem. We see the initial drug deals in Peru and Ecuador and the decision to produce coca in Colombia, rather than having the country just serve as a transit point. We see the impact of U.S. policy decisions and of the U.S. market for drugs; we see the chaos caused by the traffickers' fear of being extradited to the United States: "Better a grave in Colombia than a cell in the United States."

Miguel Cabañas, an associate professor at Michigan State University who studies the popular cultural representation of drug trafficking, observes, "The narcotelenovela [*sic*] is attractive to audiences not only because it offers a window into the world of criminality but also because it contains global themes and shows the dark side of globalization."[5]

Some criticize narconovelas because they allegedly glamorize the narco lifestyle and apologize for the drug trade. *El Espectador* columnist Mario Fernando Prado, in a June 2012 opinion piece, observes that "the development of such novelas reveals that the result of drug trafficking is always prison, death or destruction. It is one misery after another so that no viewer would want to follow this path." Colombian psychologist José Antonio Garciandía agrees, arguing in the Colombian magazine *Semana* that "telenovelas are not legitimating anything, they are simply showing what is already informally legitimated in the national culture."[6]

But *Pablo Escobar* is more than just about the drug trade; it is about how the drug trade engulfed an entire society, including its basic institutions such as the courts, the Congress and the press. It is that all-encompassing effect with which Colombians are only now coming to terms.

The Obitel 2013 report observes,

> Fiction like *Pablo Escobar: el patrón del mal* . . . in which specific historical events represent a country, but which are exhibited in many others, are part of a symbolic and interpretative repertoire which make collective memories that transcend the boundaries of the original country.

It points out that the telenovelas and films about the Holocaust, World War II or 9/11 become "shared memory resources."[7]

The Pablo Escobar story—which like all telenovelas, aired five nights a week—gathered the viewer up with its plots and subplots of love, violence, vengeance and betrayal. The narconovela follows the history of Pablo Escobar from his boyhood on the outskirts of Medellín through the building of his empire to his eventual demise, cornered on a rooftop. It gives us the story of his principal victims, ranging from newspaper editor Guillermo Cano to Justice Minister Rodrigo Lara Bonilla to charismatic presidential candidate Luis Carlos Galán. We meet their families, watch them work and hope. We know what is going to happen. And yet, like in any telenovela, the story hooks us minute by minute.

The power of the story is its ability to build characters and to create identification with the viewer. That includes Escobar—intent on tumbling an extradition law to the United States, intent on making his fortune at any cost, and yet a family man, a vulnerable man, a man with pride and charisma. The viewer him/herself undergoes a process of increasing immunity to violence. In one of the earlier episodes, Escobar is having an affair with a young woman—actually what we would consider an underage woman. He takes Yesenia's virginity, and on some level, seems genuinely fond of her.

That is, until she shows up with her older brother at his hacienda Napoles, where he lives with his wife and two children, Manuela and Juan Pablo. She thinks he will be happy to learn that she is pregnant with his child. Escobar is obviously angry that she has come to his domestic space, but the resolution of the "problem" seems ambivalent until Escobar's mother Enelia divines the reason the young woman has come. "You must only have children with your wife," she storms.

This leads to a violent kidnapping scene in which Yesenia, who has already bought a crib and decorated a nursery, is snatched from her home and drugged. Doctors cut the fetus from her body and she is sent back home to recuperate in the company of one of Escobar's trusted henchmen. The abortion scene is horrific; the viewer has already participated in the girl's desire to have a child and witnessed her kind brother's support.

Violence leads to more violence. Marino, Escobar's sidekick, ends up falling in love with Yesenia. He keeps their relationship secret from his boss, fearing that he will be jealous. But Escobar's pragmatic, although perhaps exaggerated, reaction upon learning of the relationship is that Yesenia will never forgive him for the abortion and may be using Marino as a way to seek revenge. He gives Marino an ultimatum: kill Yesenia or be killed yourself. Marino, with obvious pain, complies. It is the death of one human being at the hands of someone who loves her.

Santiago and the thousands of other viewers may not think of these scenes as an exercise in collective memory. But whether intended that way or not, the abortion and the murder of Yesenia reflect the daily choices Colombians had to make during the years of the drug wars: kill or be killed; betray or be betrayed; stay or leave; collaborate or be killed, or as the popular Colombian expression describes it, "plata o plomo," take the money or get a bullet.

As the narconovela progresses, the death toll escalates and the viewer is distanced from the deaths by their sheer numbers and frequency. Toward the end, as Escobar degenerates and expresses that degeneration with a callous hunt of available virgins, he has a young woman killed because—not a virgin—she had tried to trick him with a vial of sheep's blood. It's sad, but unlike the murder of Yesenia, it's one more death in a litany of death. It's sometimes hard to remember how disposable life was during that period of Colombia's history. The telenovela reminds us.

The strength of the collective memory is reinforced by the strong role of gender in narconovelas. When I started to watch these series, I assumed that they would be somewhat like the cowboy movies I had watched as a child: the good guys, the bad guys and an occasional female love interest. So I was surprised that narconovelas had so many ambiguities and also featured so many women: mothers and wives, prostitutes and party girls, star reporters and female drug lords, hitwomen and female detectives, doctors and architects. The relationship to the women often provides a human interest element and creates ambiguities, and it also gives the narconovela a more universal appeal.

Fordham University anthropology professor O. Hugo Benavides observes:

> [O]ne of the telenovela's most important contributions to the Latin American imaginary: making women much more visible than they have been in officializing Latin American political or social statements. . . . Contrary to official media representations, women are understood in telenovelas as being vital to the maintenance and reproduction of culture and daily life in Latin America.[8]

The role of women in narconovelas also relates directly to collective memory, since it is often women who transmit those memories from mother to child. Pablo Escobar's mother is cunning and astute and much in favor of money-making, but she also remembers Colombia's *Violencia*, a ten-year bloody civil war (1948–1958) between liberals and conservatives. She sees the havoc her son is creating through the lens of someone who experienced that time of bloodshed and turmoil, and yet she is proud of the fact he has become rich and successful; she just wants him to understand certain limits. Patricia, Escobar's wife, plays a clearer role. She is the muse, the one who is against violence, the one who fears and predicts Escobar's downfall.

Although women play important—although largely supportive—roles in *Pablo Escobar, el patrón del mal*, they are front and center in many narconovelas, including *Rosario Tijeras* (Colombia, 2010), *Reina del Sur* (Telemundo, 2011) and *Sin tetas, no hay paraíso* (Colombia, 2006—there was also a 2010 Mexican remake, *Sin senos, no hay paraíso*).

Rosario Tijeras (Figure 6.2) is the story of a young girl who grows up to be a hitwoman for the drug cartels. She lives in the *comunas*, the hillside slums of

Medellín. As a schoolgirl, she is full of spunk, and when some architecture students come to visit for a project, she ends up on a dare kissing one of them whom she considers particularly cute. As a result of her actions, she gets kicked out of school (it's not just a matter of the kiss; she and her classmates take scissors to a teacher's hair when she insults them). Antonio, the object of her affections, tries to find her in a Cinderella-type quest that always results in near misses. She manages to save his life once as he is attacked by gang members and then disappears yet again.

Like most telenovelas, the story sports subplots, and subplots of those subplots. Everyone seems to be in love with everyone else. As in *Pablo Escobar*, Rosario's long-time boyfriend-pal Ferney is ordered to kill her, but this time not to prove his loyalty (although it's a factor), but to silence her because she has discovered a complex plot to cheat her boss by substituting sugar for cocaine. But instead of claiming his reward for the assassination (which turns out not to be successful), he tries to commit suicide by riding off a precipice on his motorcycle. Unsuccessful, he actually helps rescue Rosario from the hospital and nurses her to health in hiding instead of finishing her off.

Amidst all the love triangles and an abundance of hot sex scenes, the viewer is constantly reminded of the way the drug trade permeates Colombian society. When an astute woman detective and her companion figure out that Antonio knows Rosario (they have a spoken portrait of the hitwoman), they try to convince him to talk by saying that it's not just about Rosario; it's about the whole

FIGURE 6.2 *Rosario Tijeras*, 2010, Produced by Ángela Pulido Serrano, Image: María Fernanda Yépez, Sebastián Martínez and Andrés Sandoval.

Colombian drug trade and the damage it's doing to the country. It's the only quasi-moralizing scene about drugs in the whole telenovela. Only a few scenes deal directly with drugs, notably the one in which the fake cocaine is loaded into an airplane that later explodes in the air. But everything is about drugs. Antonio's father, a respectable businessman who is building a condominium complex, finds himself under investigation when underlings use his tractor-trailers to transport cocaine. The hitmen and gang members who populate the film earn their keep from the drug trade. The glitzy nightclub in which Antonio's best friend Emilio meets Rosario as a glamorous adult woman (not realizing that she is the woman Antonio has been yearning after for several years) is where Medellín's underworld and privileged youth come together seemingly without touching each other's worlds.

The women provide the links between the worlds, whether it is Antonio's confidante and sometimes-lover, Samantha, who figures out that Rosario was once the teenage girl who captured Antonio's heart, or Rosario's mother, Ruby, a hairdresser who moves on her motorcycle between the two worlds to attend to the hair of the privileged class. The telenovela constantly reminds us that the world of the tennis courts cannot be separated from the world of the dusty soccer fields of the slums. The drug trade is in the shantytown hillsides, but it is also in the elegant mansions of the rich and the well-furnished apartments of the comfortable middle class.

One of the stark differences, though, is the familiarity of the poor with death. At the funeral of a homeless, poetically eccentric man, the one who reminds her, "It is more difficult to love than to kill," and who brings her clothes and succor after she has been raped by gang members as a teenager, Rosario says, "I have seen so many people killed, so many people dead, but mostly they are young people, so many young people."

Part of the sense of collective memory—again fueled by gender and the role of women—is the constant reminder of class. Class is a contradiction—the narconovela comfortably weaves from the slums to the rich to the middle class, forming a sense of unity, of oneness. The opening shots of many episodes show Medellín an ultra-modern city with the *teleférico* (cable cars) moving toward the hillside slums with seamless elegance. But as Antonio's mother Lucía screams out at her husband's secretary Susana, when she discovers that her husband has been having a long-term affair with her and that they have a child together, "You will never have my last names and you will never have my social class. You are nothing."

It's a reminder that despite the infinite intersections of the classes, in a rigid society, there is no mobility, and that perhaps the only mobility is an illusory one: the temptations of the drug trade.

Benavides eloquently observes that the drug trade

> has led to new wealth for oppressed and exploited male urban youth [with] few other financial options. The drug trade at first also brought about a

continuation of and increase in urban political and social violence, inherited from years of war and guerrilla warfare in most of Colombia's southern hinterlands.[9]

In discussing the ever-present effects of the drug trade on society, Obitel's 2013 report writes of yet another Colombian telenovela, *Capo II*, saying,

> [The telenovela shows that] the stain of drugs has spread and embedded in everyday life in broad sectors of society. . . . [T]he boundary between what is forbidden and what is permitted, what is illegal and legal, is as fragile as it can be at certain times and circumstances underlying moral values and ethics of individuals.[10]

That statement could have been written of either *Pablo Escobar, el patrón del mal* or *Rosario Tijeras*.

Another telenovela, this one centered around Mexico, also raises issues of collective memory, gender and class: the highly popular *La Reina del Sur* (Queen of the South) (Telemundo, 2011). Although Telemundo is a U.S. network, and produced the series in conjunction with the Antena 3 network of Spain and RTI of Colombia, *La Reina del Sur* is widely perceived as a Mexican telenovela because of the starring presence of Mexican actress Kate del Castillo.

In its 2012 report, Obitel observed that in the month of May alone on Telemundo, *Reina del Sur* averaged nearly three million viewers, surpassing ABC and CBS in the hour among adults aged 18 to 34, and became the highest-rated program among men aged 18 to 34 at the 10 p.m. slot, regardless of language.[11]

La Reina del Sur, like *Rosario Tijeras*, centers around a strong woman. Teresa Mendoza, a 23-year-old woman from the rough Mexican town of Culiacán, becomes one of the most powerful drug dealers in southern Spain. She is forced to leave Mexico after her boyfriend and drug trafficking partner, *el güero* "blondie" Dávila, is killed. In Spain, Teresa meets a Galician, Santiago Fisterra, but he too is killed when his drug boat is intercepted. Teresa ends up in a Spanish jail. With the help of her former cellmate Patricia O'Farrell, the bisexual daughter of a rich Irish-Spanish family, she manages to use her knowledge and guile to become a powerful trafficker. She eventually returns to Culiacán to seek revenge.

The narconovela, like all telenovelas, is full of twists and turns, many of which would lead the viewer to think about power relationships in Mexico. For example, the man responsible for killing her first boyfriend is a campaign manager for the country's next presidential election. The man's nephew—who actually turns out to be his biological son—arranges a hit job on the candidate so his uncle/father, who is the ringleader of the Sinaloa cartel, will assume the candidacy. Threatened by the possibility that a drug trafficker might assume the Mexican presidency, the U.S. Drug Enforcement Agency reaches out to Teresa in Spain, offering her immunity if she will testify against the candidate and ruin his political chances. But at the same time, the candidate and his nephew contact Teresa, inviting her to participate in his candidacy. Their real intention is to assassinate her because she is the only living person who can attest to the candidate's criminal past.

Returning to Mexico, Teresa narrowly avoids being killed, shooting Ramiro (the nephew/son) in the chest. She testifies. The candidate is arrested and his political career is over.

Victoria Dittmar, writing in Insight Crime, an online news service that closely follows the drug trade, observes that while Teresa is upwardly mobile because of her involvement in the drug trade, *La Reina del Sur*

> seems to criticize the hard and difficult life of people involved in drug trafficking, so the show does not paint it as something to which people should aspire. The series also reinforces the idea that once inside this business, it is not easy to leave.

She adds that about the only way one can leave the drug trade is through death or vanishing.[12]

Like the Colombian telenovelas, this narconovela evokes a collective memory—or perhaps one might even say present-day collective awareness, since the drug trade and related violence is so present in Mexico. The 2011 Obitel report notes,

> Social violence suffered in Mexico is no longer an exclusive theme of the television news because, increasingly and in different ways, the telenovelas are representing the excessive violence of the criminal groups and the often excessive violence of the government in fighting organized crime.[13]

A frontal war against drug trafficking began in 2006 under the presidency of Felipe Calderón, who called the onslaught "a crusade" and "a war." Since 2006, an estimated 150,000 people have been murdered in connection with this war and more than 27,000 have been forcibly disappeared.

Violence spiralled as the army and police took on drug traffickers or suspected drug traffickers in brutal urban confrontations. The violence continues, moving from one region of the country to another, touching people's lives with fear, if not actual and sometimes random violence. Like the Colombians, Mexicans are developing a memory of the violence, almost at the same time they are experiencing it. This is, in part, because the trafficking and violence are regional, but also because the drug trade permeates society in almost invisible ways.

The nature of this collective memory works on many different levels. The viewer who watches *La Reina del Sur* night after night is pulled in by the myriad love stories, the violence, the intrigue, but also recognizes the strands of power on many levels. Teresa, who is deprived of her "princes" through violence, goes on to claim her own power as a woman and as a drug trafficker. But throughout the series, she also recognizes that she has been a victim of corruption and betrayal, and finally, in her return to Mexico, decides to do something about it.

Many ordinary Latin Americans—and Latinos—recognize this initial power-lessness in the face of the relentless violence and government inefficiency, corruption and state-sanctioned violence. It takes a woman perhaps to tell this story because in the end it is a Cinderella story without a prince, a poor girl made rich by "marrying" into the drug trade, but then embarking on a quest for justice, an errant knight's tale in which the knight becomes a courageous dame. Teresa's femininity—like Rosario's—is never called into question, and indeed, a coda to the telenovela shows her in some seaside hideaway happily pregnant.

Ironically—or perhaps not—it was a woman who wrote the screenplay for what was probably the very first narconovela in history. In 1982, Colombian screenwriter Martha Bossio wrote *La mala hierba* (Weed), based on a book by the same name by Juan Gossaín. According to Colombian media expert Clemencia Rodríguez, Bossio, a successful playwright, had dabbled in telenovelas, but refused to do more because they were too "light." Caracol Television tempted her with remaking Gossaín's book as a telenovela, and she took up the challenge.

The plot involves two families on the Colombian coast, the Mirandas and the Morales, who are caught in a web of debt, homicide and revenge. The Mirandas become involved in the marijuana boom, and the vendetta against the Morales intensifies. The telenovela had a level of violence that had not been shown up until then: one of the Morales is shot to death in a movie theatre; a five-year-old witnesses the death of a relative. Indeed, President Belisario Betancur intervened to make sure that the telenovela did not have an ending that favored the marijuana lords; the narconovela was actually extended 20 episodes so that the protagonists would lose all their wealth and not live happily ever after.

The telenovela was a precursor of the modern-day narconovelas in many ways. Like the more recent series, *La mala hierba* was not told in blacks and whites, but in shades of gray. Government authorities are corrupt, and go unpunished. Church members are less than saints, and the vendetta between the two families is violent and intractable—but at the same time understandable, given family history. And the protagonist, El Cacique "the Chief" Miranda, is a sympathetic character with a sense of humor, despite his thirst for vengeance.

Like the modern narconovelas, *La mala hierba* was swept up in controversy. Indeed, the appearance of drug traffickers on television—beyond the context of the nightly news—was in and of itself a source of irritation. As Rodríguez observed in her book on Colombian telenovelas,

> *La Mala Hierba* had struck such a note in Colombia that it was the object of censure. But it was not censure because of the family's immorality or objections to the relationship of the couple, but because it was showing a social

group (the drug traffickers) in their daily lives, in their ways of being and of seeing the world; that is, a cultural group without social legitimation had access to the television through *Mala Hierba*.[14]

The Colombian Association of Toxicology opposed the series. So did many parents' groups, and the head of the Colombian television authority Inravisión, Germán Castro Caycedo, questioned the level of violence in *Mala hierba*.

"There's no need to tell the country half-truths," author Gossaín told the newsweekly *Semana*,

> because then one would have to create an underground academy of history to tell the truth. Moreover, in Colombia, it's a fact that corruption exists and the tendency towards an easy life is not a sign of immaturity—it's a sign of hunger.[15]

Like the modern narconovela, in an effort to create a detailed rendering of reality, *Mala hierba* was one of the most expensive to be produced up until that time, filmed in Cartagena and Turbaco on the Atlantic Coast and Girardot in the country's center, as well as in Miami, with interior scenes shot in Bogotá. The wealth and power of Colombia's marijuana boom was not left up to the imagination; three yachts, Mercedes Benz automobiles, armored vehicles, Betamax (the now obsolete, but then cutting-edge, video recording system), ostentatious furniture and other luxuries were constantly featured.

This narconovela—like those that followed—is a story of power. It is a story of transformations of a family, of a region and of habits because of the appearance of the illegal drug trade in marijuana. And it was a telenovela that at that time sparked discussion about how to deal with that period of Colombian history before cocaine replaced marijuana as the principal drug export. Like the present-day narconovelas, it contributed to the formation of collective memory.

Narconovelas also invoke collective memory precisely because they are stories of power. "Narconovelas are all about the *caudillo*—the Latin American strongman—the key figure in our history and literature. They are telling us our history," Boris Muñoz, a *New York Times* editor who has written frequently on Latin American cultural subjects, commented to me. The *caudillo* is a traditional Latin American figure, one who figures prominently, for instance, in Gabriel García Márquez's *El otoño del patriarca* (The Autumn of the Patriarch), which describes the life of a fictional Caribbean strongman with infinite power. One of the funniest depictions of this archetype of this all-powerful figure is in Woody Allen's 1971 film *Bananas* in which the would-be dictator of San Marcos declares that the official language of the country will be Swedish, adding that "all citizens will be required to change their underwear every half hour. Underwear will be worn on the outside so we can check." The expectation, both in fiction and fact, was complete obedience.

Thus, the sense of hierarchy pervades the narconovelas. As in Marino's obedience to Escobar in killing Yesenia, orders must be followed. The king is the king; it is not a coincidence that in *Rosario Tijeras*, on at least one occasion Rosario actually bows to the druglord, and his henchmen treat him with utmost deference (at the same time that they are swindling him behind his back).

I've spent a lot of time in this chapter telling you about the important role of women in these narconovelas, and now I'm telling you that they are about an archetype, a traditionally important man closely associated with the male dominance of *machismo*. I don't think that's a contradiction. First of all, it's historically correct. Pablo Escobar's primary rival was César Gaviria, the president of Colombia, or perhaps the Colombian state (that part of the state he did not co-opt). Second, the important role of women is a way of talking about resistance, a way of overcoming powerlessness. Third, the drug trade (as depicted in these television series and in real life) contains an inherent contradiction.

On the one hand, dealing drugs or becoming a hit man is a way out of powerlessness. It is a way to make money quickly, providing for your mother (money for the "cucha" or mother is an important theme) and/or your girlfriends; it can change your class status and give you access to goods you could never have imagined; it provides a sense of community and brotherhood (and sometimes sisterhood); in the case of women, sometimes, it gives you the power and independent wealth usually enjoyed by men in the society; in more subservient roles, it gives you access to a more comfortable life. Rosario Tijeras—*tijeras* means "scissors" in Spanish—initially used her beautician mother's feminine tool to avenge a rape and castrate her attacker, as well as to defend herself against nasty teachers in school. But she soon exchanges this feminine weapon for the more masculine gun, overcoming powerlessness through economic security and social mobility.

But, on the other hand, involvement in the drug trade can be the ultimate form of powerlessness: the loss of the right to live. The journal *Health Affairs* recently published a study by the UCLA Fielding School of Public Health that indicates life expectancy for Mexican men between the ages of 15 and 50 across the country fell an average of 0.3 years between 2005 and 2010 because of drug-related homicides. In 2005, Mexico's homicide rate was 9.5 per 100,000 deaths. By 2010 it reached 22 per 100,000 deaths, dropping a bit in 2013, according to the World Bank.

But one doesn't need the statistics when one watches the narconovelas. Death is always present and life is cheap. The melodrama of the narconovelas is always reminding the viewer of these choices, like and unlike choices they may have to make in their ordinary lives.[16]

One of the strengths of narconovelas is that they are very specific in time and place but are also portraits of people with whom anyone can identify; it is not so much that the drug trade is humanized, but that the people who work in it at all levels become human. Thus, an Argentine watching a Colombian or Mexican telenovela is understanding a history that is very specific to those countries, but is also reacting in a very visceral way to the situations caused by the drug trade.

Brazilian media scholar Esther Hamburger notes how telenovela's melodramatic tone redefines the relationship between the political and the personal because it translates political issues into personal and familiar terms, in "terms that are meaningful in everyday life."[17]

Breasts and Beyond

That is very true for the narconovela, and perhaps there is no better example than *Sin tetas, no hay paraíso* (Without Tits, There's No Paradise). After all, what woman has not thought that if she just had bigger or smaller breasts, a smaller stomach or tighter buttocks, she could meet Mr. Right? And I suspect that many men also obsess over their weight and their muscles and whatever else men obsess over.

In the case of *Tetas*, there's some "objective" justification for Catalina's search for money to fund her breast enlargements, since the drug dealers have made apparent their predilection for buxom women. It's such an ordinary situation—trying to raise money for something you really want that you think is going to change your life. *Tetas* takes it to an extreme.

Catalina, a young woman from Pereira in Colombia's lush coffee region, decides to become a prostitute with a drug trafficker clientele to raise money for her operation. She abandons her boyfriend, Albeiro, and becomes obsessed with making more and more money, eventually—after the breast implants—marrying a retired drug lord and leading a life of luxury and violence.

But the breast implants are low quality and she has to have them removed or die; her husband abandons her and leaves her without money. She hires hitmen to kill the woman who has seduced her husband (who is the same woman who got her into the prostitution business in the first place), but then decides to commit suicide by disguising herself and having the hitmen actually carry out the deed.

Colombian writer Gustavo Bolívar, author of the best-selling novel that became the telenovela, commented that "we are assisting in the burial of the Cinderella scheme" that characterizes telenovelas. That is, the narconovela is ending the paradigm of the traditional melodrama in which a poor girl marries a wealthy, honest man and instead depicts the gritty reality of the drug trade in Latin America and the United States (and Spain, in the case of *La Reina del Sur*).[18]

I'd argue that it's not the end of the Cinderella story; it's just a different one in which Cinderella has upward mobility that comes from different sources, and there's not always a happy ending. Indeed, most often there is not a happy ending, striking a moral note into the narconovela. Just as the poor and worthy young woman gets her (rich and worthy) man and the Cinderella story ends with a glamorous wedding, the narconovela in which the poor and (un)worthy have "married" into the underworld of drugs and violence ends up at the funeral home, instead of the church.

FIGURE 6.3 *Pablo Escobar, el patrón del mal*, 2012, Directed by Carlos Moreno and Laura Mora, Image: Andrés Parra.

In *Pablo Escobar, el patrón del mal* (Figure 6.3), as in real life, a defeated, slovenly and heavily bearded fugitive dies riddled by bullets on a Medellín rooftop. Viewers who do not know the story of Rosario Tijeras from the novel of the same name might think that the ending of the narconovela was well on its way to a story-book finish. Rosario says she has renounced violence; Emilio has obtained fake passports for her and Antonio with which they can leave the country for Brazil to start a new life, but instead the end escalates to violence of the proportion of a Shakespearean tragedy with the two star-crossed lovers and just about everyone else ending up dead. *Sin tetas* ends with a violent homicide-suicide, and only *La Reina del Sur* gives a faint glimmer of hope with Teresa's pregnancy.

For all the fast car scenes and fast women in narconovelas, for all the violence and sex, there is a profound underlying morality. In addition to the not-so-happy endings (just dues), a sense of religiosity permeates the narconovelas. Rosario boils her bullets in holy water before going out to kill; she prays to the Virgin daily and venerates a statue in her home. Pablo Escobar displays a prominent portrait of a local Virgin in his home. It is not only the women who are religious. As in real life, the drug dealers and hitmen in the narconovelas have their own particular saints and prayers.

Morality often extends to the nature of the family. Although everyone is having an affair with everyone else and some of the love partners (Susana, the secretary in *Rosario Tijeras*, for example, or even Regina, the broadcast journalist lover of Pablo Escobar) seem to be more sympathetic characters than the wives, it is the wives who win out. Family ties trump justice or even business. When El Rey de los Cielos ("the king of the skies") reluctantly orders Rosario killed after she has murdered his brother, he declares "a brother is a brother." And that is despite the fact that he has come to realize that his brother has betrayed him by doing secret deals, and that Rosario has been telling the truth in denouncing him. Morality is not simple, but eventually it comes down on the side of traditional values.

Perhaps it is this tension between the traditional values and the new glistening lifestyle of the underworld that taps into the collective imagination of a continent struggling with its identity, trapped between poverty and underdevelopment and the oft-painful world of relentless growth and modernization.

Building Backlash

And perhaps it is this very tension that has spurred quite a bit of backlash against narconovelas. As mentioned above in the case of *Pablo Escobar, el patrón del mal*, some criticize narconovelas as glamorizing the narco lifestyle. In 2010, for example, the Venezuelan media regulation body, CONATEL, (like the Federal Communications Commission in the United States) asked the television stations Venevisión and Televen to stop broadcasting the Colombian narconovelas *Rosario Tijeras* and *El Capo* after the programs had been on the air only a month. The request was made after the Center of Studies on Venezuela's Expansion and Development (Fundacredesa), a foundation associated with the government social protection agency, published a study called "Narco-novels. Drugs and Sex." The arguments centered around the charges that the narconovelas were not suitable for children and teenagers—and that Venezuelans tended to watch telenovelas (or narconovelas) as a family in prime time. The stations complied.

Immediately, there was a strong public reaction. Several Facebook groups were formed to bring back the shows. One of them was El Capo Fan Club Venezuela with almost a thousand members. The group offered its followers a link where they could download all the narconovela's episodes.

Another Facebook group, with 1,886 fans, was called "Venezuela wants Rosario Tijeras and El Capo back." The group's creators continuously posted questions to spur public interest in getting the telenovelas back on the air. The fans also share links where people can download the episodes or information about cable or satellite stations that broadcast any of the narconovelas.

In Mexico, a group of legislators from the House and Senate Commissions on Radio and Television has been trying since November 2016 to force all television networks to take the narconovelas off the air or schedule them after midnight so they will not be seen by children. The legislators contend that the airing of these series during prime time violates the Telecommunications and Broadcasting Federal Law because the content "promotes and glorifies violence and depicts drug trafficking and its [related] activities as an aspirational life-style" and is not suitable for children.

In response to the legislative effort, the National Autonomous University of Mexico brought together academics from the United States and Latin America to discuss narconovelas—both the telenovela and literature—in a conference entitled *Narcocultura: de Norte a Sur* (Narcoculture: From North to South). UNAM scholar Ainhoa Vásquez commented, "The majority of the narconovelas, in México and Colombia, have a very clear underlying melodramatic layer: the protagonist—the narcos—die or repent. The moral idea is evident: those who get involved in [drug trafficking] end up badly."

While the legislators debate, television channels are preparing to find a way around possible restrictions. Last November 7, Mexico's Imagen TV started advertising a program called *Perseguidos* (The Persecuted), airing at 9 p.m. Monday through Friday, prime time. It's advertised as a story of a delinquent who flees justice, but the visuals are of the narconovela *El Capo*; the advertising is the same; only the name of the telenovela has been changed so it can continue to run in prime time if legislation should go ito effect.[19]

In an interview with InSight Crime about the phenomenon of trying to censure narconovelas, Michigan State's Cabañas said that stigmatization of narco culture is an attempt to distract from the chronic problems of citizen security caused by organized crime.

"If we follow this line of thought, we realize that the [aforementioned politicians and activists] are redirecting the debate from the corruption in the country or problems with the justice system towards cultural aspects," Cabañas told InSight Crime. "The problem isn't to view it on television, it is to view it on the streets."

He added that since narconovelas combine history and fiction, viewers can see government response to the drug traffic through the stories of the multiple characters.[20]

The debate is likely to continue both in Mexico and Colombia and beyond. Netflix is scheduled to air a 60-part narconovela about the life of the Colombian hitman Jhon Jairo Velásquez, better known as "Popeye." Colombia's Caracol television is producing the series, based on his book *Surviving Pablo Escobar—Popeye the Assassin*. Velásquez, who left prison after serving a 23-year sentence, admits to killing 300 people and being an accomplice to the murder of 3,000 more, including the bomb intended for presidential candidate César Gaviria that took the lives of 107 passengers on a doomed 1989 Avianca flight from Bogotá to Cali. Gonzalo Rojas, who was ten when his father died on the flight, told the *Miami Herald* that he resented the surging popularity of narconovelas.

"The only thing these series have done is re-victimize the people who lived through violence," he told reporter Jim Wyss, adding that most narconovelas tweak history for dramatic effect and put the villains in a good light.[21]

Although narconovelas—including the Popeye series currently being made—tend to promote traditional values with the bad guy caught in the end, the messages viewers receive can be entirely different. A good example is *Tetas*. In a publicity blitz, Caracol stressed it wanted to bring general attention to the unsupervised proliferation of breast implants and the proven case of "prepaid girls," where lack of education, ignorance and the need to procure money bring about a fall into a context in which the body becomes the only option to obtain goals.

In other words, to make the general public aware of the situation.

But in Argentina, nightclubs began to raffle out breast implants. Teens throughout Latin America got gifts from their parents to pay for the implants—rather like nose jobs. In 2007, a councilwoman from Margaritas Island in Venezuela proposed a program called Sin Tetas No Hay Paraíso to cover the costs of breast implants for underprivileged youth from the state of Nueva Esparta.

Impassioned Facebook groups sprung up to discuss the telenovela and the wisdom of breast implants. Unlike the Venezuelan groups that advocated for the return of their telenovelas to the air, these groups sought to continue the conversation about the series in a virtual space.[22]

For many in Latin America—as these Facebook groups suggest—the narconovelas are highly personal; they relate to their everyday life (Figure 6.4). That relationship may have to do with the way the drug trade has affected their lives through economic trickle-down; it may have to do with—as in the case of Santiago in Bogotá and those with little memory of the terror—the understanding of a period that intimately touched the lives of their parents and grandparents. It may have to do with the fear and blood in today's Mexico. It may have to do with the crime on the streets in the United States related to gang activity and drug use. It may be that these narcodramas are simply good tales of life and death and survival, of upward mobility and revenge, of love and hate and fear. As much as viewers obsess about the programs and talk about them and critics complain, the narconovelas have begun national and international conversations about the subject, converting reality through melodrama into a nightly and intimate experience.

Benavides again has an insightful comment:

> [T]he structure of the narco-drama is very similar to the hegemonic reworking of the telenovela, in which an audience can believe for a couple of hours, or only several minutes, in a meaningful symbol of aliveness, which is normally censored in everyday existence.[23]

It's not only academics who find this sense of reality and aliveness in the narconovela. Prize-winning Guatemalan journalist Julie López, who has covered drug trafficking for years, observed, "The television viewer sees in the characters an ordinary person in his own neighborhood, his barrio, and understands the multidimensional nature of the narco."

She can attest to the realism of the narconovelas. She was covering a drug case in New York and spotted a customs official associated with the case in the courtroom. She approached him. He was a bit startled and asked her how she had

FIGURE 6.4 T-Shirts With Images of Pablo Escobar Are Sold on Bogotá Sidewalks. Photograph by June Carolyn Erlick.

recognized him. "From the *Señor de los cielos*," she replied, referring to "The Lord of the Skies," a 2013 Telemundo narconovela based on the life of Amado Carillo Fuentes, the former druglord of the Juárez Cartel. López, the author of *El Chapo Guzmán: La Escala en Guatemala* (El Chapo "Shorty" Guzmán: His Layover in Guatemala), added, "These telenovelas give people a chance to converse about the narcos. It becomes a conversation."[24]

Stranger Than Fiction

There's the old cliché that truth is often stranger than fiction. Telenovela's melo-dramatic structure works effectively with the narconovelas because the reality itself is often strange. In *Rosario Tijeras*, a group of people are looking at a televi-sion set when a daring escape takes place, captured by television cameras. "It's not a television series," someone gasps. "It's the news."

In an interview with journalist Nelson Hippolyte Ortega, Venezuelan teleno-vela screenwriter José Ignacio Cabrujas observes,

> Today there are news programs all too dramatic in their own right, quite convincing in showing us news that grabs us sentimentally, emotionally. . . . A telenovela focuses this reality with a certain texture, with details, with a style, but at the end of the day the story itself creates the grand event.[25]

Perhaps at no time in recent history have reality and fiction, realism and melodrama, mingled so much as with the 2015 encounter of telenovela star Kate del Castillo and Hollywood movie actor and director Sean Penn with fugitive Mexican druglord Joaquín "El Chapo" Guzmán.

Del Castillo, who portrayed the role of Teresa in *Reina del Sur*, brought Penn to Guzmán's secret hiding place (whether the purpose was to write an article for *Rolling Stone* or to obtain a movie contract has been disputed). The saga began in 2012 with a longish Tweet:

> Today I believe more in El Chapo Guzmán than I do in the governments that hide truths from me, even if they are painful, who hide the cures for cancer, AIDS, etc., for their own benefit. Mr. Chapo, wouldn't it be cool if you started trafficking with the good? . . . come on, señor, you would be the heroes of heroes. Let's traffic with love, you know how. Life is a business and the only thing that changes is the merchandise. Don't you agree?

Some outraged Mexicans accused her of defending violence and drug trafficking, and others as ardently defended her. Her father, Eric del Castillo, himself a well-known telenovela actor, defended her to the media, but privately sent her a detailed critique of her statement. "You're not Teresa Mendoza," her older sister, Verónica del Castillo, angrily reminded her. Indeed, the line from her Tweet about "life is a business" had originally been said by Teresa, the Queen of the South, in the narconovela.

The drug lord got in touch through his lawyer and asked her to make a movie about his life. Although Guzmán had a reputation for being a relentless murderer of anyone who got in his way, like Pablo Escobar in real life and the telenovelas, he was also the people's antihero, a Robin Hood of humble origins who gave to the poor of his region of Sinaloa and who defied a corrupt and bungling government. He thumbed his nose at the government of Mexican president Enrique Peña Nieto by escaping from a high-security jail through an elaborate and sophisticated mile-long tunnel—his second escape.[26]

According to Robert Draper, writing in the *New Yorker*, the lawyers explained to Del Castillo why he had chosen her: "Because you're very brave. Because you're outspoken. Because you always tell the truth, even when it's about the government. Because you come from a great family. And because he's a fan of yours from 'La Reina del Sur.'"

In his *Rolling Stone* article, Penn stresses the political, charging,

> There are both brutal and corrupt forces within the Mexican government who oppose her (and indeed, according to Kate, high-ranking officials have responded to her public statement with private intimidations), and hence, a responsibility of the greater public to shepherd those who make their voices heard.

But he also talks of the adventure, the clandestine phone calls, the trek to the jungle, the vow by the druglord to Kate that "he would protect her more than his own eyes."

He describes El Chapo as a "global pariah," and then adds in glowing terms that El Chapo rapidly rose through the ranks since becoming a drug trafficker while he was still a teenager, building "an almost mythic reputation." He describes El Chapo both as "a cold pragmatist," but as "a Robin Hood-like figure," providing much-needed services for the Sinaloa poor. "By the time of his second escape from federal prison, he had become a figure entrenched in Mexican folklore," Penn concludes.[27]

The dramatic escape and the subsequent revelation of the visits by Sean Penn and the telenovela actress only enhanced the folklore. When El Chapo was finally captured as a result of tracing communications between him and Del Castillo, authorities found arms, weapons, hair dye for his distinctive mustache and many DVDs of *Reina del Sur*.

The 2016 Obitel yearly report, in its section on Mexico, observes, "Fantasy and reality intertwined travelled the Latin world and became trending topics, helping us think about the role of reality in fiction and the role of fiction in reality."[28]

I happened to be in Colombia when the news about Kate del Castillo's El Chapo connection broke. For the Colombians, the story hit home. Although the country for the most part is no longer plagued by the Medellín cartel and racked by drug-related violence, it still grows coca, produces cocaine and participates in the international drug trade. But the brutal violence experienced in Mexico, which now has become the hub of drug trafficking, is an all too familiar story.

In a January 17 story, Colombian daily *El Tiempo* called the revelation of Del Castillo's ties to El Chapo "an earthquake" that shook not only legacy and social media, but also "Mexican society, which always feels so uncomfortable when the analysts talk about the 'Colombianizing' of Mexico."

Del Castillo is a well-respected actress in Mexico, the article pointed out, and comes from an important line of actors, but then quoted an unidentified Mexican sociologist, "Our societies have a hard time understanding how the personalities they most admire . . . end up involved in different ways with drug traffickers."[29]

That is, after all, the story of the narconovelas.

It is a story being told night after night with Latin American actors and screen-writers. It is a way of remembering; it is a way of understanding; it is a mirror to society past and present.

As Colombian screenwriter Fernando Gaitán, best known for *Yo soy Betty, la fea*, observes, "Drug trafficking is part of our history; it is better that we ourselves tell our own history."[30]

Notes

1 Alexandra J. Gratereaux, "Narco Novelas Prove a Golden Telenovela Formula for Latino TV Networks," *Fox News Latino*, April 8, 2013, http://latino.foxnews.com/latino/entertainment/2013/04/08/narco-novelas-prove-golden-telenovela-formula-for-latino-tv-networks/.

2 Maria Immacolata Vassallo de Lopes and Guillermo Orozco Gómez, eds., *Social Memory and Television in Ibero-American Countries*, Ibero-American Observatory for Television Fiction (Obitel), 2013 Yearbook, (Porto Alegre, Brazil: Editorial Sulina, 2013), p. 216. Obitel yearbooks are published in Spanish, English and Portuguese. I have followed the numbering on the English version.

3 Telemundo's July 9 broadcast of *Pablo Escobar: El Patrón del Mal* averaged nearly 2.2 million viewers, July 10, 2012, http://tvbythenumbers.zap2it.com/2012/07/10/telemundo-medias-pablo-escobar-el-patron-del-mal-averages-nearly-2-2-million-total-viewers/141131.

4 Daniela Franco García, "Asesino en serie: El próximo lunes se estrena en el Canal Caracol 'Escobar, el patrón del mal', la superproducción que cuenta la historia del crimen organizado desde cuando el auge del contrabando fue liderado por Pablo Escobar," May 26, 2012, www.elespectador.com/noticias/temadeldia/asesino-serie-articulo-349050.

5 Miguel Cabañas, "Narcotelenovelas, Gender, and Globalization in *Sin tetas no hay paraíso*," *Latin American Perspectives* 39, no. 3, May 2012, 74–87. Note that the term "narcotelenovelas" is used interchangeably by many authors with "narconovelas."

6 Mario Fernando Prado, *El Espectador*, June 15, 2012, and José Antonio Garciandía, *Semana*, October 10, 2009, are quoted from articles in the respective newspaper and magazine in Maria Immacolata Vassallo de Lopes and Guillermo Orozco Gómez, eds., *Social Memory and Television in Ibero-American Countries*, Ibero-American Observatory for Television Fiction (Obitel), 2013 Yearbook (Porto Alegre, Brazil: Editorial Sulina, 2013), p. 334. Translation is Obitel's.

7 Maria Immacolata Vassallo de Lopes and Guillermo Orozco Gómez, eds., *Social Memory and Television in Ibero-American Countries*, Ibero-American Observatory for Television Fiction (Obitel) 2013 Yearbook (Porto Alegre, Brazil: Editorial Sulina, 2013), 467.

8 O. Hugo Benavides, *Drugs, Thugs, and Divas: Telenovelas and Narco-Dramas in Latin America* (Austin: University of Texas Press, 2008), 97.

9 Ibid., 89.

10 Maria Immacolata Vassallo de Lopes and Guillermo Orozco Gómez, eds., *Social Memory and Television in Ibero-American Countries*, Ibero-American Observatory for Television Fiction (Obitel) 2013 Yearbook (Porto Alegre, Brazil: Editorial Sulina, 2013), 219.

11 Maria Immacolata Vassallo de Lopes and Guillermo Orozco Gómez, eds., *Transnationalization of Television Fiction in Ibero-American Countries*, Ibero-American Observatory for Television Fiction (Obitel) 2012 Yearbook (Porto Alegre, Brazil: Editorial Sulina, 2012), 387.

12 Victoria Dittmar, "Mexico's Narco Soap Operas Do More Than Just Glorify Drug Trade," Insight Crime, November 24, 2016, www.insightcrime.org/news-analysis/mexico-narco-soap-operas-do-more-than-just-glorify-drug-trade.

13 Maria Immacolata Vassallo de Lopes and Guillermo Orozco Gómez, eds., *Quality in Television Fiction and Audiences' Transmedia Interactions*, Ibero-American Observatory for Television Fiction (Obitel) 2011 Yearbook (Rio de Janeiro, Brazil: Editorial Globo S.A., 2011), 177.

14 Clemencia Rodríguez and María Patricia Tellez, *La Telenovela en Colombia: Mucho más que amor y lágrimas*, Controversia 155, CINEP (Centro de Investigación y Educación Popular, Bogotá, Colombia, 1989), 71. Translation is mine.

15 Hamburger, Esther, "Mala Hierba Nunca Muere, Una telenovela, 'La mala hierba', divide la opinión de los televidentes," *Semana*, November 10, 1982, www.semana.com/cultura/articulo/mala-hierba-nunca-muere/882-3. Translation is mine.

16 Lucy Wescott, "Mexico's Drug War Has Decreased Life Expectancy for Men," *Newsweek.com*, January 6, 2016, www.newsweek.com/Mexicos-drug-war-has-decreased-life-expectancy-men-412351.

17 Esther Hamburger, *Politics and Intimacy in Brazilian Telenovelas* (Chicago: University of Chicago Press, 1999).

18 Maria Immacolata Vassallo de Lopes and Guillermo Orozco Gómez, eds., *Transnationalization of Television Fiction in Ibero-American Countries*, Ibero-American Observatory

for Television Fiction (Obitel) 2012 Yearbook (Porto Alegre, Brazil: Editorial Sulina, 2012), 334.

19 Pablo Ferri, *"Narco ¿qué?* México discute si restringe la emisión de series sobre traficantes de drogas a horario especial. ¿Serviría de algo?" *El País*, November 18, 2016, http://cultura.elpais.com/cultura/2016/11/18/actualidad/1479432577_601934.html.

20 Victoria Dittmar, "Mexico's Narco Soap Operas Do More Than Just Glorify Drug Trade," Insight Crime, November 24, 2016, www.insightcrime.org/news-analysis/mexico-narco-soap-operas-do-more-than-just-glorify-drug-trade.

21 Jim Wyss, "He Murdered 300: Now Popeye the Assassin is a Colombian Media Star," *Miami Herald*, November 11, 2016, www.miamiherald.com/news/nation-world/world/americas/colombia/article114199558.html#emlnl=The_Americas.

22 Héctor Fernández L'Hoeste, "Gender, Drugs and the Global Telenovela: Pimping Sin Tetas No Hay Paraíso" in Diana L. Ríos and Mari Castañeda, eds., *Soap Operas and Telenovelas in a Digital Age: Global Industries and New Audiences* (New York: Peter Lang, 2011), 165–182.

23 O. Hugo Benavides, *Drugs, Thugs, and Divas: Telenovelas and Narco-Dramas in Latin America* (Austin: University of Texas Press, 2008), 160.

24 Skype interview with Julie López, August 16, 2016.

25 Nelson Hippolyte Ortega, "José Ignacio Cabrujas: 'La muerte de la telenovela,'" *ProDaVinci*, May 16, 2010, http://prodavinci.com/2010/05/16/actualidad/jose-ignacio-cabrujas-la-muerte-de-la-telenovela/. My translation.

26 Robert Draper, "The Go-Between: The Mexican actress who dazzled El Chapo," *The New Yorker*, March 21, 2016, www.newyorker.com/magazine/2016/03/21/kate-del-castillo-sean-penn-and-el-chapo.

27 Sean Penn, "El Chapo Speaks," *Rolling Stone*, January 9, 2016, www.rollingstone.com/culture/features/el-chapo-speaks-20160109?page=8.

28 Maria Immacolata Vassallo de Lopes and Guillermo Orozco Gómez, eds., *(Re)Invention of TV Fiction Genres and Formats*, Ibero-American Observatory for Television Fiction (Obitel) 2016 Yearbook (Porto Alegre, Brazil: Editorial Sulina, 2016), 301.

29 Redacción Internacional, "La Novela del 'Chapo' y la 'reina' de la televisión," *El Tiempo* (Bogotá, Colombia), January 17, 2016, 13. Translation is mine.

30 Viviana Martínez Pérez, "De la telenovela a la narconovela," *El Universal* (Caracas, Venezuela, February 4, 2013), www.eluniversal.com.co/suplementos/dominical/de-la-telenovela-la-narconovela-107361. Translation is mine.

Bibliography

Benavides, O. Hugo. *Drugs, Thugs, and Divas: Telenovelas and Narco-Dramas in Latin America.* Austin: University of Texas Press, 2008.

Cabañas, Miguel. "Narcotelenovelas, Gender, and Globalization in *Sin tetas no hay paraíso.*" *Latin American Perspectives* 39, no. 3. May 2012, 74–87.

Dittmar, Victoria. "Mexico's Narco Soap Operas Do More Than Just Glorify Drug Trade, Insight Crime." November 24, 2016. www.insightcrime.org/news-analysis/mexico-narco-soap-operas-do-more-than-just-glorify-drug-trade.

Draper, Robert. "The Go-Between: The Mexican actress who dazzled El Chapo." *The New Yorker*, March 21, 2016. www.newyorker.com/magazine/2016/03/21/kate-del-castillo-sean-penn-and-el-chapo.

Ferri, Pablo. *"Narco ¿qué?* México discute si restringe la emisión de series sobre traficantes de drogas a horario especial. ¿Serviría de algo?" *El País*, November 18, 2016. http://cultura.elpais.com/cultura/2016/11/18/actualidad/1479432577_601934.html.

Fernández L'Hoeste, Héctor. "Gender, Drugs and the Global Telenovela: Pimping Sin Tetas No Hay Paraíso" in Diana L. Ríos and Mari Castañeda (eds), *Soap Operas and Telenovelas in a Digital Age: Global Industries and New Audiences*. New York: Peter Lang, 2011, 165–182.

Franco García, Daniela. "Asesino en serie: El próximo lunes se estrena en el Canal Caracol 'Escobar, el patrón del mal', la superproducción que cuenta la historia del crimen organizado desde cuando el auge del contrabando fue liderado por Pablo Escobar." May 26, 2012. www.elespectador.com/noticias/temadeldia/asesino-serie-articulo-349050.

Gratereaux, Alexandra J. "Narco Novelas Prove A Golden Telenovela Formula for Latino TV Networks." *Fox News Latino*, April 8, 2013. http://latino.foxnews.com/latino/entertainment/2013/04/08/narco-novelas-prove-golden-telenovela-formula-for-latino-tv-networks/.

Hamburger, Esther. *Politics and Intimacy in Brazilian Telenovelas*. Chicago: University of Chicago Press, 1999.

Hamburger, Esther. "Mala Hierba Nunca Muere, Una telenovela, 'La mala hierba', divide la opinión de los televidentes." *Semana*, November 10, 1982. www.semana.com/cultura/articulo/mala-hierba-nunca-muere/882-3.

Martínez Pérez, Viviana. "De la telenovela a la narconovela." *El Universal*. Caracas, Venezuela, February 4, 2013. www.eluniversal.com.co/suplementos/dominical/de-la-telenovela-la-narconovela-107361.

Ortega, Nelson Hippolyte. "José Ignacio Cabrujas: 'La muerte de la telenovela.'" *ProDaVinci*, May 16, 2010. http://prodavinci.com/2010/05/16/actualidad/jose-ignacio-cabrujas-la-muerte-de-la-telenovela/.

Penn, Sean. "El Chapo Speaks." *Rolling Stone*, January 9, 2016, www.rollingstone.com/culture/features/el-chapo-speaks-20160109?page=8.

Redacción Internacional. "La Novela del 'Chapo' y la 'reina' de la televisión." *El Tiempo* (Bogotá, Colombia), January 17, 2016, 13.

Rodríguez, Clemencia, and María Patricia Tellez. *La Telenovela en Colombia: Mucho más que amor y lágrimas*. Controversia 155. Bogotá, Colombia: CINEP (Centro de Investigación y Educación Popular, Bogotá, Colombia, 1989.

Rodríguez, Clemencia, and María Patricia Tellez. "Telemundo's July 9 broadcast of *Pablo Escobar: El Patrón del Mal* averaged nearly 2.2 million viewers." July 10, 2012. http://tvbythenumbers.zap2it.com/2012/07/10/telemundo-medias-pablo-escobar-el-patron-del-mal-averages-nearly-2-2-million-total-viewers/141131.

Vassallo de Lopes, Maria Immacolata, and Guillermo Orozco Gómez, eds. *Quality in Television Fiction and Audiences' Transmedia Interactions*. Ibero-American Observatory of Television Fiction (Obitel) 2011 Yearbook. Rio de Janeiro, Brazil: Editorial Globo S.A., 2011.

Vassallo de Lopes, Maria Immacolata, and Guillermo Orozco Gómez, eds. *(Re)Invention of TV Fiction Genres and Formats*, Ibero-American Observatory of Television Fiction (Obitel) 2016 Yearbook. Porto Alegre, Brazil: Editorial Sulina, 2012.

Vassallo de Lopes, Maria Immacolata, and Guillermo Orozco Gómez, eds. *Transnationalization of Television Fiction in Ibero-American Countries*, Ibero-American Observatory of Television Fiction (Obitel) 2012 Yearbook. Porto Alegre, Brazil: Editorial Sulina, 2012.

Vassallo de Lopes, Maria Immacolata, and Guillermo Orozco Gómez, eds. *Social Memory and Television in Ibero-American Countries*, Ibero-American Observatory of Television Fiction (Obitel), 2013 Yearbook. Porto Alegre, Brazil: Editorial Sulina, 2013.

Wescott, Lucy. "Mexico's Drug War Has Decreased Life Expectancy for Men." *Newsweek.com*, January 6, 2016. www.newsweek.com/Mexicos-drug-war-has-decreased-life-expectancy-men-412351.

Wyss, Jim. "He Murdered 300: Now Popeye the Assassin is a Colombian Media Star." *Miami Herald*, November 11, 2016. www.miamiherald.com/news/nation-world/world/americas/colombia/article114199558.html#emlnl=The_Americas.

CONCLUSIONS

Looking Backward and Going Forward

During the Brazilian dictatorship in the 1960s, many Brazilian writers and journalists found themselves censored and unemployed. Few venues existed for speaking out in repressive and politically tumultuous times.

These talented and, in many cases, highly progressive creators found a home in Brazil's expanding telenovela industry. And they brought to the small screen on a nightly basis the topics Brazilians couldn't talk about otherwise.

Telenovelas have long been the hemisphere's response to the growing pains of development, the fierceness of repression, the questioning of identities. Amidst the protracted kisses, the emotional cliffhanging mysteries of who's really who, the anguish of the abandoned and the abandoners, telenovelas have forged and been forged by a uniquely Latin American culture.

Perhaps it is no coincidence that some of the most fertile and influential creators of telenovelas have been immigrants and exiles from other Latin American countries, particularly Cuba and Venezuela. For telenovelas are the voiced dreams of the outsiders becoming insiders. Telenovelas break down walls, whether they are the real borders between Latin American countries, or between Latin Americans and the Hispanic community in the United States, or the less visible borders between Latin America's megacities and the sprawling rural areas of plains, deserts, mountains, jungles and valleys.

In a region where women were (and sometimes still are) often seen through the lens of machismo, which assumes that the male is dominant and with more rights than women, women became the protagonist of daily dramas. And at a time when many more men than women were employed in formal jobs, women screenwriters fashioned their telenovelas to make the women stars.

James Barrett "Scotty" Reston of the *New York Times* once wrote, "The people of the United States will do anything for Latin America, except read about it."

Indeed, Latin America has all too often been absent from the global discourse. And so, even more sadly, have women.

So one gets a powerful two-for-one when Latin American telenovela stars emerge as global heroines. Mexican pop star Thalia Sodi, for example, who starred in the 1994 *Miramar*, visited the Philippines and was received by crowds outnumbering those who came out to receive the pope on his visit there. Mosques in the Ivory Coast were said to have issued the call to prayer early so the enthusiastic telenovela audience would not miss the evening *Miramar* episode. When Veronica Castro, the star of the Mexican telenovela *Los ricos también lloran*, visited Russia, she was received at the Kremlin by then-president Boris Yeltsin. She may or may not have been aware of all the posters and teacups emblazoned with her image and collected by ordinary Russian fans.

The successful projection of female and Latin American identity in the global context also strengthens the influence of telenovelas in the pan-Latino context. What is recognized abroad often becomes even more important at home. And telenovela stars often use their heroine status to take up popular causes. For example, when the 22-year-old Brazilian telenovela actress Daniella Perez was brutally murdered, her scriptwriter mother authored a telenovela about missing children and subsequently spurred an effective social service campaign on their behalf.

Telenovela actresses are listened to. Alicia Machado, a Venezuelan telenovela star turned Miss Universe, played an important role in the 2016 U.S. election when Donald Trump's insults and harassment of her because of weight gain became public. Long before Democratic presidential candidate Hillary Clinton brought up Trump's treatment of Machado, the telenovela actress (she's currently in the Colombian telenovela *La ley del corazón* [The Law of the Heart]) had spoken out about eating disorders and bullying.

Whether it's through overt social change campaigns or a more subtle holding up a mirror to Latin American identity, telenovelas are a vehicle for putting subjects on the table that aren't ordinarily talked about. The topics can be as far ranging as sexuality, sexual identity, race, corruption, class and the drug culture.

It's not even necessarily that telenovelas are politically correct. If that were always so, Betty in *Betty la fea* perhaps wouldn't have got a makeover and would have gone on to head her former company anyway. Isaura in *Escrava Isaura* would have fled to the free slave community with fellow slave André, married him and then in a super-counterfactual sweep, led an uprising that led to the abolition of slavery in Brazil—instead of finding true love with white Brazilian nobility (albeit an abolitionist).

As I began to imagine counterfactual politically correct scenarios, I remembered the spate of feminist and fractured fairy tale books that came out as a result of the cultural revolutions in the United States in the 1960s and '70s. I can't say I remember any of those stories, whatever their political and literary merits. But I will always remember (and sometimes misremember, as I discovered in the process of writing this book) *Cinderella* and *Little Red Riding Hood* and *Jack and the Beanstalk*.

Telenovelas are like fairy tales in that way. They tap into primal emotions. They tap into archetypes. They hold up a mirror to our desires and our fears and our multiplicity of identities. And despite the fact we may have read the fairy tales in school, or had them read to us at bedtime, they are part of an oral tradition handed down to us directly by our parents, grandparents and teachers, or indirectly through myriad cultural references.

As I researched this book, I was slightly surprised by the number of times I was told that someone had not seen a telenovela and yet s/he could intelligently discuss the plot and its impact. Telenovelas are a pervasive part of everyday conversations in both public venues like buses and beauty salons and in private venues like the dinner table. In that way also, they are like fairy tales—seeping orally into the general knowledge.

One can argue against the portrayals in telenovelas, just as there are myriad arguments against some of the depictions of fairy tales. But that very act of arguing against a portrayal deepens the capacity to think about social issues.

Like fairy tales, telenovelas make up part of the fabric of historical memory in Latin America and beyond. In some cases, that characteristic is quite literal. Young Colombians learn about the terror of the drug trafficking era of Pablo Escobar through narconovelas. Brazilians learned of the cruelty of colonial-day slavery through telenovelas like *Escrava Isaura*. Argentina's telenovela *Montecristo* riveted the country with its portrayal of the subject of the forcibly disappeared. And, of course, these telenovelas move beyond borders, creating a kind of collective historical memory and historical knowledge among Latin Americans, who might not have learned about the history of their neighbors otherwise.

Yet there is a different but related historical memory that does not rely so much on recounting the facts of the past, but by creating shared experiences. For many Colombians, the telenovela *Café, con aroma de mujer* (Coffee with Scent of a Woman) marked the first time they became aware of the beauty of coffee country and began to perceive it as an integral part and driving force of the nation. Angelika Rettberg and Enrique Chaux, a Boston-educated couple who are now university professors in Bogotá, remember seeing the telenovela during a field trip to Cuba. "We would walk past every house and the doors would all be open, and everyone was watching the same novela, *Café*. As we walked past each house, we could follow the episode without any difficulty," recounts Rettberg. The experience continued in Boston, she remembers, as the couple walked along the Charles River—this time with the telenovela on a Walkman listening device. There was a sense of sharing—with the Cubans, with the Colombians back home, with each other, forming a part of their memories and experiences.

In a similar manner, women remember learning about rape or domestic violence at a specific point of time through a telenovela. The depiction on the small screen of these issues gave girls the courage to broach these subjects with their mothers. The repetitive nature and shared experience of telenovelas lead to this collective memory of certain episodes or themes just as if they were actual historical events. They become part of one's history.

In part, this may account for the popularity of telenovela remakes and reruns. Of course, networks find it less expensive to rerun telenovelas, and production companies are counting on the success of a remake of an already popular telenovela (but sometimes remakes do flop). But more than that, reruns and remakes manage to evoke a particular point of time, the experience of watching then and now. When the 1988 Colombian telenovela, *Los pecados de Inés de Hinojosa* (The Sins of Inés de Hinojosa) was rerun in the context of Colombian television network R.T.I.'s 60-year anniversary, the program still caused controversy with its lesbian kiss—despite all that had developed with the gay rights movement in the course of the years. And when *Por estas calles* was shown again to Venezuelans, political pundits and ordinary folk were quick to relate it to the present-day situation in Venezuela, not only talking about the telenovela casually, but also organizing panels to discuss it.

To a certain extent, one can make the same argument of the strength of historical repetition for popular movies: *Gone with the Wind*, *Casablanca* or *The Wizard of Oz*, for example. These movies also evoke archetypes; very often they are remembered as being seen in a very specific time and place and stage of one's own personal history. There are similarities, but the viewing experience is different. Telenovelas air night after night in prime time, seen as a collective experience, often viewed with others and later shared with others. The imprint of the watching experience is there, the tension and expectation of waiting for the next episode, the speculation, the conversations, the emotions. Telenovelas are an integral part of Latin American life and a quintessential Latin American creation.

That's not to say that telenovelas are stagnant and will always remain the same type of melodramas. We've already seen that the narconovelas—which do not generally have happy endings—break with the traditional telenovelas in that sense. And while for decades, Latin American telenovelas have been widely popular in Eastern Europe and parts of Asia and Africa, now Turkish telenovelas are becoming all the rage in Latin America. Series like *1001 Nights* and *El Sultán* are overtaking some locally produced shows. At the 2016 meeting of the Ibero-American Observatory of Television Fiction (Obitel), members noted that Turkish people share many of the same cultural values as Latin Americans, including the emphasis on family and religion. The Turkish telenovelas tend to be more conservative, showing little flesh and overt sex. Yet, they are very romantic, and the men tend to hark back to a more chivalrous and less egalitarian way of being. Many Latin Americans think the Turkish series are more appropriate for family viewing than the overtly sexual and often violent Latin American narconovelas, for instance.

It's not an either-or situation. Obitel panelists observed that the Chilean telenovelas have had difficulty with exports because even fellow Latin Americans find their accents challenging. But the Turkish telenovelas are being dubbed in Spanish in Chile, which some say may lead to a rejuvenation of the Chilean industry.

Just as Turkish telenovelas are having their influence on Latin America, Latin America has revolutionized U.S. television viewing. For a few decades now, telenovelas have had a significant presence in the U.S-based Hispanic channels. And many English speakers have watched them, whether to learn Spanish or to quench a cultural curiosity. But now telenovelas have created derivatives and hybrids on English-language television. U.S. channels, Netflix and Amazon Prime have partnered with Latin American networks to create series like *Narcos*. Hybrids, which, unlike telenovelas, are shown on a weekly basis and have no fixed end dates, are increasingly popular; *Ugly Betty*, based on Colombia's *Betty la fea*, and *Jane the Virgin*, based on Venezuela's *Juana la virgen*, are two prime examples.

And like their Latin American cousins, they take up controversial subjects: sex, immigration, inadequate parenting, standards of beauty, gay identity, Latino identity, social class and intergenerational conflict. In a time in the United States when identity politics are under attack, these programs simply remind us of the diversity of how the United States looks today. Just as telenovelas hold up a mirror and put women forth as powerful protagonists, these hybrids do so and more. They remind us of the generations and of the love and of the struggles and the respect of Latinos and Latinas. They remind us of immigration and the accents and the struggle to fit in. They show us who we are.

Some ask if the telenovela is dying. Busy families have less time to watch together or just want to watch different programs in a multi-television household. But telenovelas are not dying; they are morphing to express the Latin America of today and, by extension, the Latino world of today, whether it be in Boston or Buenos Aires.

Whether in Latin America or the United States, families do often watch telenovelas or the new hybrids together. They talk about them at home and at the office. But sometimes viewers just remember the times they watched telenovelas with their grandmothers as they binge watch on Netflix or taped television or YouTube. And then they post their observations on their Facebook page or a blog or tweet developments to their friends. They can communicate with fans in other countries; they can form virtual clubs; they pressure for one ending or another, expressing eternal love or rabid dislike of one actor or another. The communication is fluid, active and new. There are telenovelas that are being written to watch on smartphones. Plots are quicker, sometimes more male-oriented and always audience-driven.

Things are changing with telenovelas, and yet they are the same. Whether they are Colombian or Argentine, Turkish or Latino hybrid, whether they are watched on television or the telephone, telenovelas bring their viewers a mirror. They are a curious blend of fantasy and reality, melodrama and just plain drama; even the Turkish novelas with their romantic vision and family values seem a projection of Latin America against a different and more exotic stage.

When Brazilian writers, facing censorship in their newspapers and books, found a way to talk about social issues in telenovelas, they were by far not the first to use the daily series toward social change. But their creativity in facing censorship made for powerful dramas with perhaps more depth than ever seen before in the genre.

In an exhausting world in which a reality television star turned president has banned certain immigrants, threatened to build a huge wall to keep out our Mexican neighbors, pledged to deport thousands of Latinos and insists on America First, can a telenovela be far behind?

Stay tuned.

INDEX

Page numbers in italic indicate a figure on the corresponding page.